D0105976

LIVING ABROAD IN
SOUTH KOREA

JONATHAN HOPFNER

PRIME LIVING LOCATIONS IN SOUTH KOREA

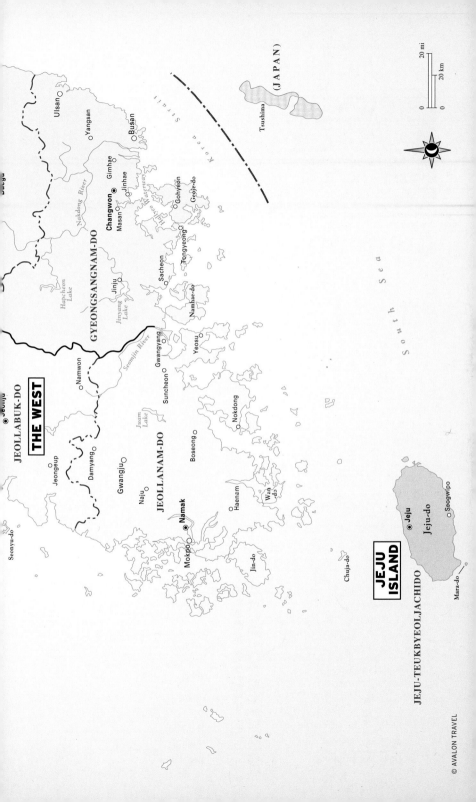

Contents

At Home in South Korea... 6

**WELCOME TO
SOUTH KOREA**............ 9

▶ **Introduction** 10
  The Lay of the Land. 11
  Social Climate 14

▶ **History, Government,
  and Economy** 19
  History 20
  Government................. 26
  Economy................... 29

▶ **People and Culture** 31
  Ethnicity and Class 32
  Customs and Etiquette 33
  Social Values 36
  Gender Roles 36
  Religion.................... 38
  The Arts 41
  Sports and Games........... 44

▶ **Planning Your
  Fact-Finding Trip** 45
  Preparing to Leave 46
  Arriving in South Korea 48
  Things to Do................ 51
  Sample Itineraries........... 52
  Practicalities 60

DAILY LIFE 65

▶ **Making the Move**.......... 66
  Immigration and Visas 67

  Moving with Children. 69
  Moving with Pets 72
  What to Take 73

▶ **Housing Considerations** ... 76
  Types of Housing............ 77
  Renting.................... 80
  Buying..................... 84
  Household Expenses......... 85

▶ **Language and Education**... 86
  Learning Korean 87
  Education.................. 92

▶ **Health** 96
  Hospitals and Clinics......... 98
  Insurance 99
  Pharmacies and Prescriptions.. 100
  Preventive Measures......... 101
  Environmental Factors 102
  Disabled Access............. 103
  Safety 104

▶ **Employment** 108
  Teaching English 109
  Self-Employment............ 111
  The Job Hunt 115
  The Work Environment....... 118
  Labor Laws................. 119

▶ **Finance** 120
  Cost of Living............... 121
  Banking.................... 125
  Taxes..................... 130
  Investing................... 131

▶ **Communications**. 133
   Telephone Service. 134
   Internet. 136
   Postal Service 138
   Media 139

▶ **Travel and Transportation**. . 141
   Map 142
   By Air 143
   By Train 144
   By Bus. 146
   By Boat. 146
   By Bicycle. 147
   Public Transportation 148
   Driving 150

**PRIME LIVING
LOCATIONS**. 155

▶ **Overview** 157
   Map 156

▶ **Seoul** 서울. 163
   Map 164
   The Lay of the Land. 166
   Daily Life. 169
   Where to Live. 172
   Getting Around 177

▶ **Gyeonggi-do** 경기도 179
   Map 180
   The Lay of the Land. 181
   Daily Life. 183
   Where to Live. 185
   Getting Around 189

▶ **The East**. 191
   Map 192

   The Lay of the Land. 193
   Where to Live. 194

▶ **The West** 205
   Map 204
   The Lay of the Land. 206
   Where to Live. 207

▶ **Jeju Island** 제주도. 217
   Map 216
   The Lay of the Land. 218
   Where to Live. 222
   Daily Life. 224

RESOURCES. 227
   Consulates and Embassies 228
   Planning Your
      Fact-Finding Trip 230
   Housing and
      Real Estate Agents 230
   Making the Move 230
   Language and Education 231
   Health. 232
   Employment. 232
   Finance. 233
   Communications 233
   Travel and Transportation 234
   Prime Living Locations 234
   Glossary 239
   Phrasebook 241
   Suggested Reading. 247
   Suggested Films 248

INDEX. 249

At Home in South Korea

After decades in which South Korea languished in the shadow of larger neighbors, it's safe to say the secret is out. The country's pop culture has taken the Internet by storm, its gadgets fill pockets from Boston to Beirut, and its people helm some of the world's leading think tanks. Couple that with an economy that continues to expand at rates the indebted West can only dream of, and it's easy to see why foreigners are flocking to South Korea in ever greater numbers. Yet for all this, the diminutive peninsula jutting from China's eastern flank toward the islands of Japan remains something of an enigma, and its bellicose northern half still tends to dominate global headlines. At least compared to places like Hong Kong or Singapore, nonnatives are thin on the ground. This makes a visit to South Korea an exercise in the unexpected for most new arrivals, as it was for me over a decade ago.

In a way, that's for the best, because it's a place with a knack for confounding expectations. Many of the pleasant surprises will be immediately apparent—striking mountain landscapes, top-notch infrastructure (built in barely a generation!), healthy, inexpensive, and delicious food and drink, a vibrant foreign community, and a local populace happy to help foreign residents make the most of all of these things.

But perhaps the biggest surprise of all is the deep emotion, the sense of attachment, this relatively small country can evoke. That may be because of its history, the way it dragged itself into prosperity against unimaginable odds. Or the culture, a rich bedrock of ritual that continues

to govern much daily interaction. But in the end I've come to believe it's because few other places on earth cram in such contrasts. The neon-drenched streets and clamor of Seoul give way in a few short hours to emerald rice fields or gaily painted temples nestled in secluded valleys; fortune-tellers pitch their tents outside trendy boutiques (and often draw more customers); lush, almost tropical summers are followed by near-arctic winters; joyful abandon and deep melancholy engage in a continual tug-of-war in the Korean art.

The constant interplay, and frequent struggle, between modernity and tradition mean life in South Korea can sometimes be bewildering, even frustrating—for Koreans themselves, never mind foreign visitors. The country's turbulent past still manifests itself in troubling ways. As a former "Hermit Kingdom," closed to the outside world, it is still coming to terms with its place in a globalized age—and its expanding foreign population.

But development and change are virtually hardwired into the national psyche, and the government and the South Korean people continue to make significant strides in improving the legal and social climate for the country's expatriate residents. There's arguably never been a better time to enjoy the opportunities—and ability to astonish—that are South Korea's stock-in-trade. Arrive with an open mind, and be prepared to explore—and enjoy.

▶ WHAT I LOVE ABOUT SOUTH KOREA

- The culture and pastimes on tap. Most countries boast long-standing traditions, but South Koreans go out of the way to make theirs accessible to non-natives. Whether you're keen on meditation, martial arts, tea, calligraphy, traditional drumming, online gaming, or even starting a business, you'll find well-established support networks here that will help you explore your passion and make new friends in the process.

- The sense of discovery. Much of Korea has yet to be seen by visitors. Take to the roads and you're bound to be treated to the rare feeling of stumbling upon something truly new--well, to non-Koreans anyhow. You'll also find locals who go out of their way to be hospitable to the few foreign visitors that do turn up.

- A customary level of service that makes just about everywhere else seem uncivilized by comparison. Meals nearly always come with a bottomless array of accompaniments, pubs ply loyal customers with complimentary snacks, and purchases at markets, grocery stores, and even gas stations will often result in an extra treat or two being tossed into your shopping bag by a pleased proprietor trying to encourage you to come back. And all this is in a country where tipping is virtually unheard of.

- Autumn. The crisp temperatures, radiant foliage, and azure skies of late September to November are a delight, and perhaps the only time of year when foreign residents understand the national tendency to wax poetic over the seasons.

- The mountains, especially the way locals take to them each weekend in the thousands, usually decked out in carefully color-coordinated hiking gear and enough equipment to make an Everest climber envious. As many peaks are dotted with temples and ruins, exploring them is as much a cultural experience as an athletic one.

- *Ondol.* These networks of pipes carry hot water under every home, warming the floor (but nothing else) to near frying-pan temperatures, which keeps your mattress toasty even as the wind howls and the snow falls outside.

- A broadband infrastructure that's nothing short of phenomenal. The network is always on, dizzyingly fast, and comparatively cheap.

- The countryside. This is still a rural culture at heart, and outside the crowded cities there's an abundance of lovely scenery, fantastic produce, and some very friendly people.

- The socializing. South Koreans approach play the same way they approach work: very seriously. Nights out are usually lengthy affairs that include gut-busting communal meals, plenty of drinks, singing, and good cheer. And whoever is hosting is highly unlikely to let you pay a cent.

- Public transportation. It's completely possible to jump on a taxi, bus, and even a bullet train with complete confidence that you'll be ferried wherever you need to go on time and in comfort at a very low price.

WELCOME TO SOUTH KOREA

INTRODUCTION

A small rocky outpost in a volatile neighborhood, South Korea is situated among far larger powers that have traditionally received a lot more attention. But it's a far more complex place, geographically and socially, than its size and rather muted global profile suggest, and taking some time to learn about this ancient country and its people is one of the best preparations you can make for a successful life here.

Let's be blunt: Although it shares some traditions with neighboring China and Japan, and has more recently been a devoted student of Western economic and pop culture, South Korea is different—very different. It's one of the most ethnically homogeneous places on earth, but interracial marriage rates are skyrocketing. It prides itself on its technology yet clings to traditions that often appear outdated. It's technically in a state of war yet calmly goes about its business. People race to stuff themselves into crowded cities but get misty-eyed over mountains and autumn leaves. Non-Koreans may be viewed with sincere admiration, suspicion, or utter indifference, sometimes all on the same day.

So it's natural that this place can surprise, confuse, and yes, irritate foreign residents. But arming yourself with knowledge and a flexible attitude will better position you to enjoy the positive aspects of living here, and there are many. The locals can be almost overwhelmingly friendly and hospitable. Food and drink are generally a fantastically

good value. You'll soon get used to having just about any convenience you can think of at your doorstep 24 hours a day. And despite the occasional posturing from its isolated counterpart to the north, this is a very safe country with a rich history and landscape to explore. Arrive with an open mind, apply liberal doses of patience, and you're sure to soak up loads of exciting (and sometimes bizarre) experiences, form lasting friendships, and develop a great deal of respect and affection for a place that has managed to preserve its identity against almost overwhelming odds. Just remember that you're far more likely to be changed by South Korea than you are to change it.

The Lay of the Land

South Korea consists of the southern half of the Korean Peninsula, which juts out from China's northeast toward Japan's southern islands. Flanked by the Yellow Sea to the west and the Sea of Japan (or the East Sea, as the Koreans would prefer everyone called it) to the east, and bordered to the north by the tightly sealed Demilitarized Zone (DMZ) that separates it from North Korea, South Korea is effectively an island itself. With a total area of around 100,000 square kilometers (38,600 square miles), the country is about the same size as Hungary or Portugal. Some 70 percent of the peninsula is covered by mountains, which make for some inspiring scenery but also leave little land to cultivate or settle on; hence the population is largely clustered in a few dense cities.

The largest of these agglomerations is the capital, Seoul, which lies in the northwest just a few dozen kilometers from the inter-Korean border. Seoul is hemmed in by mountains and bisected by the broad Han River, which flows through the northern stretch of the country before emptying into the Yellow Sea near the west coast city of Incheon, a major port and industrial center.

Other major waterways include the Nakdong, which stretches from the country's center to the southeastern port of Busan, South Korea's second-largest city. With its seaside perch and many hilltop homes, Busan enjoys one of the country's more unique locations; it is the nexus of the southern industrial heartland, which also encompasses the nearby towns of Ulsan and Daegu. This region developed a reputation for grit and pollution in the rapid urbanization of the 1970s and 1980s, but tighter environmental regulations have improved things greatly. The northeastern province of Gangwon, by contrast, was and still is known for its green spaces and the alpine vistas of the Taebaek mountain range.

The lush coastal plains of the west serve as South Korea's agricultural center, a place characterized by wide expanses of rice fields, orchards, and tea plantations, as well as sizable cities such as Gwangju and Jeonju.

Much of the South Korean coast is rocky and windswept, though the southeast in particular boasts a few pleasant sand beaches. Scattered in the surrounding oceans are dozens of picturesque islands, the most renowned of which is Jeju, an oval-shaped outcrop 100 kilometers (60 miles) south of the peninsula that draws holidaymakers with its balmy temperatures and distinctive geological features, including a network of lava caves and cone-shaped Mount Halla, a dormant volcano that is the country's highest peak.

hills outside Yongin, Gyeonggi-do

COUNTRY DIVISIONS

South Korea is divided into nine provinces (*do*), one of which, Jeju-do, has special autonomous status. While provinces have directly elected their own governors since 1995, the power of provincial administrations remains limited, and most major policies are implemented at the national level. Provinces are further subdivided into counties (*gun*) and cities (*si*) as well as villages or townships. Distinct from the provinces, six major cities of more than one million people—Incheon, Busan, Daegu, Daejeon, Gwangju, and Ulsan—have been designated *gwangyeoksi* or metropolitan cities, meaning they are administered separately from the provinces around them. Towering above them all is the capital, Seoul, the only place in the country to bear the *teukbyeolsi* or special city title, which effectively elevates it to provincial level. Major cities are further split into districts (*gu*) which are made up of smaller neighborhoods (*dong*).

WEATHER

The country's four distinct seasons are a great source of pride to South Koreans, and while it is true that they can be differentiated easily, some last a lot longer than others. South Korea has a temperate climate characterized by sweltering humid summers and chilly winters—but the all-too-brief spring and autumn are just about perfect. Despite its limited size, there's a fair amount of climactic variation from one end of the country to the other, with the southeastern port of Busan five degrees warmer in winter on average than Seoul in the north.

Spring comes to the peninsula in mid-March to early April in a shower of blossoms and foliage, with temperatures rising rapidly until June, the onset of summer, when they average over 20°C (68°F). While the country isn't as vulnerable to flooding or typhoons as some of its southern neighbors, late June and early July are often ruled by the *jangma*, the local name for a seasonal monsoon that dumps most of the national annual rainfall in a few short weeks and pushes humidity up to 80 or 90 percent. August and most of September are also hot and fairly sticky, with temperatures peaking at around 30°C (86°F). By October the peninsula has dried out somewhat, and autumn is well under way; it is a glorious time of year when the air is crisp, the skies clear, and the mountains are swathed in vivid shades of gold and red. This usually lasts just a few weeks until mid-November, when temperatures drop and winter begins to take over. January and February are the coldest months, with strong winds, temperatures regularly dipping below 0°C (32°F), and snow not uncommon in northern areas or at higher elevations.

FLORA

South Korea's complex topography has made it home to a wide variety of plant life, with more than 4,000 plant species and around 1,000 varieties of trees. Most of the peninsula's mountains were thickly forested, but war, rapid population growth, and development took a severe toll on these resources, with virtually all natural tree cover stripped away by the 1960s. Since then the tide has turned somewhat. Four decades of ambitious planting programs and the designation of about 20 national parks restoring many of the country's hills to their previously green state—although very few old-growth forests remain.

Needle-leaved trees such as pine and fir are common, as are oak, ash, and sumac. Fruit trees, including apple, pear, and persimmon, are cultivated nationwide, and the warm shores of Jeju-do are home to more than 70 species of broad-leaved evergreens. Groves of bamboo, much loved in Asian cultures for its strength and resilience, are also found throughout the country. Among the more common varieties of flowers are roses, orchids, and chrysanthemums, and the brilliant pink cherry blossoms that herald the coming of spring. South Korea's national flower is the *mugunghwa* ("eternal flower") or rose of Sharon, a pink or lavender hibiscus renowned for both its beauty and ability to withstand harsh conditions. The flower blooms continuously from summer to autumn, and *mugunghwa* blossoms appear regularly on government and military signs and seals.

FAUNA

While South Korea was once a haven for a wide variety of large mammals, including tigers, bears, and deer, deforestation and hunting—often for animal parts used in traditional medicine—has drastically reduced the animal population over the last century or so. The tigers are gone, although a few are still believed to inhabit the remote mountain stretches of North Korea, and only small numbers of black bears, roe deer, and Siberian musk deer remain, mainly in national parks such as Jirisan and Seoraksan. Wild boars, wolves, foxes, rabbits, and squirrels are more common.

Due to its position on the migration route of the bird species that flee Manchuria and Siberia in the winter for the warmer climes of Southeast Asia, South Korea is something of a haven for bird-watchers. There are only around 50 varieties indigenous to the peninsula, but another 400 or so visit regularly. Residents include the black-billed magpie and Eurasian tree sparrow, while hooded cranes, vultures, geese, and falcons make regular stopovers at wetlands such as Suncheon Bay in the southwest.

Interestingly, arguably the most ecologically rich area on the peninsula is the DMZ dividing the Koreas. With any kind of human presence in the area—4 kilometers (2.5 miles) wide and 248 kilometers (155 miles) long—strictly forbidden for the last 50 years, animals and plants have been free to take it over, making it one of the world's best-kept swaths of temperate land. It is home to around 50 species of mammals, including the leopard and rare Asiatic black bear, as well as at least two endangered types of crane. While some environmentalists and officials have mulled transforming the Zone into a nature reserve when the two Koreas eventually reunite, its fate remains highly uncertain—like most post-reunification scenarios.

Social Climate

It's easy enough to view South Korea and the Korean people as a monolithic entity. The country has no significant minority groups, and the people share only a handful of surnames. The lives of most citizens are governed by a nearly identical series of experiences and milestones—intensive tutoring and do-or-die school entrance exams for children, mandatory military service for young men, marriage and children for young women—and most people strive to work at one of only half a dozen large companies that dominate virtually every segment of the economy. A relatively rigid hierarchy based heavily on the Confucian ideals of respect for authority and filial piety continues to dictate the relations between government and citizen, employer and employee, husband and wife, and parents and offspring.

With such a common pool of experiences to draw on, South Korean society, not surprisingly, is highly cohesive. People tend to harbor similar beliefs and outlooks, and are also quick to band together in the face of real or perceived slights or threats. This single-mindedness was a major contributor to the country's meteoric rise from the ashes of the Korean War, and it means there's little evidence in South Korea of the alienation or tensions that sometimes plague larger, more diverse nations. But it also means the country can be highly intolerant of different lifestyles or opinions, and tough on those on the lower tiers of the social ladder—namely women, young people, and the poor.

Look a bit closer and it becomes apparent that South Korea is a more varied place than initial impressions suggest—and that it is in a state of massive flux. Some of the country's divisions have existed for generations, such as those between the wealthy labor-shy nobility (*yangban*) of the past—now represented by the Seoul elite—and the working underclass. People from the heavily industrial Gyeongsang provinces of the southeast and their counterparts in the southwestern Jeolla provinces—historically a hotbed of insurgency and left-wing sentiment—have for centuries viewed each other with such unbridled suspicion that they'll still hesitate to marry someone or vote for a politician from the opposite side. And residents of Seoul have long looked on places outside the capital with a certain degree of disdain.

These frictions have been augmented by a host of new tensions that have accompanied South Korea's rush into modernization and increasing prosperity. Elderly people gripe that the young have let traditions slip, by, for example, daring to smoke in front of their seniors or neglecting to support their aging parents. The current generation, having no experience with war or hardship, can't understand why older folks are always harping on about the need for discipline and a modest lifestyle, or sticking to formalities that no one else seems to have time for. Fewer youth—and politicians—seem to be willing to toe the government's official line that the North Koreans are the enemy, directing their anger instead toward the larger powers they believe have conspired to keep the Koreas apart. An increasing number of young women are ignoring the wishes of their parents and getting married late, if at all, and having only one or two children when they do. Rather than rushing to the carmakers and shipbuilders that gave their fathers jobs for life, young men are pursuing riskier but more personally fulfilling careers in areas like animation and electronic gaming. As recently as 20 years ago, passports were issued only reluctantly, but trips abroad are no longer exclusively the domain of the rich and connected. More South Koreans are coming into contact with—and marrying—foreign nationals, challenging the country's heavily race-based identity. It's anybody's guess how these struggles will play out, but what does seem certain is that South Korea is on its way to becoming a very different place.

SOUTH KOREA AND FOREIGNERS

Unfortunately, much of South Korea's contact with foreign nations has been of the negative variety. Most of the peninsula's earliest exchanges were with neighboring China, which was alternately a rival and a "big brother" of sorts to which Korea's rulers paid tribute in return for China allowing their shifting territories to function quasi-independently. But not every empire was so amenable; from the 13th to the 20th centuries Korea endured a nearly constant barrage of attempted conquest, invaded and ruled on and off by the Mongols, Chinese, and Japanese. A move by the battle-weary nation to close its borders to the outside world in the early 19th century was repealed under pressure from trade-hungry Western powers. Some of the Korean wariness of outsiders turned out to be justified; most of the world stood by as Japan took over the peninsula in the early 20th century, and there was a similar lack of protest when World War II ended and newly independent Korea was divided into what were essentially U.S. and Russian client states. The Korean War of 1950-1953 involved massive numbers of foreign troops on both sides, and a significant U.S. military presence remains in South Korea to this day, proof to some of the two nations' stalwart alliance but a major source of resentment to others.

Since so much of South Korea's foreign relations have been characterized by strife, betrayal, and bloodshed, it is perhaps understandable that views on foreigners are somewhat mixed. On the one hand, South Koreans are immensely curious about other countries and highly appreciative—envious, even—of their assets and achievements. They desperately want foreigners to have a positive impression of their nation and are deeply concerned about the way the country is portrayed to the outside world. The result, desirable or not, is that expatriates tend to come in for plenty of special treatment. Nearly every foreign resident will have a story or two to tell about being offered assistance when they looked lost, strangers pressing umbrellas into their hands when they were stuck in the rain without one, or restaurant servers bringing them free extras. Any foreign resident showing a genuine interest in the country—by learning a few Korean phrases, for example, or enjoying the local cuisine—will find no shortage of delighted would-be guides, friends, or teachers. The former "Hermit Kingdom" also seems to have both feet squarely in the globalization camp: Learning English is a priority for most of the population, new foreign restaurants spring up in Seoul every weekend, and much fuss is now made about the need to build a more multicultural society.

On the other hand, a lot of old suspicions and resentments die hard. With some

ماشاءالله

© CRAIG D.C. LEWIS

An Islamic clothing shop in Seoul testifies to Korea's growing multiculturalism.

justification, given the country's turbulent history, South Koreans sometimes seem to feel the world is out to get them, or at least to hold the country back. Any perceived insult or injustice—Japan's claim to a set of islets that South Korea insists are its territory is a current example—can send the entire nation into what looks like paroxysms of rage, sparking angry outpourings in the media, protests on the streets, and other behavior that looks downright xenophobic. Foreign nationals will sometimes find their countries singled out for criticism or be roped into emotional debates about wrongs that the South Koreans view as grave but that they know little about. These sorts of exchanges tend to be most charged when they involve the two countries that have influenced South Korea's modern history the most—the United States and Japan, which are regularly cast as bullies in any bilateral issue or dispute. Foreigners may also find that locals react somewhat defensively to talk that (intentionally or not) denigrates South Korea or compares it to other places—a casual remark that one prefers Thai to Korean food, for example, may elicit stony silence.

Some foreign residents find the regular extolling of South Korea's supposedly unique characteristics or achievements, both by the media and South Koreans themselves, a tad tiring—and indeed, heartfelt dissertations on the nutritional value of the local staple kimchi or the "scientific" properties of the local script tend to lose their appeal when you've heard them dozens of times. Some also find that while South Koreans are big proponents of the "when in Rome" philosophy—meaning that foreigners should conform to local cultural norms—they seem to stick to the "Korean way" wherever they happen to be, and genuinely believe their culture is one that non-Koreans will never "get."

It's difficult to deny that Caucasians sometimes receive better treatment than visitors of other ethnic backgrounds, especially at the hands of officials or employers. This is mainly the result of a naive but still common view that "developed" nations have more to teach South Korea and that their people are therefore more deserving of respect.

Japanese and U.S. nationals may find some South Koreans are less than enamored of their home countries due to the checkered history Korea shares with both places, but this prejudice rarely manifests itself as anything serious. Basically South Koreans find *all* foreigners equally confusing and curious.

While it is not much of an issue in Seoul, foreigners in less cosmopolitan parts of the country may experience what some have termed the "freak" factor. Non-Koreans are a relatively rare sight in many places and can find themselves being stared at, trailed by schoolkids shouting greetings, or otherwise singled out for attention, which can be traumatic or a lot of fun, depending on the mood of the victim.

So how does one deal with these sometimes exasperating experiences? First, don't take it personally—most South Koreans have little trouble differentiating between individuals and their nation or government, and any negative sentiment directed toward where you happen to be from is almost never intended as a personal slight. Second, practice understanding—this is a country that has suffered at the hands of larger nations more than most, and it is still to some extent rebuilding its pride and identity. Third, remember that the South Koreans are relatively new to all this—overseas travel was rigorously controlled for years by dictatorial governments, and it's only in the last decade or so that the country has had a sizable contingent of nonmilitary foreign residents, so it's natural that some of the interactions between foreigners and locals can be a bit gaffe-prone and awkward. And finally, remember that despite what the government and some media outlets may lead you to believe, many South Koreans are highly conscious of their country's failings and discuss them exhaustively—it's simply a dialogue that, for reasons of language and pride, foreign nationals are rarely involved in. South Korea has become a much more diverse and tolerant place over the last few years, and it will become even more so as non-Koreans become a greater part of the social fabric.

Foreign Population in South Korea

The number of non-South Korean nationals in the country passed the 1.4 million landmark in 2012 and now accounts for almost 3 percent of the population. By far the largest minority group in the country is Chinese, representing almost half of non-South Koreans, followed by U.S. nationals, Vietnamese, and Filipinos. Many of the country's Chinese residents and a sizable number of expatriates from Western countries are of Korean descent. Most non-South Koreans are concentrated in a few districts of Seoul and surrounding Gyeonggi Province, but there are also significant numbers in the port of Busan and industrial centers like Ulsan.

Until relatively recently, most of the Western foreigners in South Korea were soldiers, missionaries, or English language teachers (and sometimes a combination of all three), but the country's growing wealth and internationalization has seen a spike in the number of foreign executives—increasingly in the employ of local firms—as well as independent foreign entrepreneurs, consultants, and restaurateurs.

A couple of local social issues have also helped spur a rapid expansion in the foreign population, legal and illegal, since the late 1990s. First, with domestic labor getting increasingly more expensive and fewer educated South Koreans willing to buckle down and do the backbreaking factory work that the nation's export success was originally built on, more and more local manufacturers are forced to look for their employees abroad, particularly elsewhere in Asia. Second, the country's widening gender disparity—men outnumber women by a significant percentage—and the reluctance of many South Korean women to marry into rural families has created a thriving business in the import of foreign brides, especially from China and Vietnam, whose people share many physical and cultural traits with the locals.

The ballooning number of foreign residents has forced the country to grapple with identity questions in a way that was unthinkable just a generation ago; it used to be that being South Korean meant having Korean blood, but now a lot of people aren't so sure. For the most part, South Koreans seem to be dealing with the changes in their country with characteristic speed and vigor. The national and local governments have steadily rolled out initiatives to make everyday life easier for non-Koreans, including on-demand translation services and one-stop offices that can help confused foreigners with everything from filling out tax returns to signing mobile-phone contracts. Crisis centers have been established to help foreign laborers facing legal or other issues, and many cities now run free classes to acquaint nonnatives with the Korean language and culture. Even issues such as discrimination are being addressed, in ad campaigns and television programs that highlight the issues faced by multiracial families. Biracial Koreans, in the past viewed as one of the more shameful legacies of the Korean War and consequent U.S. troop presence, are no longer unrepresented in the media or music scenes. South Korea is still a long way from being a cultural melting pot, but it has made some recent admirable advances for a place that for centuries defined itself by its stubborn resistance to all outside influence.

HISTORY, GOVERNMENT, AND ECONOMY

Every country has suffered its own misfortunes, but South Korea has been privy to more than most. Its roots stretch back thousands of years, but as a small and relatively reclusive state, it was constantly buffeted by larger forces, with its attempts at development and unification regularly interrupted by prolonged periods of war and conquest. The turmoil of the last century has left it a divided nation with a short history of stability and self-government. But while there's an ample amount of tragedy in South Korea's past, there's also plenty to inspire. It has steadfastly held on to its independence and cultural identity despite numerous attempts to quash both, transformed itself from a poverty-stricken, largely agrarian society into a prosperous exporter of cutting-edge technology in a couple of generations, and traded heavy-handed dictatorships for a functioning (if sometimes messy) democracy with a healthy respect for human rights and a free press.

A basic understanding of how this astonishing metamorphosis took place, and the despair and extensive struggle on which modern-day South Korea has been built, will prove invaluable in any attempt to figure out some of the country's cultural quirks or

why Koreans act the way they do. This is one place where some knowledge of history may very well improve your quality of life, for there are few nations where history has as direct a bearing on the present.

History

PREHISTORY AND THE THREE KINGDOMS PERIOD

Korean legend has it that the nation was founded 5,000 years ago by the off-spring of a divinely assisted tiger and a bear, but most anthropologists tend to disagree. Instead they trace the country's origins to a loosely associated assortment of town-states dotted throughout the present-day Korean peninsula and Manchuria and populated by the descendants of wandering Siberian, Manchu, and Mongol tribes that developed into a relatively unified empire between 700 and 400 BC Gojoseon, as the first Korean quasi-state was known, was a force to be reckoned with, regularly provoking conflicts with the feudal states of northeastern China. It was known to the Chinese as the land of "barbarians of the east." Unfortunately it eventually took on one battle too many and lost most of its northern territory to Han China, which basically confined the state to the peninsula and hastened its disintegration.

From Gojoseon's demise, several independent states with clearly defined borders and ruling dynasties sprang up. The three that came to dominate the peninsula by the 1st century AD were Goguryeo, which spanned the northern section of the peninsula and parts of Manchuria; Baekje, which occupied much of the south and west; and Silla in the east. The Three Kingdoms Period, as the era is known, was a relatively stable time that saw the rapid proliferation of laws, literature, and religion, much of it imported from neighboring China. The three states pursued independent strategies with regard to their neighbors, with Goguryeo regularly skirmishing

a depiction of a mythological tiger-like guardian, Seoul

© ALEXANDER TROFIMOV/123RF.COM

with China, Baekje establishing ties with the Japanese, and Silla grooming a strong army to fend off the other two states and marauding Japanese invaders.

In the end it was Silla's approach that seemed to win out; by the late 7th century it had sealed an alliance with Tang-Dynasty China and easily overran its two competitors. When its Tang partners turned on Silla in an effort to seize the entire peninsula for themselves (probably their plan from the beginning), Silla warriors managed to press them back into Manchuria. While Silla failed to win all of Goguryeo's lands from the Chinese, it did have the rest of the peninsula under its control, and after the Tang Dynasty formally recognized Silla's claim to the territory it held in the early 8th century, a period of relative tranquility and rapid cultural flowering began in Korea's first genuinely united kingdom.

BIRTH OF A MODERN STATE

The unification of the peninsula under the Silla Dynasty, which lasted until around AD 900, was a cultural and political golden age in which the seeds of a genuinely national consciousness were planted. Taking a lesson from its former Chinese allies, the Silla monarchy established a fairly rigid aristocracy-led bureaucracy, a system of taxation, and a nationwide military. Buddhism became the new state's official religion, resulting in a flurry of temple-building and contributing to the development of exquisite art and ceramics. The kingdom was internationally engaged, regularly passing relics and artistic techniques on to Japan and trading with envoys from the Muslim world.

Unfortunately the peace was short-lived; peasant revolts sparked by the ruling classes' growing corruption made Silla an easy target for a takeover by the remnants of the northern Goguryeo kingdom, which seized power over the peninsula in AD 935. The Goryeo Dynasty, as it was renamed, ushered in another couple of centuries of calm in which ties with China were improved and Silla's ruling aristocrats were replaced with civil servants who attained their positions through a rigorous system of examinations. The government entrenched this system throughout the country by appointing bureaucrats to oversee regional capitals and creating a national education system. The stability that resulted allowed Goryeo academics and artisans to concentrate on achievements such as celadon pottery and metal movable-type printing. When trouble did come, it was from external forces—in 1231 the Mongols overran Goryeo as part of a wider conquest of China and transformed it into a vassal state. By the 14th century Goryeo had regained some degree of independence, but it never recovered its past glory. Its rulers were overthrown in the 1390s by a renowned general, Yi Seong-gye, who disagreed with an order to strike against Mongol forces in China.

Yi's ascension to the throne in 1392 ushered in the Joseon Dynasty, which endured until the early 20th century. During this time the country as it exists today began to take shape, with the capital relocated to present-day Seoul and provincial boundaries established that remain largely untouched. Confucianism displaced Buddhism as the state religion and resulted in a rigid social hierarchy and deference to authority that is still visible to some extent today. In the mid-15th century, Sejong, considered the greatest of Korea's kings, developed and promulgated the hangul script. This was a significant achievement that saw literacy skyrocket as people were no longer required to learn complex Chinese characters, the only writing system Korea had had up to that time, to express themselves.

monument to King Sejong, who is credited with creating hangul

The Joseon Dynasty was a time of strife as well as successes. In the late 16th century Korea suffered a massive Japanese invasion that saw many of its cities occupied and plundered, with many of its greatest cultural properties looted or destroyed. Assistance from China and Korea's unmatched naval skill eventually managed to send the Japanese home, but those battles were swiftly followed by attacks from the Manchu tribes, who were on their way to establishing control over China. The near-continuous battering convinced Korea that the outside world was a nasty place, and prompted it to shut its borders nearly completely for much of the 17th to 19th centuries, a time when it earned the "Hermit Kingdom" nickname. In 1875, Japanese pressure obligated Korea to open some ports to Japanese vessels, and it signed its first diplomatic treaty with the United States a few years later.

THE JAPANESE OCCUPATION

The last years of the 19th century saw a larger foreign presence on the Korean peninsula, with China, Russia, and Japan vying for influence, and the hasty introduction of modern infrastructure such as rail lines as well as electricity and hospitals in major cities. Japan's decisive defeat of Russia in the brief (1904-1905) Russo-Japanese War quickly established it as the dominant power in the region and gave it the confidence to force Joseon's then-ruler, King Kojong, to sign a treaty that effectively gave Japan control of the country. In 1910 the Japanese annexed Korea outright.

Japan's nearly four-decade-long occupation of the peninsula haunts Koreans to this day. It could be argued that the rapid modernization overseen by the Japanese paved the way for South Korea's later industrial success, but whatever incidental benefits it brought, Japanese rule was a clear attempt to crush the country and its people. Koreans were forced to adopt Japanese names and the Shinto religion; the teaching and even speaking of Korean were prohibited. Thousands of Koreans were roped into Japan's World War II effort as soldiers, laborers, or sex slaves. The peninsula was ruthlessly stripped of its resources, and any outbreaks of dissent quickly evoked a violent response.

THE KOREAN WAR AND POSTWAR DIVISION

Japan's defeat in World War II brought its rule over Korea to an end, but not the freedom so many Koreans were craving. Seeing the Koreans as insufficiently prepared for self-government, the United States and Russia agreed to split the country at the 38th parallel, with the United States overseeing the withdrawal of Japanese troops and preparations for elections south of the line and Russia doing the same in the north. This division quickly became entrenched, and in 1948 the northern half declined to participate in the elections held in the south that led to the creation of the Republic of Korea, soon recognized by the United Nations as Korea's sole legitimate government. Immediately after the establishment of the republic, the North Koreans set up their own Soviet-modeled government in Pyongyang.

While there's still some debate over how the Korean War (1950-1953) broke out, most historians point the finger at a June 1950 breach of the 38th parallel by North Korean troops. At this point they were far better armed and equipped than their South

BLUFFING AND BOMBS

If one were to believe the bellicose rhetoric that pours out of North Korea, the Korean Peninsula is teetering constantly on the brink of war. Dire threats are de rigueur for the North's state media, which regularly promises to reduce the South to a "sea of fire" and overthrow its government of "puppets" and "stooges." Worse, this blustering is sometimes punctuated by real action, such as North Korea's shelling of an island off South Korea's west coast in late 2010, which drove tensions to heights not seen since the Korean War. The death of North Korean leader Kim Jong-il in 2011 and the transfer of power to his young son, Kim Jong-un, added to worries about stability in the North and what it may do next. Some have justifiable concerns about living next to such a prickly neighbor, especially with South Korea's largest city and nearly half the population less than an hour's drive from the border.

Predicting the moves of a country as seemingly irrational as North Korea is a job for experts and analysts, and even they regularly get it wrong. Nonetheless, pretty much everyone is in agreement that the North's posturing is more bark than bite, calculated at squeezing concessions out of its negotiating partners. The sad fact is that stripped of all credibility, genuine allies, or diplomatic clout, periodic tantrums are about the only tactic the North has left at its disposal.

With around two million troops clustered around the border (including almost 30,000 U.S. troops in South Korea), the possibility of a full-scale conflict can never be completely ruled out, but it's worth remembering in the five decades since the Korean War not once has there been a return to serious conflict, even after other apparent tipping points like a North Korean bomb attack in Myanmar in 1983 that killed much of South Korea's cabinet or fatal naval clashes in the West Sea in 2002. The North has frequently demonstrated a healthy pragmatic streak, and many believe its ruling regime would be highly unlikely to hasten its own demise by pitting an aging army against superior opposing forces.

Whether the security situation on the peninsula worries you or not, be sure to register with your embassy when you arrive in South Korea. Many embassies make efforts to keep their nationals briefed on any major developments and to advise on courses of action or even arrange evacuation in the event of serious trouble. After that, take your cue from the locals, whom you'll soon notice rarely get worked up about acts by their northern neighbor that have the rest of the world wringing its hands.

Korean counterparts, and they pushed to the southern stretches of the peninsula in a few weeks. Led by the United States, the UN quickly stepped in to help South Korea. A bold move by the U.S. Army to launch an invasion north of the main mass of North Korean troops, at the beaches of Incheon, helped it quickly seize North Korean territory nearly all the way to the Chinese border, prompting China to send its own troops in to help the North Koreans drive the Americans back. The fighting reached a stalemate roughly around the 38th parallel, where it had all begun, and in 1953 the North Koreans, Chinese, and UN representatives (but not South Korea) signed an armistice agreement ending hostilities and making the 38th parallel a de facto border. The move separated thousands of families, and it remains one of the more tragic outcomes of the Cold War. While both Koreas claim to aspire to reunification, infrequent talks on the issue have made little progress.

TRANSITION TO DEMOCRACY AND THE CONTEMPORARY ERA

South Korea's first president, Syngman Rhee, was an autocratic figure who pursued a policy of close relations with the United States, which maintained a military presence in the country after the war. He dealt ruthlessly with any perceived challenges or expressions of discontent, arresting dissidents and crushing leftist and student uprisings, which the government viewed as tantamount to support for North Korea. By 1960, outrage at Rhee's heavy-handedness had boiled over, and the violent suppression of a protest in the port town of Masan sparked nationwide riots that eventually forced Rhee to resign and flee into exile in the United States.

New elections propelled Rhee's former foes into power. The Democratic Party took a more relaxed view of student and union activities and, in response to public demand, launched a purge of police and military officials involved in crackdowns under the Rhee administration. But that proved too much for some military officers, who in 1961 launched a coup led by major general Park Chung-hee. There was little resistance to the overthrow of the civilian administration, which was consumed with infighting and had done little to address the country's dire poverty. By contrast, Park, who won elections staged in 1963, made the economy and national development his main priority. Park continued South Korea's tradition of dictatorial leadership and has a controversial legacy, but he is generally regarded as the father of Korean industry. The government provided billions of dollars in support to export businesses, infrastructure, and factories, prompting a massive shift in the population from the countryside to major cities and from farming to activities like mining and manufacturing.

Park survived protests, threats to his rule, and even botched attempts on his life by North Korean agents, but he was assassinated in 1979 by his own chief of intelligence. Park's death saw an outpouring of student and labor activism as many South Koreans wanted an end to authoritarian government, but martial law was quickly declared by another senior army officer, Chun Doo-hwan, who arrested opposition politicians and oversaw the military response to a popular uprising in the city of Gwangju in 1980 that killed hundreds.

South Korea would have to wait until 1992 for a genuinely civilian president. A series of elections and persistent resistance had by that time made the army's involvement in politics unsustainable. The country's new leader, former opposition politician

KOREA'S EXPAT RESISTERS

South Koreans and foreign residents alike are often unaware that Korea has produced a few notable expatriate communities of its own, at least a couple of which have exerted a profound influence on the country's history.

In 1919, after nearly a decade of Japanese rule over the Korean Peninsula, inspired by a swelling resistance movement in Seoul, a core group of dissenters established a Korean government in exile in Shanghai, China, which later moved inland to Chongqing. While it was not recognized by any major powers, it still proved itself a substantial force, establishing a "liberation army" that fought beside the Allies against Japanese troops in World War II. Syngman Rhee, its first president, later became the first leader of postwar South Korea, and the South Korean constitution recognizes the provisional government as the nation's legitimate regime for the Japanese colonial period.

Neighboring Japan has a sizable Korean population, many descendants of conscript laborers or migrants who settled there in the first half of the 20th century. One of the first—and quickly one of the most notorious—groups formed to protect the interests of Korean immigrants in what was then a fairly hostile environment was the General Association of Korean Residents in Japan, commonly known by its Korean-language abbreviation Chongryon, which took shape in the aftermath of the Korean War.

Made up largely of citizens of the prewar united Korea who did not elect to take up South Korean nationality—the only Korean government Japan would recognize—the organization had socialist leanings and quickly allied itself with North Korea, launching a campaign to persuade Korean immigrants to restart their lives in the "workers' paradise." Nearly 90,000 followed the call, some bringing Japanese spouses, but many met only hardship, starvation, and if they voiced discontent with the situation, imprisonment.

Although it has branches throughout Japan that provide services such as employment assistance and legal advice to Korean residents, and runs schools and banks, Chongryon is much more than a community organization. With Pyongyang and Tokyo maintaining no official ties, the group functions as a sort of de facto North Korean embassy, and contributions from its members and businesses are a major source of cash for the reclusive state.

Unfortunately for North Korea, Chongryon's influence seems to be on the wane. The group's core message of Koreans retaining their independence and identity has started to ring hollow with young Koreans assimilating relatively easily into a more accepting Japanese mainstream, and fewer parents want to send their children through Chongryon's schools, which base their curricula on North Korea's rigid state ideology. Mindan, another ethnic Korean association with ties to South Korea, now has a higher portion of Japan's Korean population as members.

Kim Young-sam, launched legal actions against many of its former military rulers and took some tentative steps to reach out to North Korea and its remaining communist allies. These efforts continued under his successor, Kim Dae-jung, once condemned to death by the Chun administration, who steered the country through the 1997-1998 Asian economic crisis and held a historic summit with his North Korean counterpart in 2000 that earned him the Nobel Peace Prize. Kim Dae-jung was followed by Roh Moo-hyun, a former labor lawyer who often found himself at odds with the United States in his efforts to improve relations with North Korea further.

Public fatigue with (relatively) left-wing presidents led to the election of former tycoon Lee Myung-bak in 2007, who won office on pledges for a business-friendly administration that would revitalize the economy. Lee's admirers credit him with keeping the country on a relatively even keel throughout the 2008-2009 global financial crisis and boosting South Korea's international profile by hosting events like the G20 summit of world leaders in 2010. He also did much to restore South Korea's frayed ties with Washington, not least finalizing a free trade pact with the United States that came into effect in 2012. Others, however, charge him with coddling big business and adopting an overly hard-line stance on North Korea that has left inter-Korean relations at their frostiest in decades. In December 2012, voters took the landmark step of electing the country's first female president, Park Geun-hye (daughter of the assassinated General Park). Park is also a conservative, but has pledged to build a more caring, inclusive society, and while some attribute her victory to nostalgia for her father, it's a further sign that a democratic political culture is now firmly entrenched.

Government

South Korea is a constitutional democracy, but as pundits have frequently commented, it is a democracy with Korean characteristics. Traces of the traditional Confucian view that a nation's leader wields the "mandate of heaven" and is not to be questioned endure, particularly within the political establishment, meaning presidents tend to be "strongmen" and political parties relatively weak, divided, and constantly shifting. Although great strides have been made in the battle against corruption, political patronage remains common, and the ties between politicians and big businesses are still robust. The country's massive civil service is a largely closed shop that women and the disadvantaged still struggle to find their way into.

Thankfully, arrayed against this is a fairly cynical and demanding public that has a long history of protesting against—and ousting—governments seen as indifferent, bullying, or crooked. The citizenry's readiness to organize and take to the streets, and the fact that elections are a genuine test, tend to keep politicians' more excessive instincts in check.

GOVERNMENT STRUCTURE

The South Korean government is outlined by the country's constitution, revised several times since 1948, and divided into executive, legislative, and judicial branches. Political power is largely concentrated in the executive branch, headed by the president, who is directly elected for a single five-year term with no possibility of reelection. The president is the commander in chief of the armed forces and has an impressive list of powers, including appointing a prime minister who serves as the president's chief adviser and takes control of the country if the president is unable to govern. The president can also pick the heads of all major ministries, declare war or martial law, grant amnesties, and overrule some of the decisions of the National Assembly.

A state council comprising the president, prime minister, and chiefs of major ministries such as foreign affairs and trade, economy, and unification is charged with drafting core policies and approving important budgetary or military proposals. The

© CRAIG D.C. LEWIS

military recruits in Seoul

council and ministries are supplemented by "independent" agencies, many of which actually report to the ministries or the president himself. These include the anticorruption, tax, intelligence, and science and technology bodies.

The legislative branch of government is represented by South Korea's National Assembly, which is located in Seoul and has 300 members currently representing four main political parties, along with a handful of independents. Most are elected from single-member constituencies around the country in general elections that take place every four years. The assembly has steadily gained strength in the last decade and now has the right to nix some of the prime minister's appointments and to investigate alleged incidents of government malfeasance. It is responsible for debating government budgets and new or amended legislation.

The country's judicial branch is led by the Constitutional Court, which oversees impeachments or cases involving the review of the constitution, and the Supreme Court, the final avenue of appeal in South Korean legal cases. The selection of justices is split among the president, National Assembly, and Supreme Court chief justice, but the president has the most say in the matter.

At the local level, governors and assemblies are directly elected for provinces, major cities, and districts, but they enjoy little autonomy, with the national government firmly in charge of most judicial, educational, and security functions.

POPULAR PERCEPTIONS OF GOVERNMENT

In a couple of words, popular perceptions of the government are not good. Generations of harsh or ineffectual leaders, more than a few of whom helped themselves to the national coffers, have convinced many South Koreans that the government is not a force to be trusted. The mass media is happy to play to these perceptions with stories of brawling assembly members and official malfeasance. Much like in other countries, authorities are regularly pilloried for selling out to foreign or business interests,

The Central Government Complex in Seoul is home to several government agencies.

sometimes culminating in now largely Internet-based campaigns that organize street demonstrations or other forms of action.

At the same time, the government tends to be the first place people turn in times of economic or social upheaval. When the country is facing real or perceived external threats, such as the financial crisis and subsequent International Monetary Fund bailout of 1997, South Koreans are quick to rally around their leaders, and much of the traditional mistrust of authority subsides.

THE GOVERNMENT AND EXPATRIATES

South Korean authorities, especially outside Seoul, are generally not accustomed to dealing with expatriates, but they are learning quickly. A dearth of foreign-language services in important agencies such as immigration and taxation has been addressed with the introduction of forms, websites, and help lines for non-Koreans, although there are still some problem spots.

For most expats, contact with the government is minimal and handled largely through their employers. Those who have to deal with South Korean officialdom directly generally find civil servants polite and efficient enough, although they tend to be sticklers for the rules. Bureaucratic corruption undoubtedly still exists, but blatant demands for under-the-table payments to process or expedite paperwork are largely a thing of the past.

Some authorities, particularly the police, have been criticized by the foreign community for an alleged tendency to side with locals in any Korean-foreigner dispute. Whether this is the result of communication issues or genuine prejudice is difficult to say, but it is another reason to avoid conflicts with locals whenever possible, and to have a good Korean friend or two who may be able to intervene on your behalf in case of an incident.

Economy

South Korea's breakneck transition from agricultural backwater to export powerhouse is sometimes referred to as the "Miracle on the Han River," and indeed it looks like a supernatural achievement. In the 1960s, when leader Park Chung-hee kick-started the country's industrialization, it had a per capita income of less than US$100 per year, shoddier infrastructure than its northern counterpart, and ranked beside Africa's poorest nations on most development indexes. A couple of generations later, per capita income has shot up to around US$30,000, and South Korea is the fourth-largest economy in Asia and the 13th largest in the world, a major global builder of infrastructure and a producer of some of the most advanced and in-demand products on the international high-tech market.

The "miracle" was achieved thanks to a cozy relationship between government and big business, particularly for the *chaebol* or conglomerates that still dominate most segments of the economy, as well as an enviable national work ethic. None of this is to imply South Korea didn't face adversity on its meteoric rise—in 1997 the Asian economic crisis sparked a mass capital exodus that devastated the country's currency and foreign reserves, forcing it to turn to the IMF and embark on a restructuring program that is still the source of some resentment toward foreign business interests. The country is now grappling with slowing global growth as well as increased competition from lower-cost producers, especially China. But given its past achievements, it is clearly not a nation to count out.

EXPORTS AND MAIN INDUSTRIES

Exports have been at the center of the government's economic strategy since the 1960s and now account for around half of the economy. The country's companies have shed their collective image as "copycat" makers of relatively low-end vehicles and electronic products and are widely recognized as leaders in their fields.

Major exporters include Hyundai Motor Group, the world's fifth-largest carmaker; Samsung Electronics, the number one producer of memory chips and arguably the only serious contender with Apple in the global smartphone market; and LG, a manufacturer of household appliances and flat-panel TVs.

South Korea has also been the global leader in the shipbuilding sector since wresting that title from Japan a few years ago, and it is now home to the world's top three shipyards. Other key industries include steel, dominated by producer POSCO, and construction, with companies such as Hyundai Engineering and Construction regularly competing for major building projects elsewhere in Asia and the Middle East.

FOOD AND AGRICULTURE

Once the main form of economic activity, agriculture's share of the economy has waned, and it now accounts for a mere 3 percent or so of gross domestic product. That said, the industry still carries enormous symbolic significance, and the government has erected barriers to some food imports and has subsidized farms heavily to keep them alive as more young people flee the land for life in the cities.

South Korea is virtually self-sufficient in terms of rice production. It also raises and even exports a limited amount of domestic produce, including cattle, apples, pears, chilies, cabbages, and ginseng. The country additionally exports some prepared food-stuffs for sale abroad, such as instant noodles, snacks, teas and wines.

INTANGIBLE ASSETS

Government and private-sector efforts to diversify South Korea's manufacturing-dependent economy have borne some fruit. Its top-notch broadband infrastructure and tech-savvy young population have made the country an important production site and test bed for animation and online gaming, which, by some accounts, up to a third of the population engages in regularly. The explosive popularity of smartphones has also seen a surge in the mobile app development industry, and a few homegrown apps, such as messaging service KakaoTalk, have made a splash internationally.

Perhaps the biggest (and largely unexpected) triumph has been the rapid spread of South Korean pop culture. Long admired in Asia, thanks in no small part to the power of social media, South Korean films, TV serials, and music have recently garnered a truly global fan base, with "K-pop" concerts and flash mobs now a semi-regular fixture in Europe and North America. This has further bolstered the country's already growing tourism industry as eager fans flock to South Korea to check out video and film sets or their favorite stars' haunts.

THE ECONOMY AND FOREIGNERS

More than a few foreign companies have learned the hard way that the economic realm is where South Korea's nationalist instincts most regularly assert themselves. While successive governments have begun to chip away at them, plenty of seemingly arbitrary rules exist that limit or bar foreign participation in key industries. One example was a (since repealed) requirement that all mobile phones sold in the country use a home-grown standard, which significantly delayed the debut of Apple's iPhone in the South Korean market—in order, some cynics whispered, to give Samsung time to catch up.

Foreign businesses also often find themselves scrutinized more carefully than their local partners by the government, the media, and the public. Attempts to take over or "restructure" local companies are frequently viewed with suspicion—as U.S. private equity firm Lone Star found out, after having to extricate itself from the country after buying, then moving to profit from the sale of, Korea's main foreign exchange bank, a struggle that lasted years. Other market entrants have had difficulty dealing with the country's frequently activist unions.

That being said, plenty of foreign companies are highly successful in South Korea—the proliferation of fast-food chains alone is evidence of that—and Koreans can be highly adaptable when it comes to new products or new ways of doing business. The companies that have flourished here have found a sensitive public relations strategy and a little cultural awareness go a long way.

PEOPLE AND CULTURE

South Korean culture can be tough for the outsider to grapple with. It's heavily influenced by the country's early contact with China and Japan but contains elements that its Asian neighbors would find almost unrecognizable, shaped by the nation's very unique experiences with shamanism and subjugation and its relentless recent march to prosperity.

On the surface it can be a very space-age, highly Westernized place—there are few countries that are better wired or where the Internet and next-generation mobile phones have as prominent a role in everyday life and social debate. South Koreans, especially the young, seem to have wholeheartedly embraced most of the trappings of globalization, including lattes, hot dogs, hip-hop, and designer clothing labels. Take away the signs in hangul script and parts of Seoul and other big cities could easily be mistaken for New York, Berlin, or Calgary.

But newcomers shouldn't be fooled by appearances. The Koreans adopt plenty of the trappings of other cultures but are staunchly determined to preserve and pass on their own. Many of the unspoken rules that continue to govern relations between managers and employees, husbands and wives, and Koreans and the rest of the world remain largely unchanged from centuries ago. The lives of many continue to be swayed

by traditions, beliefs, and rituals some foreign residents find outdated, puzzling, and even offensive.

To add to the disorientation, some aspects of Korean culture are undergoing profound and rapid change as the country completes its transition to affluent democracy and boosts its engagement with the outside world. The local ways may occasionally confuse, but thankfully frankness, good humor, and world-beating hospitality are also common Korean traits, and a little politeness never fails to go a long way.

Ethnicity and Class

Exactly where the Koreans came from and who they are still a matter of some debate, but most experts agree that the people are descended from Altaic tribes who migrated from the Lake Baikal area in Siberia, with ethnic links to the Mongolians, Turks, and Chinese. South Korea is highly homogenous and has no sizable ethnic minorities beyond a small population of current or former Chinese nationals, many of whom are of Korean descent and so integrated that they're largely invisible.

Only recently has there been a sharp rise in interracial marriages, mostly in rural communities where there's a surplus of relatively poor farmers but a shortage of local women for them to settle down with. International marriages now account for around 10 percent of the total, with most foreign brides and grooms coming from other Asian nations such as China, Japan, Vietnam, and the Philippines.

CLASS

During the Joseon Dynasty, Korea was a highly class-conscious and inequitable place, with the royal family and *yangban* nobles enjoying lives of leisure on the backs of those not fortunate enough to be part of the bureaucracy. But the ensuing decades of Japanese colonization and war all but wiped out the former gentry and their landholdings, and by the time modern South Korea took shape, having noble lineage no longer commanded much respect. Most South Koreans can still trace their families back for generations and take some pride in doing so, but with the exception of a few famous clans—the Pyeongsan Shins, for example—having *yangban* blood doesn't confer any special advantages or even raise any eyebrows.

If anyone has replaced the *yangban,* it is the families who control the country's great *chaebol* or conglomerates and therefore a massive chunk of the nation's wealth. Their descendants regularly pop up in top schools (if they're not packed off to study abroad) and the pricey boutiques of Seoul's Apgujeong district. Concerns about inequality, particularly in terms of educational and job opportunities, have snowballed in recent years, exacerbated by economic uncertainty and the government's relatively low social spending.

KOREAN SURNAMES

Korean family names provide a good indication of just how homogenous the country is. Around half the population shares one of the three most common surnames—Kim, Lee, and Park—and there are only about 250 surnames in use. The vast majority of surnames are derived from Chinese characters that are also common last names in China; this is, however, seen as a result of past Korean leaders adopting and distributing Chinese-style names, rather than evidence of blood relations.

Within each surname group there are dozens of different clans or roots (*bon*), each usually associated with a particular town or geographic area. Women generally keep their family names after marriage, but any children will adopt the father's.

REGIONAL RIVALRIES

Standardized education and the development of a national identity have done much to blunt regional enmities in South Korea, but they still exist. The most pronounced are those between the people of the east (Gyeongsang) and southwest (Jeolla) areas, a division that has existed in one form or another since the Three Kingdoms Period more than a millennium ago. In recent decades Gyeongsang has developed a reputation for being an industrious, relatively wealthy place, home to many of the nation's leaders and some of its most powerful corporations. Largely agricultural Jeolla, on the other hand, was regularly dismissed as poor and backward, a breeding ground for student radicals and communist sympathizers. These stereotypes and interregional resentment were often nurtured by politicians, and they sometimes flared into open conflict, such as an uprising in Gwangju in 1980 that saw citizens wrest control of the city from the central government. Jeju Island has also traditionally regarded itself as distinct from the mainland and was a hotbed of dissent when the nation was newly formed.

Regional tensions are now largely confined to the odd off-color joke, however, and while they may creep into some South Koreans' hiring or marital decisions, they are unlikely to present a problem or even be apparent to most expatriates.

Customs and Etiquette

Korean etiquette is a thorny issue for many foreign residents, mainly because initially there seems to be a distinct lack of it. Behavior that would be seen as rude or inconsiderate in most Western countries—someone barging their way into an elevator before anyone's had a chance to get off, talking loudly on their mobile phone in an enclosed space, or jumping ahead of other people in a queue—is not uncommon here, and has been known to ruin many an expatriate's day. While these kinds of experiences can never be welcomed, it can help to understand some of the thinking (or lack thereof) that lies behind them.

In a sense, the basic Korean rules of conduct could almost be viewed as opposite to the Western ones. North Americans and Europeans are generally reserved and self-conscious around strangers but loosen up a bit in the presence of family or friends. For Koreans, relationships are everything—and if you don't have a relationship of some kind with someone, whether through family, work, school, or marriage, they're not worthy of much consideration. Koreans therefore tend to give little thought to how they treat or are perceived by strangers, but they are incredibly conscientious, even formal, around their friends and relatives.

There are also cultural factors at play. Confucian tradition gives the aged status

LOST IN TRANSLATION

There are a few concepts in Korean that can't be translated easily into other languages and are a struggle for nonnative speakers to get a grip on. Two just happen to be vital aspects of the national identity, so it's worth trying to understand them.

The first, *han*, is an emotional state that is unique (or so it is believed) to Koreans and that underpins a lot of the culture and daily interaction. It is roughly defined as a mix of profound sorrow and simmering resentment over the suffering and injustice that everyday life sometimes piles on people, and which has characterized so much of Korea's history.

This might sound like a horribly morbid feeling, but it's somewhat bittersweet, tempered by a healthy stoicism and grim determination to endure any misfortune. *Han* is evident in much of Korea's art, especially its poetry, music, and film, where themes of despair and retribution often dominate. It's also what many say lies behind the very open displays of emotion sometimes seen on South Korea's streets.

The second, *jeong*, refers to a form of trust or enduring bond developed over time between individuals—parents and their children, boss and employee, friends—and among Koreans collectively. People who share *jeong* will demonstrate a certain degree of loyalty and consideration to one another and make sacrifices for their partners in *jeong* if necessary. Acts of kindness or honesty are often explained by saying the person who performs them "has *jeong*."

As with *han*, there isn't a genuine English equivalent for the word; *jeong* has elements of love and affection but possesses a far weightier sense of obligation and is not always entirely positive: a wife might suffer the abuse of a husband in silence, for example, due to the *jeong* the two share.

Interestingly *jeong* isn't an exclusively Korean concept. The word is derived from a Chinese character that's also used to denote similar ideas in China and Japan, though both places apparently put less stock in *jeong* as a whole.

above just about everyone else, and you'll notice a lot of the more "assertive" behavior comes from older people, especially older men, who may see taking that seat on the subway or getting served before anyone else as their natural right. Memories of postwar scarcity, as well as a highly competitive society, have created what the locals call a *ppali ppali* (literally, "hurry, hurry," or "me first") culture in which people sometimes feel they have no choice but to act selfishly to get what they need.

But of course the South Koreans do adhere to rules of etiquette, and a basic knowledge of these will be of considerable help to any non-Korean looking to establish friendships or do business here. The barrage of personal questions (Where do you work? How old are you? Are you married?) that often accompanies an introduction is not meant to be intrusive; it's simply a means to establish where you rank on the social scale and how you should be treated. Bowing does not carry the same weight it does in, say, Japan, but a polite nod of the head in greeting or saying good-bye, particularly to people who are older or outrank you at work, is always appreciated. Gifts and business cards should always be given and received with both hands, and studied carefully before being put gently aside—never in a pocket or bag. Asking someone if they've eaten is a polite greeting or expression of concern; by no means is it an invitation to lunch. Compliments are frequently extended and just as often politely rejected by the intended recipient.

Invitations or requests, particularly from superiors, are rarely refused outright. There are a host of subtle nuances and unwritten regulations that govern the full spectrum of Korean interaction, but as a foreigner you're partially exempt, and there's no need to worry about mastering all of them. Be humble, smile a lot, don't do anything you wouldn't do at home, and you should be just fine.

DINING CUSTOMS

Few venues can be as much of a cultural minefield as the dinner table, and even though many South Korean dinners are raucous alcohol-fueled affairs, there are still norms to be observed. With the exception of quick lunches, nearly every meal is communal; soups and servings of meat are designed to be shared by all, and groups of diners will quite happily tuck into the same dishes with no apparent hygiene worries. Meals are usually accompanied by a complimentary cast of side dishes (*panchan*)—seasoned or pickled vegetables, seaweed, eggs, and the like—that can be refilled free of charge. Steel chopsticks and spoons are the standard cutlery, but most restaurants will be able to provide forks on request. People will usually wait for the oldest or most senior person at the table to begin eating before digging in themselves; this is also usually the person who will be paying, as splitting the bill remains a relatively new (and somewhat distasteful) concept in South Korea.

In the past, meals were for nourishment and not social occasions, and to this day many older people will want conversation over the table kept to a minimum. Beyond this, however, just about anything goes—in fact, many Koreans believe high-volume eating (slurping noodles, smacking lips, and so on) expresses appreciation for the food. While you'll generally be responsible for feeding yourself, when drinking alcohol you should never fill your own glass—this will be taken care of by your neighbor, and you should keep an eye on those around you and fill their glasses in return if needed.

© YUKO AOKI

Bibimbap (mixed rice and vegetables) is one of the most popular dishes in Korean cuisine.

Social Values

As in other East Asian countries, the concept that exerts the most influence on daily interactions in South Korea is that of *chemyeon,* or face. This is a difficult idea to put across in English, but it could loosely be defined as the need to maintain a certain air of respectability, and being conscious that others are constantly striving to do the same. This means the polite Korean will take great care to ensure that he doesn't cause someone to "lose face," intentionally or otherwise, by exposing a lack of knowledge or shortcoming on their part. Thus a considerate person might turn down a dinner invitation from a older friend he knew to be short of money, since the older party would have to bankroll the whole evening if he wanted his own *chemyeon* to be maintained. Other examples would be no one in an office pointing out a gaffe in a speech by the boss, or taxi drivers not admitting they have no idea where your destination is—that would be a loss of face. *Chemyeon* also sometimes means telling people what you think they want to hear in order to minimize the chances of disagreement or an embarrassing scene. To Westerners born and raised on notions of straight talk and speaking their minds, face can be an alien—and infuriating— invention, while South Koreans find the foreign insistence on being frank and verbalizing emotions odd if not downright rude.

Closely connected to the concept of *chemyeon* is *nunchi,* which literally means "eye measure" but is better translated as the ability to accurately gauge the mood of a person (*kibun*) or the atmosphere of a place or situation (*bunuigi*). Someone with *nunchi* is quick to react to nonverbal cues and will act in a way that ensures the "face" of those around them and a harmonious atmosphere are maintained. Saying someone possesses good or "quick" *nunchi* is a very great compliment, and remarking that someone lacks it is basically another way of saying they're socially inept.

If a Korean feels their *chemyeon* has been lost or the norms of *nunchi* disregarded, things can disintegrate very quickly, and the legendary national temper makes its way to the surface. The public displays of anger and shouting matches occasionally seen on the streets of Seoul usually begin over a perceived lack of respect or loss of face; thankfully these are almost always more bluster than substance, and most locals settle down as quickly as they get worked up.

Gender Roles

Women have made significant strides over the last few years, but as a whole South Korea is still very much a male-dominated place and is given low rankings on international gender equality indexes. Much of this has to do with the legacy of Confucianism, which elevated men to the superior position and taught that the place of women—especially mothers—was in the home. Traditionally in any marriage the man was the breadwinner, and the woman was responsible for caring for the children and keeping the house in order—an arrangement that still dominates today. Many women give up their careers as soon as they have their first child, and many local companies remain reluctant to hire all but the youngest women since women are widely expected to abandon a job as soon as they get pregnant.

However, women have always been far more influential than they appeared—they normally have complete control of the family finances, for example—and the old structures are rapidly breaking down as young women demand more freedom and rising costs make two-income families a necessity. There's a sizable and increasingly vocal population of female business leaders, and in late 2012 the country voted in its first female president, Park Geun-hye. The government has also demonstrated a greater willingness to address gender issues through actions such as the establishment of a ministry to advance gender equality.

Traditionally, women tend to the children and the home.

GAY AND LESBIAN CULTURE

"Don't ask, don't tell" would serve just as well for South Korea's national slogan when it comes to gays and lesbians. While there certainly is a gay community in South Korea, the country's generally conservative nature means it's far less visible than those elsewhere, and public displays of affection between members of the same sex are virtually nonexistent. Same-sex relations are not illegal per se, and (discreet) gay couples rarely face any form of targeted abuse or harassment. This is less an indication of tolerance, however, than the inability of many South Koreans to believe that homosexuality exists in their country. Same-sex relations have become something of a hot topic with the emergence of openly gay celebrities such as Hong Seok-cheon, but this has yet to translate into widespread sympathy for gays or any kind of cohesive movements for gay rights.

What does pass for a gay scene in South Korea is concentrated around a few small but very vibrant club districts in Seoul and Busan, where gays will find no shortage of curious local (and foreign) men and women to mingle with.

Religion

Religions have swept over South Korea at various times much like a succession of waves crashing on a shore, resulting in a polyglot land where people practice a healthy variety of faiths (and sometimes a couple of different ones at once). Traditionally a tolerant place when it comes to matters of the spirit, South Korea guarantees freedom of religion in its constitution, and the country has managed largely to avoid the religious conflicts and divisions that have caused so much suffering in other parts of the world.

SHAMANISM

Shamanism has been practiced in Korea since prehistoric times, and there is evidence of links to similar rituals throughout Siberia, Mongolia, and northern China. Less a religion than an amalgamation of folk beliefs and rites, shamanism seeks to appease or enlist the help of the spirit world through human, usually female, mediums known in Korea as *mudang*. Mediums can either inherit their powers or receive a "call" that bonds them to the spirit world and is impossible to ignore.

For centuries shamanism was derided and even actively oppressed by leaders who saw it as nonsensical or primitive, but it has enjoyed something of a resurgence recently and is now recognized as a legitimate part of the country's cultural heritage. While few South Koreans would call themselves shamanists, shamanist shrines are found in temples and on mountains around the peninsula, and *mudang* are regularly called on to perform ceremonies to bring prosperity to a town or business, or to soothe the spirits of the dead. These events, known as *gut,* typically involve singing, dancing and elaborate costumes. The medium usually falls into a trance in which she speaks with the spirits and passes on the requests or wishes of the people assembled.

© YEON-SOO KIM/DREAMSTIME.COM

Shamanist totems still greet entrants to some villages.

BUDDHISM

© CRAIG D.C. LEWIS

drum in Buddhist temple

Buddhism was introduced to Korea by Chinese scholars in the 4th century and is currently the professed religion of around a quarter of the population. It is based on the teachings of Siddhartha Gautama, a scholar born around 563 BC in modern-day Nepal. Gautama, now known as the Buddha, turned his back on a life of luxury to search for a way to end suffering and break the cycle of recurring births and deaths, which he discovered could be transcended through disciplined living and meditation. Korean Buddhism is of the Mahayana (Great Vehicle) school, which emphasizes the liberation of all beings rather than the individual attaining enlightenment. It has been heavily influenced by *seon* thought (known as *chan* in Chinese, or Zen in Japanese), which views direct experience and meditation practice as more important than scripture or theoretical knowledge. The country's main Buddhist sect, the Jogye order, allows both men and women to be ordained as Buddhist monks or nuns; those taking vows are expected to follow a series of precepts that prescribe vegetarianism and celibacy.

For laypeople, things are less structured; they may (but are certainly not required

KOREAN SUPERSTITIONS

Behind South Korea's modern veneer there are a number of beliefs handed down from antiquity that continue to hold sway. Here are some common superstitions to be aware of—and though they might seem irrational, so is discomfort with the number 13 or black cats.

• Names in red: Avoid writing names (including your own) in red ink—this is the color traditionally used to write the names of the dead and could imply that you wish the person the same fate.

• The number 4: As the number four shares the same pronunciation ("sa")

as the word for death in Korean, it has negative connotations, and in many buildings and elevators fourth floors are omitted altogether.

• Running shoes: Shoes should never be given as a gift, particularly to a romantic partner, as shoes are designed for movement and will cause them to run away.

• Lucky pigs: Pigs are a symbol of wealth and abundance, and if you're lucky enough to dream of one, it means there's some money headed your way—time to buy a lottery ticket perhaps?

to) visit temples to pray or to listen to sermons, and also to celebrate special dates on the lunar calendar such as Buddha's Birthday.

Buddhism reached its historical apex in the late 7th century, when it became the de facto state religion for the better part of seven centuries. This was followed by a period of suppression under the Joseon Dynasty that confined most temples to distant mountain valleys, where most remain today. Having produced much of the country's artistic and architectural wonders, the religion occupies a special place in the Korean psyche, but in recent decades it has been overshadowed by the rapid spread of Christianity, which is generally perceived as more modern and dynamic. The Jogye runs "temple-stay" programs and international *seon* centers in South Korea for foreign residents who are interested in studying Buddhist practice.

CHRISTIANITY

Next to the Philippines and East Timor, South Korea is the most Christian country in Asia, with Christians of all major denominations representing around a third of the population. While Christianity was a relative latecomer, first promulgated by Catholic and Protestant missionaries in the 1800s, it quickly won the hearts of a largely poverty-stricken and downtrodden population with its messages of heavenly rewards and equality in the eyes of God. Esteem for the religion grew further as church resources were poured into promoting literacy and building modern hospitals and educational institutions. Koreans were also grateful for the support shown by Christians for the country's independence struggle and the ensuing battles against dictatorship. Its association with democracy and development has helped the religion cultivate its inclusive, forward-looking image.

Christianity's success here is visible in the thousands of neon crosses dotting major cities' skylines, as well as the fantastic popularity and wealth of U.S.-style "megachurches" like the Yoido Full Gospel Church in Seoul. A significant number of the Christian faithful belong to smaller sects that place great value on winning new converts, so street preaching and fairly aggressive proselytizing are not uncommon—in fact South Korea produces more missionaries per capita than any other nation besides the United States. If you're not interested, a polite but firm "no" is enough to dissuade most would-be saviors. Be aware that meal, volunteering, or social invitations from total strangers sometimes turn out to be religious events.

© CRAIG D.C. LEWIS

Christianity is a major presence in South Korea.

The Arts

South Korea has a rich and long-running artistic tradition that has tended to be over-shadowed by those of its larger neighbors internationally. But those who delve into it are often surprised and pleased to find it possesses plenty of unique qualities of its own, including an emphasis on simplicity and harmony with the natural environment. The country's artistic output has gained more global recognition with the emergence of a daring new generation of South Korean visual artists and filmmakers, some of whom have translated the country's obsession with technology into thought-provoking new works and formats.

LITERATURE

Traditionally the domain of the educated elite, Korean literature was, until the 19th century, largely composed in Chinese characters and consisted of epics, poems, and historical records modeled on Chinese patterns. As the hangul script gained prominence

A KOREAN TIDE?

While the country has had years of success selling computer chips, ships, and cars overseas, it has only been relatively recently that South Korea has realized it can market its pop culture abroad as well.

In the late 1990s, local and Chinese observers alike were surprised to discover South Korean movies and soap operas attracting massive audiences in China, which traditionally has been an exporter of culture to its smaller neighbor. Journalists in Beijing struck by the surging popularity of South Korean film, food, and fashion coined a new phrase, "the Korean Wave" or *hallyu* in Korean pronunciation, to describe this phenomenon. The wave didn't stop at China, with sentimental Korean serials such as *Winter Sonata* and *Jewel in the Palace* and the country's impeccably groomed boy bands finding a ready audience throughout much of Southeast Asia, the Middle East, and even Central America. The fad arguably reached an apex when "Gangnam Style," a satirical dance-pop number performed by portly Korean rapper Psy, became one of the most watched videos on YouTube and topped charts as far off as the United Kingdom—a feat more manicured K-pop stars have yet to manage.

Academics have come up with various hypotheses to explain the Korean craze. Many have argued the relatively wholesome content and some of the themes explored in Korean dramas—intergenerational conflict, history, filial piety—strike a chord with a generally conservative Asian audience; others that developing countries like Vietnam look up to South Korea for its economic prowess, and Korean fashion has become one way to reflect their motivational aspirations. It doesn't hurt, of course, that K-pop tunes are catchy and most South Korean stars flawlessly sculpted (Psy, arguably, aside).

Whatever the reasons for the wave, the government and businesses have been quick to capitalize on it, sponsoring concerts abroad, setting up "Hallyu-wood" theme parks, and organizing tours of famous soap opera sets for groups of starstruck Asian housewives. The question now is whether the wave will prove to be an enduring trend or a brief fad. There are already signs of a backlash: Chinese and Taiwanese broadcasters have moved to limit the amount of Korean content hitting local airwaves, and *manga* (comic books) disparaging Korean culture have appeared in Japan.

and the country began to assert its independence, a more native literary tradition developed, some of it harking back to premodern folk and agricultural themes, and some of it rooted heavily in the nation's struggles with war, division, and rampant industrialization. Low book prices and the South Korean search for knowledge have stoked the popularity of reading and made writers relatively respected figures in South Korean society, but unfortunately only a small portion of the country's works are translated or made available abroad. Among the country's best-known writers are Park Kyung-ni, whose epic *The Land* chronicled the nation's modern history from Japanese occupation to the separation of the two Koreas, and Ko Un, a poet whose vivid, earthy work has won him many admirers overseas. Novelist Kyung-sook Shin has risen to international prominence with *Please Look After Mom,* a recounting of a mother's sacrifices during Korea's rapid urbanization that has sold more than two million copies globally and won the 2011 Man Asian Literary Prize, hopefully paving the way for the translation of more contemporary Korean literature in the process. The work of Korean diaspora authors writing in English, such as Krys Lee and Chang-rae Lee, has also met with considerable success.

VISUAL ARTS

South Korea is perhaps most renowned for its pottery and ceramics, characterized by their unadorned grace and delicate glazing. The textures and themes found in Korean pottery are echoed in traditional painting, which emphasizes bold, almost spontaneous brushstrokes, sparing use of colors, and natural themes. Most historic works depicted landscapes or Buddhist themes, but there was also a thriving undercurrent of folk art that was freer in its use of color and form and dealt with more whimsical topics.

More contemporary artists have drawn inspiration from international movements such as impressionism and surrealism as well as emerging technologies and indigenous tradition. This fusing of creative impulses gave rise to avant-garde darlings such

© GREGORY JOHNSTON/123RF.COM

Korean pottery is sometimes decorated with bold brushstrokes, as seen on these traditional kimchi pots.

© CRAIG D.C. LEWIS

traditional music performance

© CRAIG D.C. LEWIS

modern music performance

as painter Kim Whanki and multimedia artist Nam June Paik, who turned heads with his thought-provoking video installations.

MUSIC

Korean music is deeply rooted in shamanist and agricultural traditions and still echoes with the sounds of ritual drumming and the cries that urged farmers to work in the fields. Local instruments include the *gayageum* (zither), *daegum* (large flute), and *buk* (barrel drum). Its extremes can be witnessed in *nongak,* an onslaught of relentless joyous percussion that marked rural celebrations, and *pansori,* a stark form of opera featuring a drummer and single singer who will stretch a narrative out for hours in a voice that runs the gamut from sorrowful crooning to eerie croaks and celebratory yelps.

Younger Koreans, of course, are more partial to contemporary pop, which in its current incarnation is roughly split between heartrending ballads and more upbeat dance, hip-hop or electro numbers. Korean boy and girl bands are immensely popular throughout Asia, and, increasingly, worldwide, but there's little to distinguish them from those found just about anywhere else.

FILM

Since the late 1990s, after a lengthy spell in the cinematic wilderness in which it was difficult for them to attract even domestic audiences, South Korean directors have returned with a vengeance, and in fact the country is now one of the few in the world where local rather than Hollywood films dominate the box office. Much of this is thanks to the formidable talent exhibited by the likes of Kang Je-gyu, whose blockbuster spy drama *Shiri* heralded the new wave of South Korean cinema, and Park Chang-wook, whose unflinching meditations on the nature of violence and revenge are typified by the brutal but riveting *Oldboy*. Kim Ki-duk, whose uncompromising work has touched on everything from the Buddhist cycle of life to battered housewives, is something of a staple on the global festival circuit, taking the coveted Golden Lion at the 2012 Venice Film Festival with loan shark fable *Pieta*.

Sports and Games

The diligence with which South Koreans follow their national team in global competitions, as well as local athletes with professional sports careers abroad, is testament to the pride the country takes in its all-around athletic prowess.

While multiple traditional sports, including *ssirum,* a form of wrestling, and the martial art *taekwondo,* are still practiced, these days South Koreans seem far more enthusiastic about imports. Soccer is probably the most widely watched and played sport, followed by baseball and basketball. All these sports have national professional leagues with teams in each major city sponsored by prominent local companies. Several South Korean soccer and baseball players have made it to the roster of major teams abroad, and local archers and golfers are also known for their domination of the global stage. As past (and future) hosts and top performers, South Koreans take their showings in international competitions such as the World Cup and the Olympics very seriously, and if events like these are on, it will seem like the entire population is talking about nothing else.

baseball on the big screen, Seoul

PLANNING YOUR FACT-FINDING TRIP

A well-planned research trip is one of the best possible introductions to South Korean life, and should be seen as mandatory if you're seriously contemplating a move here. Books or the Internet can point the way, but it's just not possible to make any sound judgments about the country without experiencing it firsthand.

It's obviously important to explore the city you'll call home, but tack on a few extra days for leisure and exploration of some other parts of the country if possible, particularly historic towns like Gyeongju and Andong, which offer a much-needed glimpse into Korea's soul. Also be sure to set aside some time to get acquainted with the local food and especially the nightlife—this is a place where the workday often bleeds over into the evening, and even if you're a teetotaler, you're likely to find outings vital in cementing bonds with local friends and colleagues.

Preparing to Leave

WHAT TO BRING
Documents

A passport is obviously required to enter South Korea, but for most people that's all the paperwork they'll need—nationals of the United States, Canada, and most European countries are permitted to visit without a visa for periods of between three and six months. Try to travel on a passport that's valid for at least another six months—this isn't a strict requirement, but those that expire sooner tend to attract more attention from immigration officials, and you'll need one anyway when you eventually apply for a long-term visa.

It's also a good idea to bring the international contact information for any travel or medical insurers you've signed up with as well your as banks and credit card companies in case you're involved in an accident or your wallet goes missing. No vaccinations are required to enter South Korea, but many doctors recommend signing up for the standard shots for travelers to Asia—and hepatitis A and B inoculations in particular—before departure. If you have to take prescription medication into South Korea, be sure to bring along copies of your prescriptions to fend off any questions from curious customs officials, and to show doctors or pharmacists if you need to replenish your supply.

Clothing

The rules here are to bring as little clothing as possible, and pack whatever makes you comfortable. With the exception of the depths of winter, South Korea's climate is relatively mild, so there's little point in stuffing suitcases full of sweaters, and any extra clothing you need will be easy enough to find locally, at least in Seoul. Remember, South Korea is a fairly conservative place, and the locals put great stock in appearances, so err on the side of formality in selecting what outfits to bring. If you're planning on meeting any future business associates, pack at least one suit. A comfortable pair of shoes will be needed to walk South Korea's often uneven streets and to tackle walking in the hills.

Miscellaneous

Again, try not to cram your bags with supplies to prepare for every eventuality—there are very few things you won't be able to pick up locally if needed. If you're strict in your choice of toothpaste, soap, or other toiletries, bring enough to last through your trip as some brands will no doubt be unavailable, and you're unlikely to be familiar with the local versions. A travel guide and phrasebook are recommended to assist in getting around and interacting with non-English speakers. In South Korea you don't exist without a business card, and even if you don't have one, it's worth getting a few printed up and bringing them with you, especially if you're going to be doing a lot of socializing. A camera and journal will make it easier to record your impressions and share them with friends and relatives back home.

Money

Setting a budget for your trip is a highly personal choice—South Korea can be just

© RAGSAC/123RF.COM

visa and Korean currency

about as dirt-cheap or stratospherically expensive as you want it to be. If you're pre-pared to stay at small inns (*yeogwan*) or hostels, stick to public transport, and survive on relatively simple local dishes—rice rolls, noodles, and the like—you could survive on US$70 or so per day. On the other hand, if you're sticking to higher-end hotel chains, eating in nicer Korean and foreign restaurants, and taking cabs everywhere, each day will cost you US$300 or more. Most people find themselves somewhere between these two extremes. Remember to bring extra if you plan on doing a lot of shopping or drinking, both of which can up your spending considerably.

What form you bring your money over in is also a matter of personal preference. Traveler's checks offer some protection against theft but are not readily accepted any-where other than banks or major hotels. Cash of course has the broadest appeal, but unlike in other countries in Asia, it isn't really king—credit cards are widely used throughout South Korea, and these days even the smallest shops and restaurants are wired to accept them. If you have an ATM card with a Plus or Cirrus logo, you can also withdraw funds (in won) from your home account at international bank machines here; however, these machines can be harder to find outside of Seoul and Busan. Major currencies such as U.S. dollars, U.K. pounds, and Japanese yen can be exchanged for won at the airport, banks, large hotels, or private money changers in areas like Seoul's Namdaemun Market. Banks and hotels tend to be the most dependable, but private money changers sometimes offer slightly more favorable rates.

When to Go

If you have a choice, there's absolutely no contest—fall (roughly late September to November) is when South Korea is at its best, with day after day of clear blue skies, stunning foliage, and crisp (but not cold) temperatures. Spring (late March to June) is a close second, with similarly moderate temperatures and an abundance of blos-soms, but it is sometimes marred by the clouds of yellow dust that make their way to the peninsula from northern China. Summer is hot, muggy, and wet, and winters can be bleak and cold, particularly in the northern parts of the country, but neither season is harsh enough to warrant avoiding a visit altogether if they are the only times you're free to go.

Try to avoid traveling to South Korea during the Seollal (Lunar New Year) and Chuseok (harvest festival) holidays, the dates of which vary according to the lunar calendar but which generally fall in January-February and September-October, respectively. For the week surrounding each holiday, flights and train tickets will be fully booked, the roads packed, and many shops and offices shut down as millions of South Koreans make the journey back to their hometowns.

Arriving in South Korea

ARRIVALS AND CUSTOMS

A handful of visitors make their way to South Korea by boat, but the vast majority land at one of the country's international airports, most frequently Seoul's Incheon International. The procedures at all international entry points are relatively quick and painless, and nearly identical.

As stated earlier, visas are not required for most foreign visitors, but everyone has to fill out an arrival card that will probably be given to you along with a customs form on the plane prior to landing. The arrival card is a simple document with a few boxes that have to be filled in with details such as your name, passport number, home address, and the purpose of your visit. To avoid complications it's best to just write "tourism," "holiday," or the like here until you have local employment or residency status, as any other response is likely to result in a protracted conversation with an immigration officer—the South Koreans are fairly sensitive about foreign nationals stopping by to scout out job opportunities.

There are usually separate immigration queues for locals and foreigners, and the lines for both can be long but move quickly enough most of the time. After you reach the counter and your passport and arrival card are inspected by the immigration officer, a small note with your arrival date and the length of your permitted stay will be stamped into your passport.

Customs checkpoints are usually set up after the baggage claim area, with officers standing by to collect the customs forms handed out on the plane earlier. These contain a few simple questions about whether you're carrying contraband such as drugs, guns, or pornography (hopefully the answer will be no); fresh fruit, vegetables, or meat (most of which can't be brought into South Korea); or alcohol or tobacco in excess of the duty-free allowance, currently around one carton of cigarettes and one liter of spirits. If you've answered any questions in the affirmative, customs officials will want to inspect your luggage and may seize anything they find objectionable; otherwise you'll probably be waved on through. Travelers are sometimes singled out for random inspections, especially if they're carrying large amounts of luggage. If this happens to you, smile and stay cooperative, and you'll be on your way soon enough.

CAUSE FOR CELEBRATION

South Koreans never need much of an excuse for a party, and the country's calendar is crammed with festivals celebrating historical events, esteemed local produce, and even just the existence of a few places. They can be a lot of fun and often bring some much-needed attention and tourist dollars to the nation's remoter corners. Here's a list of a few of the higher-profile annual events; check with the Korea Tourism Organization for additional and up-to-date event information.

- **Hadong Wild Tea Cultural Festival** (May): Held among the scenic tea plantations of the south, the first place tea was cultivated in Korea, this event allows visitors to sample and buy fine green teas from specialist producers and to study tea ceremonies and cultivation.

- **Boryeong Mud Festival** (July): The mudflats of the coastal city of Boryeong are said to be rich in minerals good for the skin, and thousands flock to the beach here every summer to slather themselves in the stuff in a variety of ways. Mud baths, mud wrestling, mud slides—the list goes on. This festival is one of the main events on the youngish expat crowd's social calendar and tends to be pretty hyperactive and booze-fueled; the less party-inclined may want to give it a miss.

- **Gangjin Celadon Festival** (July/August): Korean ceramics have built a justifiably high reputation over the centuries, and this festival in the celadon production center of Gangjin is a good opportunity to view and purchase work from some of the country's finest living artisans or try your hand at sculpting your own.

- **Andong Mask Dance Festival** (September/October): This event in the history-rich Andong area showcases Korea's masked dance traditions, one of the country's oldest forms of entertainment. It has grown more international in scope, with foreign troupes now regularly invited to perform.

- **Chungju World Martial Arts Festival** (September/October): A must for enthusiasts, this event draws practitioners of a range of martial arts from around the world who participate in lectures, demonstrations, and, of course, some no-holds-barred competition. This being South Korea, indigenous martial arts such as *taekwondo* receive top billing.

- **Jinju Lantern Festival** (October):The southern city of Jinju was the site of major Japanese sieges of Korea in the 16th century, and this festival commemorates the battles fought there. But the tone is far from martial; instead giant, colorful lanterns that depict a variety of scenes and landmarks from Korean history float down the city's river in illuminated splendor. The festival also includes exhibits of lanterns from other countries and lantern-making programs.

- **Busan International Film Festival** (October): For a week or so Busan's Haeundae Beach gives Los Angeles a run for its money as directors, acting talent, and financiers from throughout Asia and beyond flock to what has become the region's premier film event. A busy screening schedule and crammed roster of parties and receptions add to the general buzz and make it easy to see why this festival seems to get bigger every year.

airport bus stop

TRANSPORTATION

After you complete the immigration and customs formalities and have finally been released into the arrivals area, it's time to organize transport to the city center—which at Incheon International, as with most South Korean airports, is a fair distance away. While authorities have tried to crack down on the practice, visitors are still frequently approached in arrivals areas by men offering taxis or help finding hotels—any such offers, no matter how persistent or persuasive, should be turned down, since they'll inevitably come at a higher price.

Instead, make your way to the nearby express bus counters, where you can arrange for bus tickets to just about any major point in the city, or designated taxi stands outside, where there will be separate ranks of deluxe and regular cabs waiting to ferry passengers into town. Train travel from Incheon International directly into Seoul is also now a possibility with the high-speed Airport Railroad (AREX), which stops in a few key neighborhoods north of the Han River with links to Seoul's extensive subway network, terminating at Seoul Station. This comes in both regular (3,850 won) and nonstop express (8,000 won) varieties—while it's only slightly faster, the latter has far more comfortable seating arrangements and is the only real choice for travelers carrying substantial amounts of luggage. The express train takes just 43 minutes to reach Seoul Station, but for people heading to the suburbs or districts south of the Han River, express buses are still likely to be the faster option outside rush hours. Bus fares from the airport to most destinations are around 20,000 won, and taxis run about 60,000-80,000 won. If you decide to take a cab, try to make sure to bring a contact number for your destination or the address in Korean script; many drivers speak little or no English, and non-Koreans often struggle to pronounce placenames correctly.

Things to Do

While exploring a new place is bound to be a lot of fun, keep in mind this isn't a sightseeing excursion, and make sure to fit in some activities that help you form a genuine picture of what it's like to live in South Korea, even (or especially) under less-than-ideal conditions. Some suggestions would be visiting a district office to see what kind of programs they offer for new foreign residents, shopping for fresh produce at a wet market—where you're often forced to bargain—rather than a department store, braving a busy subway station at rush hour, frequenting a restaurant with no English menu, or taking public transportation to a smaller town in the provinces where they don't see many foreigners.

South Korea being as safe as it is, and South Koreans being as helpful as they are, you can tackle these kinds of challenges without fear of what will happen, and breaking out of your comfort zone a little will give you far more rewarding opportunities for local interaction than confining yourself to expat enclaves or a hotel room.

© JONATHAN HOPFNER

festival at the National Palace Museum in Seoul

Sample Itineraries

South Korea is not a large country, and transportation is swift and efficient, making it easy to cover a lot of geographic ground in a very short period. To truly get a sense of the place, however, it's best to take it slow, giving yourself ample time to walk the streets, dip into restaurants or markets on a whim, test out the public transit, and plan an excursion or two to rural areas or historical sites to better understand the country's roots.

If you already know where you're going to be living or working, a week should be sufficient to explore your new home and some of its surroundings. If not, two weeks to one month should give you enough time to form an impression of most of South Korea's key cities and decide which might make the best base of operations for you.

ONE WEEK

With only a week to spare, it's probably best to concentrate on a specific location—in this example, Seoul, which is large, dynamic, and complex enough to keep anyone busy for far longer than that. A similar amount of time in Busan would allow you to check out some of the areas popular with expatriates—such as Haeundae and Pusan National University—and perhaps fit in a side trip to Ulsan or the culture-rich city of Gyeongju. It would also be enough time to make your way around Jeju Island with lengthy pit stops in the main cities of Jeju and Seogwipo. Or you could pick a region and divide the week among its main centers, heading south from Seoul to visit Daejeon, Gwangju, and Jeonju to the west, for example.

Day 1

After a night recovering from what's bound to be an exhausting flight, get up early and

© JONATHAN HOPFNER

cherry blossoms in culture-rich Gyeongju

head straight for Gyeongbokgung Palace in the central district of Jongno-gu before the inevitable hordes of sightseers arrive. This is primarily a tourist site, to be sure, but also the heart of old Seoul and one of the best places to begin getting a sense of how the city is laid out. The palace is surrounded by some of Seoul's most historic and character-crammed neighborhoods, so take the time to explore them. A short stroll from its eastern walls will bring you to the charming, Samcheong-dong district, where cafes, galleries, and boutique shops are housed in a mix of historic and eye-catching contemporary architecture. Follow the main strip toward the entrance to quiet Samcheong Park and veer right, and you'll soon be in the heart of Bukchon Hanok Village, one of the few patches of Seoul where *hanok,* or traditional Korean homes, still exist in significant numbers. With their snug courtyards and delicately curved eaves, these properties have attracted more than a few foreign residents, and you may want to drop in on a neighborhood real estate agent if you feel the lure of *hanok* life—but since many of these places are beautifully restored and equipped, bring an open checkbook. Just south of the village, on the other side of Anguk subway station, is the Insa-dong area, popular with visitors (and residents) for its craft and souvenir stores as well as traditional restaurants and tea shops. This is a great part of town for new arrivals to get acquainted with Korean food, since most restaurants see a fair number of tourists and go out of their way to cater to non-Korean speakers.

If you continue south from the main Insa-dong road, passing Tapgol Park on your right, you'll soon hit the Cheonggyecheon, a restored waterway that runs over eight kilometers through the city center. Follow it west and you'll soon see the massive (some would say garish) sculptured shell that marks its entrance from Sejong-daero, one of Seoul's main arteries for centuries. Just north of this intersection is the Kyobo Building. An excellent bookstore in the basement is stocked with material for Korean language learners, English-language newspapers, and city event magazines such as *Seoul*; pick up a few to see what Seoul has to offer in an average week. Since the store is popular with expatriates and English-speaking locals, there's a fair chance you'll also end up meeting someone to discuss city life with.

From here you've got a couple of possible ways to explore Seoul's bustling retail scene. If it's high-end boutiques and mammoth department stores you're after, head straight south past the wavelike City Hall building to the Myeong-dong district, which heaves with shoppers until the late hours and has plenty of bars and restaurants to relax in when the credit cards are (almost) maxed out. For a cheaper, more local, but also slightly more chaotic option, a short taxi or subway ride east to Dongdaemun Station will put you in the middle of one of the city's largest markets, Dongdaemun, with the Gwangjang and Bangsan Markets also just blocks away. Dongdaemun Market focuses on clothes while the latter two carry more food and household supplies, but each spans multiple blocks, buildings, and floors, and together they contain just about anything anyone could want to set up a new home. Browsing (or better yet, buying) will give you a taste of the bargaining process and how much South Koreans pay for standard goods—prices at markets are often substantially lower than those at megamarts or department stores. Cap off the day by sitting down for a bite and a drink in one of the markets' food sections, which serve up a spectacular range of good-value street snacks and are a favorite spot for the locals to blow off steam after work.

© CRAIG D.C. LEWIS

While in Seoul, you can use the subway to get around.

Day 2

It's time to familiarize yourself with Seoul's always-hot housing market. Take the subway to Noksapyeong Station and resurface next to the entrance to the Itaewon strip. Spend an hour walking the length of the street, stopping in one of the cafés along the way, for a glimpse of the center of Seoul's expatriate community. Finish at the Yongsan International School at the eastern end; if you have you have school-age children you may want to arrange a quick tour with the administrative staff.

Double back to the nearest intersection, where you'll see a few real estate agents. Most agents in this area will have a number of places throughout Yongsan district on their books. Have a chat with them about what's available, and feel free to check out a few apartments, but remember not to make any final decisions before you've talked to multiple agents—quotes sometimes differ from one to the next. If time permits, take a bus or cab up the hill to the Hyatt Hotel—just outside the hotel is an entrance to Namsan Park, which has some reasonably unstrenuous walking trails that offer sweeping views of the city. If you'd prefer a dose of culture, just downhill from the Hyatt is the striking Leeum Samsung Museum of Art, which houses much of the enviable collection of the Samsung conglomerate's founding family, as well as rotating exhibitions by contemporary local and international artists. When evening hits, make your way back down to Itaewon's main drag to sample some of the area's legendary (and occasionally notorious) nightlife. The district's diverse range of restaurants, bars, and clubs collectively probably boasts the highest concentration of expats in the city, and many are welcoming, convivial places for a chat with current Seoul residents.

Day 3

Get a look at Seoul's more modern face by heading south of the river to the affluent Gangnam district. A walk along bustling Tehran-ro, one of corporate Korea's epicenters, is a good reminder of just how prosperous the country has become, and can be followed by a visit to the rather incongruously located Bongeunsa Buddhist temple, an island of tranquility in an area that is busy even by Seoul standards. Gangnam is an important shopping destination, and several modern-style malls and megastores are located here, including the COEX center, E-mart, and further south, Costco. Poke your head into one of these places for a crash course on the costs of imported food, and if you're considering living in Gangnam, visit a few real estate agents. After dark, prepare to splurge a little and visit one of the trendy restaurants or lounges in Garosu-gil, a nightspot and designer-dotted street in the Sinsa-dong area, to mingle with some of Seoul's trendsetters.

Day 4

Regardless of whether you've decided you have to live in the city center or are staunchly determined not to, a trip out to Seoul's suburbs is worth taking, if only to witness how South Korean cities are developing. Go to the nearest rapid (red) bus stop and take a commuter bus bound for Ilsan, which should take about 45 minutes to reach from downtown Seoul. Upon arrival, head for the massive Lake Park near Jeongbalsan, a relatively successful example of urban planning that boasts bike paths, jogging tracks, artificial islands, and even a singing fountain. The park is ringed with plush new apartment complexes that are also worth a look; property agents in the area will be more than happy to show you around but may not speak much English. There's no need to head back to Seoul for dinner—the nearby Lafesta and Western Dom shopping/entertainment complexes house a variety of boutiques, restaurants, and nightspots that rival almost anything in the capital.

Day 5

To prove Seoul isn't all business, spend the day exploring the Daehangno or Shinchon/Hongdae university districts, both accessible by subway—you could even try to cram both into a single outing, although they're relatively far apart. Both have a slightly bohemian feel, pleasant pedestrian areas, and an abundance of youth-centric boutiques, cafés, and pubs, but the Shinchon/Hongdae area is better known for cutting-edge galleries and clubbing, while Daehangno is famous for its outdoor sculpture, theaters, and street-side performances. Anyone on the hunt for low-cost housing would do well to talk with some of the real estate agents in these areas, as both have accommodations geared toward student-sized budgets. You should also stop by the campuses of the main schools, such as Yonsei University in the Shinchon area, if you're considering taking language or other courses in Seoul. Parents may also want to visit the Seoul Foreign School in nearby Yeonhui-dong, seen as one of the city's preeminent international schools. The area surrounding the school also has a good range of expat-friendly housing and shops.

Day 6

Hopefully having completed most of your research, devote your sixth day to some leisure pursuits. If you enjoy hiking, tackle one of the fairly unpunishing mountains in central Seoul—Inwangsan is a good pick—for fairly fresh air, spectacular views, and hidden shrines. You're highly likely to make some local friends along the way; Seoulites are rarely as relaxed or congenial as they are on the mountaintops. Seoul Forest and any of the Han riverside parks are alternative, less strenuous venues for a long, scenic stroll. If you're willing to go farther afield, a guided tour to the Demilitarized Zone separating the two Koreas or a trip west to Gangwha-do, an island littered with temples, fortress sites, and other relics, are both worthwhile trips.

Day 7

On your last day in Seoul, try to tie up any loose ends, taking the time to visit any neighborhoods you're curious about but may have missed, even if only to browse some of the advertisements pasted in the windows of property agencies to get a better idea of prices. This might also be a good time to visit the Seoul Global Center, a support facility for non-Korean residents in Jung-gu, to ask any questions that have come up on your trip and pick up some of the literature they have on utilities, banking, and other services to help prepare you for the eventual move.

TWO WEEKS

Two weeks in South Korea will allow you to spend at least a couple of days in three or four major cities, or stay longer in two places you're struggling to decide between, with a side trip or two to important scenic or cultural spots. This example takes you east from Seoul, pausing at key destinations along the way, but you could just as easily head southwest, stopping in Daejeon, Jeonju, and Gwangju, if you're interested in the western region, or fly to Jeju after spending a few days in Seoul if island life appeals to you.

Days 1-3

After recovering from your flight, spend a couple of days exploring the key sights of Seoul and perhaps visiting property agents or schools in areas you've targeted as potential homes. Make your way to Seoul Station and book a ticket on an afternoon KTX high-speed train to Daejeon. Spend the evening in the Dunsan-dong district, the city's "new" downtown, which features a vibrant retail scene and several cafés and bars frequented by the city's foreign residents. The next morning, have a taxi take you around the outlying Daedeok Innopolis zone, centered on the country's foremost science and engineering institution, the Korea Advanced Institute of Science and Technology (KAIST). The government envisions the area as a cluster for scientific and technological research and industry, and it's already home to a sizable community of foreign students and academics. A number of the institutions based here offer long-term accommodations, and there are also real estate agents available to assist potential residents. Stop off for a soak at the renowned Yuseong Hot Springs, a vast complex of bathhouses with therapeutic pools that is a great introduction to South Korea's burgeoning public bath culture, before returning to Daejeon's train station to board the KTX to Daegu.

Day 4

After a night of rest, explore Daegu's up-and-coming Suseong-gu district, where there's a high concentration of educational institutions and, consequently, foreign teachers. If you're looking for a younger (and cheaper) scene, the Kyungpook National University area in the north of the city is known for its low-cost housing and abundance of nightlife. Take the afternoon to climb Palgongsan Mountain on the city's outskirts—it's a fairly easy trail—to the Gatbawi Buddha at its peak, where hundreds of worshippers flock each day in the hope it will grant their wishes. Return to Dongdaegu Station to board the KTX for Busan, or explore the always-busy Rodeo Street area in the city center if you'd like to spend some more time mingling with city residents.

Days 5-6

The port city of Busan, South Korea's second largest and home to the largest foreign population outside the greater Seoul area, warrants a couple of days of exploration. After a night in a hotel, preferably in the Busan Station area, cross the road and take a stroll through the Texas Street/Chinatown neighborhood. The area can be a bit racy at night but, with its odd mix of tourists, sailors, and Russian and Chinese-owned businesses, is a good illustration of the city's cultural blend during daylight hours—as well as a fine spot for a brunch of noodles or dumplings. A walk to the summit of nearby Yongdusan Park, topped with the Busan Tower, will highlight the city's scope and afford some sweeping views of the busy port, or you can take the subway straight to the new city center of Seomyeon and drop by some real estate agents and department stores to collect some data on prices in the area. Late afternoon and evening should be devoted to exploring the somewhat ramshackle, but atmospheric, old downtown and the waterfront Jagalchi Market, treasured by locals for its flapping-fresh seafood.

Spend the next day in the Haeundae Beach district, where many of Busan's expatriates make their homes. Always associated with relative prosperity, this area's taken on an even glitzier cast in recent years with the addition of Shinsegae Centum City, currently the world's largest department store, and the Busan Cinema Center, home base of Asia's largest annual film festival. Busan Foreign School is also located in Haeundae, so you may want to tour its facilities if you have school-age children, or arrange some viewings of the district's shiny new seaside condominiums for an idea of the size and quality of accommodations on offer. If time permits, take a taxi to magnificent

Busan is South Korea's second-largest city.

Beomeosa Temple, but be sure to return to the streets around Haeundae's beachfront or nearby Dalmaji Hill for a wide selection of restaurants and nightspots and a look at how Busan's well-heeled socialize.

Days 7-8

Make your way to Busan's express-bus terminal and board a bus for Ulsan, about an hour to the north. Even if you're not considering it as a place to live, the city is worth a look as a testament to the power and dynamism of South Korean industry. Spend some time in the Samsan-dong and Bangojin foreigners' compound areas if you're looking for an idea of costs and what it's like to live in Ulsan as an expatriate; or wander the energetic Ulsan University and Jung-gu (old downtown) districts, which have well-stocked traditional markets, good local cuisine, and plenty of opportunities to mingle with Ulsan's generally young and affluent population. In the morning, board another bus for Gyeongju, and spend at least a day getting to know South Korea's historical heart. There are several impressive temples, tomb sites, and ruin-littered mountains to visit, and the town itself is a very pleasant place with friendly people and some of the country's top *hanjeongsik*—the Korean version of the banquet—restaurants.

Day 9

Assuming you're not cultured out, grab another express bus north to the town of Andong, which, like Gyeongju, is another pillar of Korean tradition. Modern Andong is a fairly nondescript midsize South Korean town, but nearby Hahoe village has been left virtually untouched for the better part of two centuries and is perhaps the country's finest example of a traditional agricultural community. The village is still inhabited, so after some sightseeing it's quite possible to sit down for dinner at a restaurant there or stay in one of its lovely old homes.

Days 10-13

Another express bus north through the picturesque Sobaek mountain range will bring you to the city of Gangneung on South Korea's northeast coast. It's a fairly long journey, so you're likely to be in need of some sustenance; proceed directly to the waterfront for some of the city's justifiably renowned seafood. From the next morning, you'll have a few options: more time in Gangneung if you're mulling a move here and want to check out housing options, or heading farther up the coast to Sokcho and the stunning peaks of nearby Seoraksan National Park to see South Korea's best-preserved pockets of wilderness. If you'd like to evaluate other possible living destinations in Gangwon Province, travel west of Gangneung to Wonju, about a two-hour journey, then spend a night there before proceeding north to Chuncheon, where you can walk around the city's lakes and sample some of its famous *dalkgalbi* (spicy marinated chicken) to get a feel for life there.

Day 14

If you don't feel the need to rest prior to your upcoming journey or to wrap up some unfinished business in the capital, the trip from Chuncheon to Seoul is a brief one and will leave you enough time for a quick look at a neighboring city like Incheon or Suwon if you're considering living near the capital but not in it.

NORTH KOREA EXCURSIONS

A trip to South Korea's reclusive and frequently hostile northern neighbor may not be everyone's idea of a dream holiday, but more than a few adventurous travelers are keen for a look at one of the world's most isolated and inaccessible states. As one would expect, just buying a plane ticket and turning up in Pyongyang is all but impossible, but contrary to popular belief the North Korean government welcomes tourists provided they stick to some fairly rigorous rules.

Anyone looking to visit the North will have to arrange (and pay for) the entire trip in advance through a specialist agency such as Koryo Tours (www.koryo-group.com), which has a history of successfully negotiating the North's touchy bureaucracy. Visa applications from journalists and citizens of any current targets of North Korean ire (frequently Japan and the United States) are sometimes rejected. The fairly substantial tour fees will usually include transportation between North Korea and Beijing, China, as well as all accommodations, food, and guides, since tourists are required to be accompanied at nearly all times. Trips typically take in Pyongyang, the capital, and some nearby sights but can be tailored to the individual. Many try to time their arrival with events like the annual Arirang Festival mass games, during which North Korean officials tend to be more receptive of outsiders.

For a brief spell it was possible to visit North Korea directly from the South via two tours run by South Korea's Hyundai Group, one to the scenic Kumgang Mountains near the east coast and the other to the North Korean city of Gaesong, just north of Seoul. Both were basically day trips that were immensely popular with South Koreans and widely hailed as a concrete example of the two countries' warming ties, but they have been suspended since late 2008 due to deteriorating relations and an incident in which a South Korean tourist who allegedly went astray was shot and killed by a North Korean soldier. There's regular talk of the tours being revived, but at the time of writing both remained on hold. Check with the Hyundai Asan Company (tel. 02/3669-3000, www.hyundai-asan.com) or the Korea Tourism Organization (nationwide hotline 1330, www.visitkorea.or.kr) for the latest details.

ONE MONTH

One month would permit you to circulate virtually the entire country at a reasonable pace, perhaps combining the two-week itinerary above with a trip through the southwest—stopping in the major cities of Gwangju and Jeonju—to the port of Mokpo, where you could board a ferry to Jeju Island to spend some time there before flying back to Seoul. If you're already set on living in a particular destination and feel you've finished exploring it fully or simply don't want to do much traveling, the extra time could be used to enroll in Korean language classes at an institution such as Seoul's Yonsei University, which would give you a big head start when it comes time to live here.

Practicalities

Almost any South Korean town will have an adequate range of accommodations available for various budgets, though some places obviously have a lot more choice than others. Generally, accommodations can be divided into a few major camps—luxury hotels, which are, with a few exceptions, found only in major cities and cost around 150,000 won per night and up; "tourist-class" hotels, roughly equivalent to a three-star hotel in the United States, which are more widespread and start at about 70,000 won; and lower-end "love hotels" or *yeogwan* (inns). The former get their name because they're often used by couples in search of privacy, but they aren't necessarily sleazy; some are in fact cleaner and better-appointed than the aforementioned tourist-class lodgings. Rates start at around 30,000 won per night. Homestays or guesthouses, known as *minbak*, are also a possibility, although they are common only outside of urban areas.

Hotels are generally similar to those in Western countries, although at many you may be given the option of an *ondol* (Korean-style) room, where you sleep on a soft mat on the floor. Rates are often hiked on weekends and holidays, but at other times it may well be possible to negotiate the rates downward.

SEOUL
Accommodations
In a city with a lot of top-class hotels, the stylish **W Hotel** (175 Achasan-gil, Gwangjin-gu, tel. 02/465-2222, www.wseoul.com, doubles from 235,000 won) is widely viewed as the best, or, with its futuristic design touches and popular lounge, at least the most interesting, but it is a fair distance from the city center. Giving it some new competition in the eye-catching stakes is the colorful **IP Boutique Hotel** (737-32 Hannam-dong, Yongsan-gu, tel. 02/3702-8000, www.ipboutiquehotel.com, doubles from 200,000 won) which enjoys a choice perch on the main Itaewon drag. For more local flavor try **Rakkojae** (98 Gye-dong, Jongno-gu, tel. 02/742-3410, http://rkj.co.kr, from 250,000 won including breakfast and dinner) in the historic and very central Bukchon area, which rents out snug rooms in a beautifully restored *hanok* (Korean house). The **Fraser Suites** (272 Nagwon-dong, Jongno-gu, tel. 02/6262-8888, http://seoul.frasershospitality.com, one-bedroom units from 200,000 won) serviced apartment complex in Insa-dong is a good choice for long-term stays or visitors with families. Cheap but still reasonably cheerful options include the homey **Namsan Guesthouse** (50-1 Namsan-dong 2-ga, Jung-gu, tel. 02/752-6363, www.namsanguesthouse.com, doubles from 50,000 won), or, in the student-heavy Hongdae district, the **Stay Korea Guesthouse** (566-4 Yeonnam-dong, Mapo-gu, tel. 02/336-9026, www.staykorea.co.kr, doubles from 50,000 won).

Food
You'll never be more than a few feet from something to eat in Seoul; the only challenges are making a decision and (sometimes) deciphering menus. **Samwon Garden** (623-5 Sinsa-dong, Gangnam-gu, tel. 02/548-3030, www.samwongarden.com), an upscale Korean restaurant in the posh Apgujeong district, offers a good overview of the country's best-loved dishes. **Baru** (71 Gyeongji-dong, 5th Fl., Jongno-gu, tel.

ACCOMMODATIONS KOREA-STYLE

© BRIAN DEUTSCH

love hotel, Jeollanamdo

Standard hotels in South Korea, especially in Seoul, are some of the most expensive on the continent—paying the equivalent of US$300 for a pokey room is not uncommon, and there's a noticeable shortage of quality mid-range accommodations along the lines of those provided by business hotel chains in other countries.

This gap in the market is addressed somewhat by a couple of very local alternatives: love hotels and *minbak*, a sort of cross between a guesthouse and a homestay.

Few love hotels would be brave enough to call themselves that, but they're basi-cally standard motels or *yeogwan* with a few added touches to appeal to romance-minded couples—curtained car parks for privacy, themed rooms with soft lighting and fancy bedding, and "inspirational material" on the television. However, even if you're traveling solo, they can be an extraordinarily good value. Most are found in city centers, and since competition tends to be fierce, they regularly attempt to upstage each other in terms of cleanliness and facilities. Nice toiletries, Internet-connected PCs, and purified water dispensers are standard in most love hotel rooms, and some places offer deluxe suites equipped with Jacuzzis and massive flat-panel televisions for around 80,000 won a night, less than a three-star Seoul hotel.

Minbak are more commonly found in the countryside and resort areas. They are basically private homes that accept guests, the closest thing South Korea has to bed-and-breakfasts. They can vary widely in terms of design, quality, and service, from a tiny bedroom next to the owner's to large expansive properties with individual cabins. Meals are not usu-ally served (though you can always ask) and room rates are usually in the 30,000-80,000 won range.

You may also come across "pensions" and "condos" while traveling in South Korea—the former is basically another term for *minbak*, though they tend to be more upmarket. "Condo" is taken from the English *condominium* and refers to large resort complexes in tourist areas offering units with multiple bedrooms and kitchen facilities.

02/2031-2081, www.baru.or.kr) is an atmospheric eatery near Insa-dong that specializes in Buddhist-temple vegetarian cuisine. For Western comfort food, try **Do Ha Gun** (109 Sagan-dong, Jongno-gu, tel. 02/3210-2100), a lovely French-Italian restaurant in a traditional Korean house in the heart of historic Seoul, or **Vatos Urban Tacos** in Itaewon (181-8 Itaewon-dong, 2nd Fl., tel. 02/797-8226, www.vatoskorea.com) for an imaginative take on Mexican cuisine and killer cocktails. The Hongdae/Shinchon axis a good place to try out the street snacks, cheap barbecue, and pastry shops beloved by budget-conscious students.

THE EAST
Accommodations

In Busan the **Westin Chosun Busan** (737 Woo 1-dong, Haeundae-gu, tel. 051/749-7000, www.chosunbeach.co.kr, doubles from 245,000 won) is the grand old lady of hotels on Haeundae Beach, or try the immaculate and convenient **Toyoko Inn** (1203-15 Choryang-dong, Dong-gu, tel. 051/466-1045, www.toyokoinn.com, doubles from 71,500 won), which has additional branches in Seomyeon and Haeundae. In Ulsan the **Lotte Hotel** (282 Samsan-ro, Nam-gu, tel. 052/960-1000, www.lottehotelulsan.com, doubles from 210,000 won), in the fast-developing Samsan-dong area, is probably the best top-end choice, while the centrally located **Ulsan Hotel** (110-10 Sinjung 2-dong, Nam-gu, tel. 052/227-6300, www.ulsanhotel.co.kr, doubles from 80,000 won) is another decent pick. In Daegu the **Novotel Daegu City Center** (11-1 Munhwa-dong, Jung-gu, tel. 053/664-1101, www.novotel.com, doubles from 160,000 won) is as well-positioned as its name implies and gets favorable reviews, while in Daejeon the **Hotel Riviera** (444-5 Bongmyung-dong, Yuseong-gu, tel. 042/828-4001, www.hotelriviera.co.kr, doubles from 200,000 won) is nestled among the city's research institutes.

Food

Given its seaside location, Busan is unsurprisingly all about seafood. For the freshest at very reasonable prices, visit the **Jagalchi Market** (Nampo-dong 4-ga, Jung-gu, tel. 051/245-2594) where you can select something from the catch on the ground floor, and it'll be prepared for you in a restaurant upstairs. The Haeundae Beach area has a number of upmarket, cosmopolitan restaurants, clubs, and pubs, such as the relatively

© RUFINA K.E. PARK

Busan is known for its fresh seafood.

new **Tap and Tapas** (17-1 Gunam-ro, Haeundae-gu, tel. 051/808-1027, www.tapntapas. com). In Ulsan, the old downtown, Jung-gu, probably still has the best selection of mainly Korean restaurants per square foot, as well as the **Royal Anchor** (10 Seongnam-dong, Jung-gu, tel. 019/599-7590), a British-style pub that's something of an expatriate institution. In Daegu, Rodeo Street has a colorful assortment of local, Indian, Italian, Mexican, and other restaurants. Also in the area is **Traveler's Bar & Grill** (24-7 Bongsan-dong, Jung-gu, tel. 010/4591-4869, http://travelersbar.com), a foreign-owned and operated establishment that's got plenty of Western comfort food and attracts a healthy number of foreign residents. Daejeon is not known for its cuisine, but there is a cluster of generous *hanjeongsik* (Korean banquet) restaurants in the Bongmyeong-dong area that are worth a try, as well as a number of Western chain-style eateries in the busy Dunsan-dong area near the central government complex. **Santa Claus** (1-28 Gung-dong, Yuseong-gu, tel. 042/825-5500) is probably the most consistently popular expat watering hole.

JEJU ISLAND
Accommodations
The holiday capital of South Korea, Jeju is choked with places to stay, but prices tend to be higher than they are on the mainland. In Jeju City, the **KAL Hotel** (1691-9 Yido 1-dong, tel. 064/724-2001, www.kalhotel.co.kr, doubles from 300,000 won) enjoys a central location and top-notch facilities, while in Seogwipo the **Hyatt Regency** (114 Jongmoongwangwang-ro 72-beon gil, tel. 064/733-1234, http://jeju.regency.hyatt. com, doubles from 145,000 won) and the **Shilla** (3093-3, Saekdal-dong, tel. 064/735-5114, www.shilla.net, doubles from 400,000 won), both beachfront properties, are among the top-ranked. Prices tend to be higher in peak seasons such as July-August. The foreign-run **Jeju Springflower Guesthouse** (1046-1 Hamo-ri, Daejeong-eup, Seogwipo-si, tel. 010/6816-8879, www.gojejuguesthouse.com, doubles from 40,000 won) is a peaceful, pleasant budget option.

Food
Jeju is famous throughout South Korea and beyond for its sweet tangerines, abalone, raw fish, and jet-black pigs, whose meat commands a hefty premium. For raw fish, **Jinmimyeongga** (2072 Sagye-ri, Andeok-myon, Seogwipo-si, tel. 064/794-3639) outside Seogwipo has an excellent reputation, while **Kasantobang** (3077 Topeyong-dong, Seogwipo-si, tel. 064/732-2095) is lauded for its barbecued pork and garden-like surroundings. **Gecko's Terrace** (2156-3 Saekdal-dong, Seogwipo-si, tel. 064/739-0845), the local branch of a Seoul pub franchise, is a fair trek from Seogwipo proper, but worth the journey if you want to track down genuine Western food and atmosphere.

DAILY LIFE

MAKING THE MOVE

Picking everything up, taking the plunge, and moving to an entirely new country is never going to be an easy experience, and the need to negotiate an entirely unfamiliar bureaucracy that functions mainly in another language makes it an even more intimidating prospect. Thankfully, dealing with South Korean officialdom these days is relatively straightforward and unblemished by the questionable practices and lengthy delays that even locals complained about in the past. In many cases, expatriates are assisted through the visa and residency process by an employer, but the government's efforts to improve foreign-language services mean that it's perfectly feasible to do much of the legwork yourself if needed.

Besides, when it comes down to it, permits and paperwork are the least of any expatriate-to-be's concerns—saying good-byes, deciding what to take and what to leave behind, and preparing kids or pets for a new life overseas are all more complex and more emotionally draining experiences. Just keep in mind that any trepidation is soon bound to give way to excitement at having an entirely new country to explore, and that the wealth of new experiences and friends that await should take a lot of the sting out of separation.

Immigration and Visas

TOURIST AND SHORT-TERM VISAS

South Korea has a liberal immigration system that allows citizens of most countries to enter for short social or recreational stays without applying for any visas in advance. While the exact amount of time a visitor is permitted to remain in the country is left to the discretion of immigration officers, in general U.S., British, and other European Union nationals showing up at entry points can expect to be cleared to stay for three months, and Canadians for up to six months.

Those who don't qualify for visa-free access to the country or who would like to secure a visa in advance can apply for a C3 (temporary visit) visa at the nearest South Korean embassy or consulate. This requires only an application form, a couple of photographs, and a copy of your planned flight itinerary, although consular officials have the right to request additional supporting documents. There are separate temporary-stay visas for those planning to enter South Korea for purposes such as business or journalism, and they involve providing additional documentation.

LONGER-TERM VISAS

Anyone residing in South Korea for more than a few weeks for purposes other than tourism or socializing will require a long-term visa. These should ideally be secured before arriving in South Korea, although it is also possible to arrange things here and then make a quick trip to a nearby country—Japan is the favorite—to pick up a visa (see *Changing Visa Types* for more details).

Visa categories, requirements, and regulations can change with astonishing rapidity, so make sure you check with the relevant authorities for the latest details. However, there are a few things that remain fairly consistent. Visas are generally valid for one year and are attached to a specific employer or sponsor; they can be renewed as long as that relationship continues. Documentation requirements vary depending on the type of visa being applied for, but nearly always involve an application form that includes a few questions on your personal details, educational or professional history, and your planned role in South Korea; résumés or academic transcripts and certifications; and documentation from your future employer or sponsor confirming your relationship. Application fees are usually in the US$35-50 range. They can take as little as a few days to process, but to be on the safe side it's best to plan for a turnaround of about two to four weeks.

Visas are roughly divided into a few different types by letter. "A" visas are assigned to people in South Korea for diplomatic or official purposes, and "D" visas are a grab bag of students (D2), factory workers (D3), and investors or employees of foreign enterprises (D8 and D7, respectively). Most foreign residents you'll run into in South Korea hold either "E" (employment) or "F" (resident) visas. E visas are subdivided into various occupations (E1 for professors and E5 for consultants, to name two), with some requiring special paperwork or qualifications. E2, the visa for foreign-language instructors, which requires applicants to complete health and criminal background checks, is the most notorious example.

F visas are unique in that most classes allow the holder to take work or switch jobs virtually at will. While in the past they were almost exclusively awarded to those with family (usually marriage) or ethnic ties to South Korea, it's now possible to get them in other ways, including making substantial investments in South Korea or holding a professional position and passing a government-created evaluation scheme that awards points based on things like age (the younger the better), education, income, and Korean language ability.

F visas are also, if desired, a path to a permanent stay. After a couple of years on consecutive F visas—two years in the case of those who obtained the visas through marriage, five years for most other categories—it's possible to apply for "F5," or permanent residency status. The F5 visa in theory never loses its validity, even in the case of divorce from or death of a South Korean partner, though it can be revoked if the holder spends an extended period of time living outside of Korea. In addition to the usual job mobility benefits, it comes with a few other perks, such as the right to vote in local elections. In theory, any foreigner resident in South Korea for five consecutive years or more, in good social and financial standing, with a solid command of the Korean language and customs, has the right to apply for South Korean citizenship, though relatively few foreign nationals manage to obtain it in practice.

Once you've entered South Korea with your visa, regardless of the type, you have 90 days to report to immigration to apply for your rather ominously named alien registration card, which will function as your ID within the country. The card takes about a week to process.

CHANGING VISA TYPES

Visas in South Korea are usually tied to one employer or sponsor, and they are fairly rigid in terms of the activities they permit—only holders of certain types of student visas are legally allowed to take on part-time work, for example. Changing your visa (or changing jobs) can therefore involve some hassles. While it's sometimes possible to hop jobs within the same visa category, if you're switching visa types, and sometimes even employers, you may need to cancel your old visa, leave the country, and reenter after receiving a new visa from a South Korean embassy or consulate overseas. The South Korean consulate in Fukuoka, Japan, is a favorite for this purpose because it's a relatively inexpensive three-hour ferry ride from the South Korean port of Busan.

If you're leaving one job in South Korea and planning to take another, immigration may ask you to provide a letter of release from your original employer before formally canceling your old visa and making you eligible to receive a new one. After a visa is canceled, you'll have only a couple of weeks to leave the country.

LEAVING AND REENTERING SOUTH KOREA

Since late 2010, foreign nationals residing in South Korea on a long-term basis (generally defined as 91 days or more) have been free to exit and reenter the country at will as long as their visas remain valid, with no need for separate reentry permits.

Once you've got an alien registration card, it can be presented to immigration officials at border checkpoints in lieu of the arrival/departure cards that arriving passengers usually have to fill out, although you'll still have to line up in the "foreigners" line. Some visa classes, including permanent residents (F5) and spouses of Korean nationals (F6), can sign up for immigration's "Smart Entry Service," which allows

REMEDIES FOR CULTURE SHOCK

Nearly every foreign resident has days in South Korea when almost everything about the place seems to be conspiring to drive you crazy. These feelings can be triggered by a wide range of things—getting bumped one time too many in a crowded subway car, facing a plate of *kimchi* for the fourth time in a day, not being able to explain to a taxi driver where you want to go. But these have the same root cause: culture shock.

Living in a place as all-around different as South Korea can be a challenge, and it's sometimes perfectly natural to feel out of place or deeply frustrated with your environment. But before you race for the exit, remember that these emotions do pass, and that you'd no doubt be having the odd bad day back home as well.

When culture shock strikes, spare no effort or expense in making yourself happy. Often it's your body and mind's way of telling you they need a healthy dose of the very familiar. Make a few long-distance calls to old friends, get on the Internet to seek out favorite music, TV shows, or movies, or splurge on that long-anticipated Italian or Indian meal. Visit an expatriate stomping ground like Seoul's Itaewon district to stock up on home comforts and mingle with some fellow foreigners, or go the other way and spend a couple of days in the countryside collecting your thoughts. Some find studying something local—the Korean language, *seon* meditation, or martial arts—helps rekindle their affection for the country. Whatever you decide on, getting out and doing something is key. Sitting at home reflecting on all the things you dislike about your new home is unlikely to improve your state of mind.

travelers at certain airports, including Incheon International and Gimhae in Busan, to complete entry formalities via automated gantries—usually much quicker than a wait in the non-Korean queues.

Moving with Children

Taking kids to the grocery store can be a trial, never mind moving halfway around the world, so be prepared for plenty of doubts—those voiced by others, and a few of your own—when you make the decision to move your entire family to South Korea. It is a monumental decision, and it's almost inevitable you'll hit some rough patches along the way, but there are very few expatriate families who take the plunge and decide they're worse off for it. Kids, like their parents, are bound to miss some aspects of home, but they will also find plenty of things to appreciate about South Korean life, from the new friends they'll make to the abundance of kid-friendly activities and entertainment. In fact, in many ways, the country is more child-centric than the West. South Korea, and indeed Asia, is also very much a place on the move, and early exposure to the region's customs, culture, and languages can help build a foundation of experience that will serve them well later.

PREPARING CHILDREN FOR THE MOVE

Children are unlikely to know much about this strange far-off place they're being shipped away to, so it's important that parents make at attempt to introduce them to

South Korea to encourage them to view the move more positively and address a few of the concerns they'll inevitably have. Unfortunately, because the country doesn't occupy the same prominence in the Western imagination as, say, China or Japan, there's less material on it out there, especially things geared toward kids. But enough should be available on the Internet and through agencies like Korea Tourism and the Korea Culture and Information Service, which have multiple outlets in the United States, Canada, and Europe, to give kids a rough idea of what to expect and a brief introduction to South Korean customs. If your children are old enough, you may want to encourage them to correspond with Korean pen pals or email pals so they can make a friend or two before they hit the ground—there are multiple agencies and websites devoted to this purpose.

It's also key to provide your children with a sense of continuity. Make sure they leave with a pile of friends' addresses so they can keep in touch, leave enough space to pack a few of their favorite books and toys, and if they have any sports or activities they enjoy, look into whether they'll be able to continue them in South Korea. Above all, whatever stresses it brings, try to view the move as an adventure yourself—most kids take cues from their parents.

SOUTH KOREANS AND CHILDREN

South Korea is an extremely family-oriented society, and children are highly prized. When they're very young, they're basically given free rein, with parents seemingly ready to cater to their every whim and rarely disciplining them for behavioral breaches. Things change dramatically when they reach school age, when they're put under immense pressure to excel academically and expected to study nearly constantly without complaint.

Western children—especially young, light-haired ones—are still something of a novelty and will be the subject of a fair bit of attention and adoration, plied with sweets, cuddled by strangers, and given a steady supply of potential playmates. Most kids enjoy the fuss, but it can be a bit exhausting at times. Since South Koreans believe it takes a village to raise a child, locals will have few qualms about touching your kids or offering them food, drinks, or snacks, sometimes without asking permission. You'll have to be vigilant if there are things you don't want your kids to eat. On the plus side, this means there's almost always someone watching out for the kids, and frequently taking them off your hands!

Children are highly valued in South Korean society.

MOVING WITH BABIES AND PRESCHOOLERS

Kids who are of preschool age and younger are the easiest to move with in the sense that they're not likely to have formed strong attachments to friends or places. While there's a fairly wide variety of toys, clothing, and baby-related necessities available in South Korea at very reasonable prices, be sure to bring some of your own, especially if you or your child are attached to certain brands, since exact matches may be impossible to find.

There are expatriate-oriented play groups in most major cities that bring toddlers together, as well as plenty of good affordable local preschools if you don't mind immersing your child in a primarily Korean-speaking environment. Many expatriates with young children comment on the importance of choosing an apartment that has a playground, or at least has one nearby. Since most South Korean homes lack yards, these are often the only places kids have to tear around in, and they also make it easy to meet friends.

MOVING WITH SCHOOLCHILDREN

At this age, kids will require more assurances about the relocation. If you know what school your child will be attending, ask if they'd be able to recommend a couple of students for your child to correspond with even prior to the move. Try to keep your children busy and help them meet new friends by signing them up for the activities or sports they enjoyed at home, assuming they're available, or for more local pursuits such as *taekwondo* or Korean language classes. Favorite DVDs, books, and exchanging emails or letters with friends and relatives can provide a much-needed connection to home.

MOVING WITH PRETEENS AND TEENS

This can be a tough age to move since relationships with peers and places are often very entrenched, but your preteens and teens can be assured there are plenty of others in this age group in the same boat, and they're likely to make friends quickly. Many also enjoy having new places to explore, and large cities such as Seoul and Busan offer plenty of shopping, game rooms, cafés, and other distractions for the teenager. South Korea's relatively safe streets mean teens can be trusted with more independence than they might be back home, and parents have little cause to worry about drugs, gangs, or guns. Alcohol and tobacco, however, could well be another story; the fact that South Koreans have a hard time working out how old non-Korean kids are and Korean society's generally permissive attitude toward alcohol and tobacco mean teenagers can often access them easily.

DAILY LIFE

Moving with Pets

It may sound callous, but it's worth thinking carefully before deciding to bring a pet to South Korea. The procedures can be troublesome and stressful for pet and owner alike, and when your pet arrives, it is likely to find less space to run around in than it had back home. Many apartment complexes and landlords simply won't accept pets at all. The whole idea of animals as companions rather than pests or sources of food is relatively new in South Korea, and therefore facilities for pets and veterinary standards are relatively undeveloped. Nonetheless, there are plenty of people who do bring their furry companions over and do just fine.

BRINGING A PET TO SOUTH KOREA

Anyone bringing a pet into South Korea has to obtain clearance from the Animal, Plant and Fisheries Quarantine & Inspection Agency, which has inspection stations at major ports of entry. Since December 2012 any animal imported to South Korea has to be implanted with an ISO-compliant microchip, which allows authorities to verify its identity and vaccination records. Animals should be accompanied by the (positive) results of a rabies-neutralizing antibody test administered by a competent authority in the country of origin from 30 days to 24 months prior to travel, unless they're from a handful of countries, including Australia, New Zealand, and the United Kingdom, that are designated "rabies-free regions," in which case no test results are required. Provided no health problems are apparent, animals older than 90 days meeting the requirements are typically released immediately, and animals younger than that subject to one day of quarantine. Animals arriving without the proper chips and papers will have to be treated and quarantined, or shipped back, at the owner's expense.

PETS IN SOUTH KOREA

Pets such as dogs, rabbits, birds, and hamsters are readily available at pet stores or at some markets, although there tends to be less variety in terms of breeds than in places like Canada and the United States. Cats are less common since many South Koreans still view them as slightly malevolent. The variety and availability of pet food, supplies, and veterinary care is increasing, but it is still limited compared to most Western countries.

If you're planning on bringing or buying a pet, be sure to make that clear during the house-hunting process; many buildings and landlords do not allow pets due to concerns about noise or hygiene. Dogs are welcome at most parks and walking trails, and since indoor space is likely to be limited, their owners should try to find an apartment close to some green space.

What to Take

The good news is that most of the essentials from your home country will be available in South Korea. The bad news is they may not be in the form or carry the brand you're used to. The range of imported goods on local shelves has surged over the past few years, but prices are very high.

Unless you're moving to a massive house and your employer is kind enough to pick up your shipping costs, it's probably best to leave most of your furniture in your home country. Many apartments are already partially furnished, and even those that aren't are unlikely to have enough space for most of the items in an average North American or European home. There's also a wide variety of furniture and appliances available locally at good prices.

Instead, devote your packing space to things with sentimental value or that are harder to come by here. Your needs will obviously vary, but here are a few suggestions:

- Foods: Western spices and condiments such as gravy mix, pickles, hot sauces, and Marmite, all of which are hard to find or are extremely expensive. Baby food is available here, but if you or your children are attached to a particular brand, you may want to bring a supply.
- Clothing: Men have less trouble, but women with a non-Asian physique should bring plenty of pants and undergarments in their sizes. Shoes and socks also tend to be on the small side for men and for women, so you may want to pack a few pairs.
- Books: Supply is less of an issue now with so many book vendors shipping internationally, but English-language books, particularly children's books, are limited and expensive, so bring as many as you can.
- For kids: favorite DVDs, toys, stationery supplies, board games, and clothing. Most of these things can be found here but are often overpriced and perhaps not in the variety you or your child will like.
- Toiletries: preferred cosmetics, toothpaste, soap, shampoo, deodorant, and tampons. Many Western brands are only available at specialty shops in Seoul and are very expensive.
- Pharmaceuticals: Most varieties of medication can be found here, but bring a few months' worth of prescription medication if possible so you don't have to worry about it while you're settling in. Many expatriates aren't satisfied with the local versions of birth control (condoms and pills), multivitamins, or herbal supplements, so pack your own.

ELECTRICITY AND ELECTRONICS

South Korea is a major producer of electronics, so it's no surprise there's a wide variety available here, although ironically prices for locally made goods are often higher than they are in Canada or the United States. Imported brands are very expensive. About the only thing you may want to consider bringing would be computers, since it can be difficult and pricey to buy a machine with an English-language operating system. Most new DVD players sold here play discs from all regions, but some gaming systems (like the Xbox 360) are region-specific, so gamers may want to bring their own to avoid compatibility issues.

DAILY LIFE

DAILY LIFE

LEARNING TO SHOP LOCAL

© SUNG KUK KIM/123RF.COM

Seoul marketplace

With the advent of Western-style grocery and superstores, shopping in South Korea is no longer a very different experience than it is back home, once you get past the shouting vendors (even the supermarkets employ these) and weekend crowds. There are, however, a couple of local realities to look out for.

The first is that bargaining is a far more common tactic than it is in the West and indeed some other parts of Asia. This applies particularly to markets and smaller shops, but it certainly isn't unheard of at larger retailers, particularly if a substantial purchase is made. Rather than negotiating for direct cash discounts (which is sometimes seen as a bit coarse), a bargainer will often seek a few extras—a tie or a couple of belts if buying a suit, for example, or a carrying case or other accessories if purchasing a digital camera. Many vendors will provide little "bonuses"

without any prompting at all, but if they don't, it can be worth asking, essentially, "Is this the best you can do?" The most commonly used Korean phrase for these types of situations is probably: *"jom kka-kajusaeyo,"* or "Please give me a deal/discount." Whatever you're asking for, keep it good-natured with a smile firmly on your face; heated arguments are rarely effective and demean both buyer and seller.

If you're a regular patron of any particular retailers or shops, it's also worth asking if they have some kind of discount or member program—these are very common in South Korea and often have more generous reward schemes than the North American or British variety, with almost any trip to the shop likely to result in some sort of sizable discount or giveaway. While there are few real barriers to non-Koreans signing up for these programs, unfortunately few local retailers provide information on them in English, so you'll probably have to enlist the help of a local friend to sign up if there is a language barrier.

Finally, all residents of South Korea should register for the National Tax Service (NTS)'s cash receipt (*hyeongum yeongsujung*) system. This basically entitles consumers to annual income tax deductions for every cash purchase they make, provided they request the retailer issue a form of cash receipt that can be tracked by the government; it is a method to reduce tax evasion. After signing up for the system via the NTS website (so far the application form is available in the Korean language only), you'll be able to request cash receipts from any retailer by simply providing your mobile phone number or the cash receipt card issued to you by the NTS. A year's worth of small purchases can add up to some significant tax savings.

South Korea uses 220 volt wiring and usually two-pronged round plugs. Transformers and converters are easy to find, so it's generally not a problem to bring appliances with different voltages or plug types.

SHIPPING OPTIONS

If you have to take more than your airline baggage allowance, you'll need to enlist some shipping help. Those with just a few boxes to send may want to consider doing the packing themselves and shipping them by standard post, which is by far the cheapest option. For large shipments, expatriates-to-be usually engage the services of an international relocation specialist such as Allied Pickfords, Santa Fe, or Asian Tigers, who will usually assist with the packing and unpacking and handle all the customs paperwork.

Prices vary—be sure to get a few quotes—but a door-to-door sea freight shipment from North America of a dozen or so boxes and three or four pieces of furniture, enough to fill a standard South Korean apartment, should cost around US$5,000 and take about a month. Prices for air freight are astronomical, but it's obviously a lot faster. It's theoretically possible to save some money by using a smaller company or doing the packing yourself, but this carries more risk, especially in terms of customs frustrations.

CUSTOMS

Customs procedures can be complex, time-consuming, and change regularly, so try to make sure you're getting some help from your employer or a savvy local agent. Foreign nationals working in South Korea are permitted to bring a reasonable amount of household goods duty free; how much constitutes a reasonable amount is generally left to the discretion of customs officers. Obviously used goods are unlikely to attract much attention, but new "luxury" items such as golf clubs or expensive cameras may be questioned or subject to tax. To qualify for this duty-free exemption, expatriates have to provide customs with copies of their passports, a statement from their employer verifying their status, bills of lading, and full packing lists.

Your shipment will be inspected by customs on arrival and then cleared for release, which usually takes just a few days but can take much longer if something seems out of order.

DAILY LIFE

HOUSING CONSIDERATIONS

Housing is one of the main adjustments expatriates will have to make, especially if they're coming from a standard North American suburb. South Korea, and Seoul in particular, are among the most densely populated places on the planet, and while Western-style homes exist in places, most people live in units of just three or four rooms in towering apartment blocks. While they may find space more limited, many foreign residents come to enjoy the convenience and security South Korean apartment life offers. For those who can afford them, there are some lovely stand-alone homes up for grabs in some areas, from rustic *hanok* (traditional houses) to modern mansions.

Since the local real estate market can be tricky to negotiate for new arrivals, many companies provide housing or assistance finding accommodations for foreign employees. If the house hunt is something you have to tackle on your own, rest assured it is possible, although you'll want to enlist the help of a Korean speaker. While housing costs are high overall, there's a range of accommodations available that spans most budgets.

Types of Housing

APARTMENT COMPLEXES

Apartment complexes house most of South Korea's population and dominate the landscape in most areas. Typically consisting of a dozen or so towering blocks, from the outside some of these have all the charm and aesthetic value of filing cabinets, but don't be put off—on the inside they're often surprisingly roomy and pleasant. Newer complexes are more design-conscious and often incorporate features such as walking paths and landscaped gardens. Playgrounds, small grocery stores, and laundries are common facilities, but pools and exercise rooms are rare. Apartments also usually have security guards and management offices that help in the day-to-day running of the complex.

A typical apartment consists of a few rooms, separated by sliding doors, with wood or linoleum floors—South Korea's muggy summers make carpets impractical—that can be heated in winter. Kitchens often function as dining rooms as well and will usually have a small stove, but ovens and dishwashers are relatively rare. Many units have an enclosed patio with a washer-dryer that functions as a laundry area. Toilets are almost always Western-style, but bathtubs are uncommon in smaller units. Garbage generally must be brought outside by tenants to a collection area where it has to be separated by type for disposal or recycling.

Since there are only a handful of companies building them, apartment layouts remain fairly similar regardless of price. The differences are more apparent in size, quality of the fittings—higher-end apartments may have touches like marble floors, big built-in closets, and Jacuzzi tubs—floor number, and location, with units on higher floors and in major cities costing the most. Prices are also higher for furnished or partially

COMMONLY USED REAL ESTATE TERMS AND ABBREVIATIONS

- *bojunggum* (보증금): deposit or "key money" on a rental property

- *budongsan* (부동산): property or real estate agency

- *imdae* (임대): for rent

- *jeonse* (전세): local rental system in which the tenant gives the landlord a large deposit (typically around 50-60 percent of the property's value) but no monthly rent is paid; the deposit is returned to the tenant at the conclusion of the contract

- *mae-mae* (매매): literally "buy and sell," typically appears on the window of property agencies that offer sale as well as rental properties

- *pyeong* (also *pyong* or *pyung*, 평): traditional unit of measurement for housing and property, equivalent to approximately 3.3 square meters (35.5 square feet)

- *wolse* (월세): literally "monthly rental," Western-style rental system in which the tenant gives the landlord a security deposit and pays rent on a monthly basis, with the security deposit to be returned at the conclusion of the contract. Note security deposits in Korea tend to be high; 5 million won is seen as the minimum even for places with low monthly rents, and putting down less will severely curtail your options.

apartment blocks in Jeollanamdo

furnished units, which make up the majority of housing targeted at expatriates and usually come at least with the major appliances (washing machine, refrigerator, air-conditioner) and sometimes much more.

Many complexes also charge tenants a management fee that supposedly covers the costs of building security and maintenance as well as heating and cooling if both are provided centrally. These can vary greatly, so make sure they're spelled out specifically in any rental contracts.

All in all, if you are not opting for the full-deposit system in which you pay a lump some up front and no monthly rent, expatriates should plan on spending at least 1.5-2 million won per month for a fairly spacious, partially furnished two-bedroom unit in a centrally located apartment complex in Seoul; that amount would go substantially farther in other cities.

VILLAS

Villa is one of those adopted foreign-language terms that has taken on a rather different meaning in Korean. Anyone for whom the word conjures up images of a luxurious country house may be in for some disappointment; in South Korea it's a sort of catch-all phrase for smaller apartment buildings or private homes carved up into apartment units. These are usually no more than three or four stories with one or two units on each floor, and they vary significantly in terms of quality, from cramped basement studios to spanking new penthouses that rival the nicest apartment. They account for most housing outside apartment blocks and usually outnumber apartment complexes in older neighborhoods.

While they can be quite nice and are similar to apartments in many respects, units in villas tend to cost less, mainly because they generally lack facilities such as security guards, outdoor play areas, and parking—no small concern on South Korea's crowded streets. Besides the price advantage, some expatriates like them for their cozier feel

WHAT WAS THAT ADDRESS AGAIN?

The unique address system that still dominates South Korean cities is often of little help in finding a destination. During the country's rapid development, building numbers were frequently assigned on the fly as plots of land were divvied up or created and thus often have no real connection to physical placement: 147-6 Hyoja-dong could be right next to 847-2 Hyoja-dong, for example.

What logic there is to old-style addresses can be outlined as follows. They'll generally include the *gu* (city district) and the *dong* (neighborhood). *Dong* vary in size and shape and major districts will include dozens, but if you've found the *dong* you need to go to, you generally won't be too far from your final destination.

So how do people get where they need to go? In the past this was a bit of a crapshoot—directions were typically given in relation to the nearest subway station or other major landmarks. With the arrival of GPS technology, however, most cabs are now equipped with navigation devices, and a lot of Koreans sport navigation-equipped smartphones on which destinations can be called up with a few keystrokes. Most cabbies will know how to get to major sights, parks,

and landmarks, but for restaurants and clubs, you should have the address written down for them in Korean, or at the very least a phone number they can call for directions.

The address system is complicated by the fact that authorities, aware of the headache the old system represents, are busy rolling out a new one that's much closer to the international standard, with building numbers that correspond to positions on a major street. There has also been an effort to name and post signage for more streets, which was previously seriously lacking. The new system has already taken hold in many areas, and you'll notice in some neighborhoods roads are clearly named with the "ro" or "no" suffix, which denotes a major street, or "gil," which indicates a smaller street running off a major one. Thus "Wausanro 12-gil" would be the 12th smaller street running off the major road of Wausanro.

This system will make getting around easier when it's consistently applied, but that's a work in progress due to be completed by 2014. Even then, as old navigation habits die hard, the old address system is likely to coexist with the new for some time.

compared to larger housing blocks. A functional (but by no means fancy) two-bedroom villa in a major city will rent for around 700,000 to 1 million won per month, but prices can sink to half this level if you're willing to consider small units in older buildings.

STAND-ALONE HOMES

It's certainly possible to find stand-alone homes in South Korea, but they're likely to be fairly rare and very costly compared to where you came from. Here expansive homes with large yards are the domain of political leaders and top-ranking executives, confined to a few very affluent pockets of the country such as Seoul's Seongbuk-dong area. Houses come in a wide range of styles, from red-brick mock English manor houses to low-slung traditional Korean *hanok* with their graceful flared roofs. On the inside, however, most are full of decidedly local touches such as sliding doors and under-floor heating.

The procedures for renting or buying a home don't differ widely from those for apartments, but the tenant is almost always entirely responsible for any maintenance costs that may arise during residence. For this reason, before signing any contracts it's advisable to be extra diligent with checking the wiring, plumbing, and so on. Most stand-alone homes available for rent in urban areas are marketed to foreign executives and diplomats, and rents, at around three million won per month and up, reflect this, although there are houses available for much less in more rural settings.

OTHER HOUSING OPTIONS

There are a few subcategories of housing you may run across in a property search. One of the most common is the "officetel," a hybrid of "office" and "hotel" that's rather oddly used to describe modern apartment complexes typically in city centers that blend mainly studio-type accommodations catering to young working professionals with a few floors of restaurants, shops, and commercial space. These are distin-

a villa in Seoul

© JONATHAN HOPFNER

guished from apartment complexes mainly by the small unit sizes and lack of grounds or outdoor space, but because they're often new and in very convenient locations, rents are around the same or even higher.

On the lower end of the scale, *goshiwon* and *hasukjip,* the former a sort of dormitory and the latter a type of homestay, target students and low-income earners with monthly rents of around 500,000 won or less. Both are typically concentrated in student districts and offer very small private rooms with shared bathing and kitchen facilities, with *hasukjip* owners often providing meals. These can be good value but are far from luxurious and will generally appeal only to a struggling single person.

Renting

REAL ESTATE AGENTS

While it's by no means mandatory, most new arrivals to South Korea find themselves either using real estate agents (*budongsan*) appointed by their companies or engaging their own. Online classified sites such as Craigslist will carry the occasional listing from a landlord or foreign residents looking for someone to take over a lease, but the amount of housing advertised directly by owners is pretty limited. Agents generally know their stuff and don't cost an awful lot, so there's no need to shy away from using one.

The recommended procedure in South Korea is to pick an area first and then an agent or two who specialize in it. If at all possible, don't commit to any housing before you put your feet on the ground and have had a chance to explore a few neighborhoods

A HOUSING TRADITION

© CRAIG D.C. LEWIS

entrance to a traditional *hanok* home

Traditional-style Korean homes, or *hanok,* were once viewed as a somewhat backward reminder of South Korea's poverty-stricken past and were regularly leveled to make way for the generic-looking but convenient apartment blocks that most city-dwellers still aspire to. Fortunately, in the last few years there has been a renewal of interest in traditional architecture and more emphasis placed on preserving the few clusters of *hanok* that remain.

This is a welcome development because there's a lot to appreciate. Though most *hanok* are far from palatial, with their graceful tile roofs and warm earthy colors they possess an understated beauty that's a welcome contrast to the country's neon-drenched cityscapes. Anyone who spends time in a *hanok* will quickly appreciate how much thought has gone into the deceptively simple-looking design of these homes. Traditionally, every square centimeter of the house is made of natural materials such as wood and earth and is designed to harmonize

with the surrounding environment. From the *ondol* under-floor heating system to wide *daechong* porches that promote the circulation of air in South Korea's muggy summers, *hanok* design features are remarkably effective and continue to inspire Korean architects to this day.

Seoul's Bukchon district and the Jeonju *hanok* village are among the country's top spots for *hanok* viewing, though you'll come across them in all kinds of places. More than a few foreign residents have been smitten enough with *hanok* that they choose to live in, build, or buy them, though with their high maintenance costs and the scarcity of some *hanok* construction materials they can be something of a labor of love. And despite their often humble appearance, the recent revival of demand means they don't come cheap—fully restored *hanok* in central Seoul, many of which are kitted out with modern conveniences like professional-grade kitchens and underground car parks, can easily run into the millions of U.S. dollars.

or living locations relatively thoroughly. Try to arrange temporary accommodations for a few weeks after you arrive to give yourself some time to look around.

Despite some claims to the contrary, agents do generally focus on a particular district or two, inevitably those they're located in. If you're house-shopping in expat-heavy neighborhoods like Seoul's Yongsan-gu or Haeundae in Busan, you'll find many agents who speak English or target non-Koreans. This can be great in terms of convenience and having them understand your needs, but it also sometimes carries the risk of quotes being inflated due to an affluent expatriate clientele. Outside of these areas, you'll probably need to enlist the help of a Korean-speaking friend or colleague; rental negotiations and contracts are not an area where you want any misunderstandings. Be as specific as you can about your requirements, and be patient—some agents try to foist their least desirable listings on new customers first—and you'll almost certainly find something you're comfortable with, since there's no shortage of housing in most places.

Remember you're not bound to any particular agent (unless your company is employing one), so check with as many in your preferred area as possible. That nice complex that one agent said was "unavailable" or "full" might just turn out to have five listings with the next guy. It's also possible to do some preliminary research online, but much of what's available is either extortionately expensive (if it's advertised in English) or misleading—in South Korea very attractive online property offers are sometimes used as bait to draw people into agents' offices, at which point they suddenly no longer apply.

Commissions are standardized at around 0.5 percent of the rental rate—every agent should have a chart of exact rates that will be applied according to the transaction displayed prominently in their office—and payable by both the renter and the landlord.

LEASES
Short-Term Rentals
Short-term rentals (defined as anything less than one year) are not common in South Korea, and agents generally won't be interested in arranging them. You may get lucky with taking over a lease for a short time from someone leaving the country, however—check websites like Craigslist and the Seoul city government's (www.seoul.go.kr) for listings.

Failing that, if you have a sizable budget, your best option is serviced apartments, of which there are many in sizable cities like Seoul and Busan. These basically function like hotels in that they can be rented by the day or month and often include perks like cleaning services, buffet breakfasts, and swimming pools, but also have standard home-like touches such as fully functional kitchens and separate bedrooms. They're a convenient option but quite expensive, with rates for a one-bedroom serviced apartment in Seoul starting at about 2 million won per month, often payable up front and with a damage deposit of up to one month's rent for longer stays.

Many serviced apartment complexes are owned and operated by hotel chains or large hospitality firms with multiple branches throughout Seoul and other South Korean cities. Some of the better-known operators with a local presence include Frasers Hospitality (www.frasershospitality.com), Somerset Serviced Residences (www.somerset.com), and Vabien Suites (www.vabiensuite.com). A quick Internet search for

"Seoul serviced apartments" or "Korea serviced apartments" will throw up dozens of other options.

It's also possible to arrange long-term discounts with most *yeogwan* (inns or motels) for stays of a couple of weeks or more. These can be fine in a pinch but won't really contribute to feeling that you're settling down.

Long-Term Rentals

The minimum lease most landlords will consider is one year, and many prefer two-year contracts, although it's often possible to leave earlier by finding another tenant to take your place. Basically renters in South Korea will be presented with two options. One is *wolse,* or monthly payment, which mimics the system found in most other countries where the tenant is charged a monthly rent and pays an initial security deposit, to be returned when the contract is completed. However in South Korea this deposit is usually fairly large—5 million won is generally seen as a minimum, and it can be tough (though certainly not impossible) to find a landlord that will accept the standard Western deposit of one or two months' rent. *Wolse* is the most common arrangement in expatriate-heavy areas and is becoming more accepted elsewhere.

Perhaps unique to South Korea, and still the norm outside of the more cosmopolitan districts of Seoul, is the *jeonse* or full-deposit system, in which the tenant puts down a significant chunk of money, typically 50 to 70 percent of the price of the house or apartment, and no monthly rent is charged at all, with the landlord instead profiting from banking or investing the sum, and again returning it in full to the tenant on completion of the rental contract. Relatively few foreigners go this route because of the amounts involved—200 million won or more for a typical middle-class home in Seoul—and the fact that banks are reluctant to extend *jeonse* loans to expatriate tenants (although those with South Korean partners may have more luck). In the past, landlords absconding with deposits was a serious problem, but they are now tracked carefully and "insured" to some extent by the government, so it has become less of an issue. This is obviously a more cost-effective option for the renter in the end and a good halfway step between renting and full ownership, but it won't appeal to everyone.

Hybrid *jeonse-wolse* arrangements are also possible and indeed welcomed by some landlords. This will all be down to the landlord's finances and your (or your agent's) negotiating skills, but as a rough guideline you can expect to knock 10 million won off the *jeonse* deposit for every additional 100,000 won you agree to pay in monthly rent—thus a landlord requesting a 150 million won *jeonse* deposit may very well settle for 100 million won and 500,000 in rent monthly. The reverse also applies—a landlord asking for a 10 million won deposit and 500,000 won monthly may knock the rent down to 400,000 won if the deposit is doubled.

Negotiating is a time-honored tactic in South Korea, and while it doesn't tend to move prices much unless the place was ridiculously overvalued to begin with, if there's something else you'd like—new wallpaper, a washing machine to be replaced with a newer model, your landlord to pick up the cable bill—it never hurts to ask.

Whatever rental agreement you sign up for, make sure you obtain certification that the landlord is the real owner of the property and is not in danger of defaulting on it, and that any contracts and deposits are registered with the local district office, which will allow you quicker redress in the case of anything going wrong. These are

apartment courtyard, Seoul

standard procedures that any agent should be able to walk you through. Also be sure to check that the contract specifies which expenses you'll be responsible for (monthly maintenance, parking fees, appliance breakdowns, etc.) and to take a few pictures of any significant property damage (large wall stains, dented appliances or floors, and so on) prior to moving in so that you won't be inadvertently billed for any damage on your way out. Once you've moved in, the agent will generally see his or her job as done, and it will be largely up to you to navigate any future disputes or issues you may have with the owner.

Buying

There are no real restrictions on foreign nationals buying property in South Korea, and most buyers go about it the same way as renters, by browsing the listings of property agents in their area of focus. The main difference is that prices are high for what you get—most Seoul apartments seen as desirable start in the 300 million to 500 million won range, enough to buy a sizable house in many other countries—and access to financing from local banks is very limited, especially if you don't work for a multinational or don't have a local significant other.

If you do decide to buy a place outright, you'll need to pay commissions, legal fees, and registration and acquisition taxes that will add around 20 percent to the property's purchase price, and complete a transfer of ownership registration at the nearest district office. Nonresidents of South Korea will also have to show that the funds for the purchase came from outside the country and register the transaction with the local land authorities.

Regardless of residential status, foreign nationals aren't generally permitted to repatriate any proceeds from the sale or rental of a property they own. Some get around this by setting up local companies, which face fewer restrictions, and buying properties through them, but the procedures for doing so are complex and likely to require some outside expertise.

Household Expenses

If the arrangements aren't already made when you move in, you'll be able to set up accounts with utility providers—water, electricity, and communications—in a few days with copies of your rental agreement, passport, and alien registration card. It's common for real estate agents and landlords to assist in this, so don't have any qualms about seeking their help. Provided you have a long-term visa, few utility vendors will seek deposits, but some, especially Internet and cable suppliers, will want you to sign up for long-term contracts that can sometimes (but not always) be carried over to your next place.

The first thing to establish is whether you have to pay a maintenance fee, and if so, what it includes—in some places it's in the hundreds of thousands of won and covers everything from water to electricity expenses; in others it's far less and includes only security services and rubbish collection (which you'd be unlikely ever to see a bill for anyway). If you're coughing up for these things separately, water costs are usually only 10,000 won or so per month and electricity around 70,000 per month, though you'll spend more if you have a big property and in the winter and summer when heating or air-conditioning may be required. Budget 30,000 won per month each for unlimited broadband Internet services, cable TV with a few foreign channels, and phone bills.

LANGUAGE AND EDUCATION

Both the Korean language and learning in general are national obsessions, stretching back into antiquity, feted with holidays and ceremonies, and agonized over by parents and their children. And both rank among the biggest concerns of expatriates, who fret about their ability to communicate with the locals and how to further their own or their children's education. These are legitimate concerns, but the good news is that there's an abundant and growing number of resources, both within South Korea and abroad, to help any new resident tackle these issues.

The South Korean education system is known for being rigid and academically rigorous, but it has been instrumental in the country's economic success and regularly tops international rankings in areas like math skills and the proportion of students pursuing higher education. A number of international schooling options also exist for parents who prefer that their children follow global curricula. Local universities have also expanded programs for foreign learners and now offer a number of degrees in partnership with schools outside South Korea.

Would-be Korean language learners will also find themselves spoiled for choice.

While studying Korean isn't absolutely necessary for a stay in the country, it certainly makes residing here an easier, and far more enriching, experience.

Learning Korean

We might as well get the bad news out of the way first: learning Korean is not easy. Experts rank the country's national language right up there with head-scratchers like Chinese, Japanese, and Arabic in terms of the amount of study required to attain fluency. It has been linked to everything from Hungarian to Japanese, yet academics still disagree on how to classify it. Throw in a unique script, multiple levels of formality, and for Westerners, alien grammar, and it's apparent why very few non-Koreans attain fluency.

The good news is that fluency doesn't have to be anyone's goal. English is now a core component of the education system (and at the center of a massive tutoring craze) so most South Koreans now have at least a passing knowledge of the language. Many important businesses and government departments have made an effort to set up departments providing services in English and other major languages, and many more can rustle up an English speaker to assist if needed, particularly in cities like Seoul and Busan. There's also no shortage of English speakers in the workplace, especially where expatriates are likely to be employed.

Of course, Korean is the national language, and regardless of what foreign residents do or where they choose to live, they'll have to resort to whatever Korean they've picked up at some point. Korean fluency may not be realistic, but Korean functionality certainly is. Hangul, the Korean script, is remarkably logical and can be picked up after a few days of study. There are no tones to contend with, and many articles or grammar points can be dropped in everyday speech without risking any misunderstanding. A few simple phrases and words will be enough to engage in small talk and handle common shopping, dining, and travel situations. For the most part South Koreans are delighted with and supportive of any attempts to speak their language—indeed the chief danger is that they'll mistake your fumbling attempts for fluency and start rattling off all kinds of sentences you have no hope of understanding.

How much Korean you'll need depends on where you work and live—those in smaller local firms or towns, for example, will find the lack of language ability more of an issue than someone working for a multinational in Seoul. Those content with "survival" Korean can usually get by with a bit of self-study, for which there's a wide range of books and Internet-based classes available, or a couple of hours per week of being tutored or language exchange sessions.

Those who have set Korean proficiency as a goal—usually long-term residents or those with serious local business interests—will require more intensive learning, either through private tutors or institutes or via one of the excellent language courses available at local universities. These involve a substantial amount of work but produce definite results and can often be fit around a typical executive's schedule.

DAILY LIFE

WRITTEN KOREAN

Until the 15th century, Korean lacked its own script and was written exclusively using *hanja,* or borrowed Chinese characters. Many of these were incorporated into the Korean language, and it's currently estimated that over 50 percent of Korean words are of Chinese origin.

AN ALPHABET OF PRINCIPLE

newspaper in a mix of hangul and *hanja* (Chinese characters)

The Korean people are immensely proud of hangul, their homegrown alphabet, which has become inextricably bound up with the national identity. It's not uncommon for foreign residents proudly to be informed that hangul is the "most scientific" script in the world. This may seem an odd claim—how can an alphabet be "scientific"?—but when one understands how hangul was developed, it's not utterly without merit.

When King Sejong ordered a committee of scholars to create an alphabet in the 15th century, their main task was to come up with something easy to learn in order to pull the masses out of illiteracy, but they managed to cram some very clever concepts into hangul's no-nonsense design. Hangul consonants are actually designed to map the shapes made by vocal organs when they're pronounced.

Thus the character ㄴ ("n") resembles the tongue touching the upper gums, while ㅁ ("m") shows two lips coming together. The basic vowel signs, meanwhile, symbolize earth, the sky, and people, the basic trinity in much Taoist and Confucian philosophy. Although these traits are unique, hangul character designs weren't created in a total vacuum, as some Korean nationalists claim; scholars have remarked on the similarities between hangul and the Mongol alphabet of the time, which would have made an appearance in the royal libraries.

Hangul's design elements, along with the way vowels and consonants can be combined to approximate almost any sound, are impressive, but nothing speaks more to the virtues of hangul than its effectiveness. Today, nearly 100 percent of South Koreans are literate, one of the highest rates in the world.

DAILY LIFE

© GINA SMITH/123RF.COM

THE LANGUAGE LADDER

Being a heavily hierarchal society, South Korea has a language to match. One of the biggest stumbling blocks for new students of Korean is the way sentence structure and even vocabulary have to change depending on to whom you're speaking. Technically Korean has half a dozen levels of politeness, but these categories can be broadly divided into *jeondaemal* (formal) and *banmal*, or casual speech. The differences are most apparent in verb endings—the very casual *kaja* versus the polite *kapshida* for "let's go," for example. They also pop up in words and expressions, such as the formal *chapsushida* versus the typical *mogda* for "eat."

Choosing the right form of speech to use with someone is important. Generally people who are older or in clear positions of authority (teachers, police, or bosses, for example) will expect to be addressed in the politer forms of Korean and may be quite offended if they're not. Children and your close friends, on the other hand, would find it strange or very humorous indeed if you spoke to them using *jeondaemal*.

That said, there's no need for undue stress about language forms. Most South Koreans understand that their language is a complex one and are very impressed with any effort by a nonnative to speak it, mistakes or no. And when in doubt, there's a sort of catchall that can be appended to any sentence to make it an acceptably polite one—the suffix *-yo*, which you'll hear often in everyday speech. Thus *ka* (go) becomes *kayo*, *mogo* (eat) becomes *mogoyo*, and so on.

The indigenous script, hangul, was unveiled by King Sejong in the mid-15th century to combat the problem of illiteracy, and it is still viewed as a masterful linguistic achievement, perfectly encapsulating all the sounds used in Korean and simple enough for most to master in just a few days. It consists of 24 letters that are arranged in syllabic blocks, resembling Chinese characters to some extent but nowhere near as complex. Learning hangul should be considered the first step in any effort to study the Korean language; it's not at all difficult and will prove invaluable in perfecting pronunciation and decoding timetables or restaurant menus.

Not surprisingly, despite some resistance from the aristocracy, the use of hangul spread like wildfire, but the status attached to *hanja* meant they continued to dominate the written language until the early 20th century. Since the 1950s the use of *hanja* has declined markedly, and Korean is now written almost entirely in the native script, which is all that most foreign students will ever have to learn. That being said, Chinese characters continue to be taught in schools, and there's still a certain amount of credibility associated with *hanja* fluency, especially in academia and the arts. Chinese characters also make regular appearances in instances where visual impact, brevity, or clarification may be required, since so many words are written and pronounced identically in Korean. Examples include advertisements, newspaper articles, and name cards. When Chinese characters are used, they appear in the traditional forms still used in Hong Kong, Macau, Taiwan, and with some exceptions Japan, rather than the simplified versions adopted in mainland China and Singapore.

Romanization—the use of Latin letters to represent Korean—is a common but still controversial affair. In 2000 the government introduced a new official romanization system that was designed to address some of the inconsistencies of the

© CRAIG D.C. LEWIS

a bridge marker written in *hanja*

McCune-Reischauer standard commonly used until then by permanently assigning corresponding Latin letters to Korean consonants and vowel combinations. While the system has definitely gained a foothold, some find it awkward and have steadfastly refused to fall into line, meaning that many Korean words, especially people's names and place-names, can and often are romanized in several different ways. A couple of common examples are Lee/Yi/Rhee, Park/Bak/Baek, and Pusan/Busan. Learning hangul is the best way to avoid confusion.

SPEAKING KOREAN

Compared to their counterparts in some other parts of Asia, expats in South Korea have it easy—there's only one national language to contend with, it's free of complicated tones, and grammar rules in the spoken language are quite lax. While there are some vowel and consonant combinations that are tricky for a non-Korean speaker to distinguish or get right, virtually all sounds used in Korean also appear in English, and pronunciation is a fairly straightforward affair.

Korean sentences generally follow the subject-object-verb order, which can confuse English speakers initially but is quickly gotten used to. In spoken Korean the subject of a sentence is often dropped altogether. Verb conjugations and tenses generally follow regular patterns, although frequently these too are abandoned, and the timing of an event or whether a sentence is a statement or question are inferred by tone or context.

One of the main difficulties to contend with is Korean's varying levels of formality; sentences should often have entirely different verb endings (and in some cases, words) depending on the age and seniority relative to you of the person you're addressing. While most locals understand non-Koreans are learning the language and are very forgiving of mistakes, failing to use the appropriate sentence constructions in such a status-conscious society can sometimes cause offense. For this reason most Korean language instructors recommend their students gain fluency in the more polite forms of Korean first.

REGIONAL DIALECTS

Standard Korean (*pyojunmal*) as spoken in Seoul is the de facto national dialect, and as it's taught in schools and dominates television and movies, it is readily understood throughout South Korea. There are distinctive regional accents, particularly in the southwest and southeast, that are a frequent source of amusement for Seoulites but are unlikely even to be picked up on by nonnative speakers. Some people on the island of

Jeju-do speak a more unique dialect that incorporates archaic Mongolian and Korean words; however even this is falling into disuse among the young.

LANGUAGE SCHOOLS

While plenty can be picked up through books, tapes, or the Internet, to attain genuine proficiency in Korean, formal instruction is a must. Within South Korea it's also a great way for new residents to meet people and approach everyday life with more confidence. Full-time immersive study is obviously the quickest way to develop Korean skills, but even a couple of hours of class per week will enable most learners to develop the vocabulary to handle common social interactions.

Before You Go

While Korean isn't studied abroad to the degree, say, Chinese is, classes can generally be arranged in major cities through language school chains such as Berlitz. Many universities, including the University of Washington, University of California at Los Angeles, Oxford University in the United Kingdom, and Canada's University of British Columbia, have Korean language and degree programs. Instruction can also be arranged through nonprofit organizations such as the New York City-based Korea Society and the Korean-government backed King Sejong Institute, which has several locations in North America and Europe.

Universities

Virtually every large city in South Korea has universities running degree and nondegree Korean language programs for foreign learners, including Busan, Ulsan, Daegu, and Daejeon. The highest concentration is, of course, in Seoul, where there are dozens of choices. Yonsei University and Sogang University generally have the best reputations for producing fluent Korean speakers.

Most universities will offer students full-time or part-time study options that are usually confined to evenings and weekends. Fees start at around 1 million won per term, and classes tend to be relatively large and fast-paced, with some amount of additional independent study required.

Language Schools

Larger cities like Seoul and Busan have multiple private language schools offering Korean language classes. The benefit of these outfits is that they tend to be far more flexible than universities and can tailor courses to the needs of specific individuals or groups. However, standards and costs vary widely, so be sure the school has a good reputation and ask about the qualifications of your would-be instructor. In Seoul, the Language Teaching Research Center and Seoul Korean Language Academy are well-established and centrally located, as is the Korean Language Institute for Foreigners in Busan.

Other Options

Increasing numbers of city and district governments offer free Korean language courses to new residents in order to help them adjust—check with your nearest district office to see if any are running. Language exchanges can also be arranged easily with a host

DAILY LIFE

of eager Koreans in your area through community centers, universities, or social net-working sites like Facebook and meetup.com.

Education

South Korea's education system is highly centralized, rigorous, and competitive, and it is the focus of a far higher proportion of government spending than in most other countries. Whether it provides good education is a matter of age-old, heated, and exhaustive debate. The general sentiment seems to be that the emphasis on structure and rote learning does a fine job of developing students' science and mathematics skills, thereby preparing them for a career in one of the country's technological or industrial powerhouses. But as the service and creative industries have grown in importance and South Korean companies compete on an increasingly international stage, many worry the educational system has failed to keep pace and that more emphasis on creativity and critical thinking is needed. Some tentative reforms have been introduced, but many of the system's features—including occasional corporal punishment and an abundance of exams—have remained unchanged for decades.

Foreign residents of South Korea are free to send their children to local schools in their area, and fees are minimal to nonexistent. Given language barriers and differing educational philosophies, however, most opt to send their children to international schools, which are found throughout the country but are especially concentrated in Seoul and Busan.

COLLEGES AND UNIVERSITIES

Students typically graduate from high school and start university at age 19, mainly entering four-year undergraduate degree programs, although young men may start later and take longer to finish a degree as they also have to complete two years of mandatory military service. Quite a high percentage of high school graduates go on to university because vocational schools have an image problem and a degree is seen as a necessary first step to a successful career.

At the end of each year, months of intensive cramming culminate in punishing university entrance exams, a heated race that decides who will seize the coveted few spots in the country's top schools. These institutions, crowned by the so-called "SKY" triumvirate of Seoul National, Korea, and Yonsei Universities, produce the vast majority of the country's top civil servants and business leaders, and gaining admission to one is basically a guarantee of prestige and prosperity.

Much like their Western counterparts, most South Korean universities offer bachelor, master's, and postgraduate degree programs. The academic calendar is typically divided into two semesters, one running February-June and the other August-December.

Most universities will accept applications from international students in September or October for programs starting in the spring semester, or in April or May for programs starting in the fall, but not all have English-language degree programs available. Universities generally require proof that an applicant has completed high school, or a bachelor's degree if a postgraduate degree will be pursued. Some universities require new students to pass a Korean language proficiency test if Korean is the language of

© BRIAN DEUTSCH

DAILY LIFE

college entrance exam day in Gwangju

instruction. Tuition fees at top universities are typically around 10-15 million won per year, and some schools have scholarships and housing support available.

There are currently around 60,000 foreign students at South Korean universities, most studying Korean language or culture programs. Degree programs often, but not always, allow students to earn credits that will be recognized abroad. Only a handful of South Korean schools—Seoul National and Yonsei top the list—have any international reputation. Prospective students worried about their degrees being accepted overseas might want to look into one of an increasing number of joint degree programs on offer at universities in Seoul, such as Yonsei's dual international studies degree with the University of Chicago.

PRIMARY SCHOOLS AND HIGH SCHOOLS

South Korean children begin elementary school (*chodeunghakgyo*) at age six, usually after one or two years of preschool. Elementary school is mandatory and, in the case of government schools, free of charge; almost 100 percent of the country's student population completes it and goes on to middle and high schools. The school year typically starts in March and ends in late February, with summer and winter breaks of around six weeks each beginning in July and December, respectively. Students usually attend classes from morning to mid-afternoon Monday to Friday. Once-common Saturday classes have been largely phased out.

Elementary school consists of six grades, with students graduating when they're 11 or 12, and it is a relatively rigorous affair. Classes cover a range of subjects, from language and physical education to arts, with a particular emphasis on Korean, math, and English.

Studies move into high gear in middle school (*junghakgyo*), which consists of three grades. Students typically enter at age 12 and finish at age 15 or 16. At most schools, strict regulations on uniforms and haircuts are enforced, and the curriculum follows

© JONATHAN HOPFNER

a middle school in Seoul

a standard format nationwide, with the core subjects of math, English, science, and Korean supplemented by the study of Chinese characters, history, and computers.

Although students tend to progress from grade to grade regardless of academic achievement, their examination scores in the final year of middle school are key to gaining entrance to top high schools and consequently universities. Therefore, they are the focus of much pressure from relatives and peers. Most students will attend *hagwon* or private academies to supplement their studies after school hours in the hopes of boosting their test scores, meaning some are studying a full 12 hours or so per day—indeed, it's not uncommon in Seoul or Busan to see young students on the subways or buses in the middle of the night, groaning under the burden of a bag full of textbooks.

The cramming reaches a fever pitch in high school (*godeunghakgyo*), which has three grades that take students about age 17-19. Studies are intense and often cover nearly a dozen subjects to prepare students for the university entrance tests at the end of their stay—the entire high school experience is colloquially referred to by some as "examination hell" and is associated with some serious social problems, such as South Korea's high rate of teen suicide. There is some variety available in high schools in terms of programs and curricula, with institutions that specialize in areas such as arts, science, or technical education. The government and educators have strained in recent years to reduce the emphasis on testing and private tuition, with limited success.

INTERNATIONAL SCHOOLS

Foreign residents of South Korea are free to send their children to local schools in their area. For elementary schools, parents can apply to the school directly with the child's alien registration certificate, but middle and high school applications have to go to the nearest municipal education office, which will decide on placement.

Due to concerns about language and integration, the majority of expatriates send their children to international schools. Seoul and Busan have the highest number, but there are schools with international programs throughout the country, with many more coming onto the scene in recent years as the country gears up to support a larger and broader foreign population. While the majority of international schools follow the U.S. system and prepare students for American colleges, there are also schools offering the international baccalaureate, and others that follow British, Chinese, Japanese, French, or German curricula. Many schools have religious (mainly Christian) roots, but most are accepting of all faiths and allow parents to opt their children out of bible or religious classes if they prefer.

Major international schools have large, relatively diverse student bodies made up of expatriate children and "returnees," or children of Korean descent who hold overseas citizenship. The government generally bars locals who don't have foreign passports or haven't spent extended periods abroad from attending international institutions. Educational standards are generally very high, and the staff is mainly made up of certified teachers from Western nations.

About the only disadvantage of international schools—and it's a big one—is cost. Tuition rates start at around 10 million won per academic year for kindergarten and rise quickly until at the high school level most parents are paying well over 20 million won per child per year, sometimes plus additional bus, activity, or book fees. The more popular international schools often have waiting lists, and registering early is important. Unlike their local counterparts, most international schools follow the standard North American academic calendar, with classes beginning in late August and ending in June, with a winter break of about one month.

DAILY LIFE

HEALTH

In just a few generations, South Korea has achieved one of the highest life expectancies in the world. This is partly a result of habits—South Koreans are by and large more physically active than the average North American, and the local cuisine tends to be low on fat and meat and big on herbs and vegetables. But the government also deserves credit for building a sophisticated and efficient health care system that has made medical care relatively affordable and accessible to all, including foreign residents. Western medicine is supplemented by a highly developed system of indigenous and Chinese-influenced medical traditions that some have found more effective in treating chronic ailments.

South Korea's achievements can't be discounted, but problems still exist. Air and water quality, although they are improving, are poor in places. Facilities for the disabled fall short of those in most Western countries. Smoking and heavy drinking are national pastimes. And expatriates may have a tough time embracing some local medical practices, such as the very public hospitals or doctors' affection for injections.

© RUFINA K.E. PARK

A TASTE OF KOREAN MEDICINE

© JONATHAN HOPFNER

haniwon, Seoul

While a solid standard of modern medical treatment is readily accessible almost anywhere in Korea, many locals prefer to fall back on much older techniques. *Hanyak* literally translates as "Korean medicine," but it's perhaps more accurate to call it Asian medicine since it's part of a far wider tradition shared by the Chinese and other cultures in the region.

Hanyak is a complex approach thousands of years in the making, but basically it views the body as a combination of elements and forces (heat, cold, life force, and spiritual energy) that cause illness when they are out of balance. Diagnoses are conducted through general observation of the patient, without the aid of instruments or lab tests.

A variety of methods are used to treat diseases and bring the patient's body back to equilibrium, including herbal formulas (typically containing things like ginseng and ginger, but sometimes more exotic ingredients like deer antler), massage, and acupuncture. Endangered animal parts such as Asiatic black bear gallbladder still find their way into some *hanyak*-inspired potions, but this is increasingly rare and frowned on by any serious traditional medicine professional.

Hanyak treatments can't substitute for the modern variety on every occasion, but interest in them has grown globally as they have been demonstrated to be very effective for some ailments, especially common ones such as colds and fatigue, and chronic conditions including allergies and muscle pain. If you are interested in trying out *hanyak,* visit a *haniwon,* or Asian medicine clinic, which are nearly as numerous as the standard variety and are also covered by medical insurance. Several comprehensive Asian medicine hospitals with English-speaking staff have also opened, including the sprawling Jaseng Hospital in Seoul's posh Gangnam district.

Hospitals and Clinics

Every sizable town in South Korea has at least a clinic, and a major hospital is never too far away—indeed, most large cities have dozens. Standard clinics can diagnose and dispense medication for everyday gripes such as colds, flu, or headaches, but for more serious health issues they will refer the patient to the nearest hospital. There's also no shortage of specialist clinics covering areas like dentistry, optometry, and children's medicine.

Hospitals offer emergency care and a wide range of medical services. The vast majority of hospitals are private institutions, often affiliated with universities, companies, or religious groups, but the government insurance system and abundance of competition tend to keep fees fairly low by international standards. Those insured under the system are free to choose any medical provider they like, so most residents end up frequenting the hospital closest to home. Standards are generally excellent, and most hospitals have top-of-the-line equipment and highly trained staff. While the language barrier can be an issue, especially when it comes to speaking to nurses or administrative staff, most doctors speak at least some English.

Most of the problems expatriates are likely to run into at local hospitals will have less to do with standards of treatment than culture. Doctors are highly respected in South Korea's heavily Confucian-influenced society and thus not accustomed to being questioned or engaging in long exchanges with patients; basically they make a diagnosis, prescribe a cocktail of medications, and that's it. There's also a clear tendency to overmedicate, at least by U.S. standards—even a quick visit to the clinic because of a cough or a runny nose is likely to result in two or three injections and a bag full of pills and powders big enough to treat an entire village.

Foreign patients may also be surprised to find that hospitals here don't place great

Hae Jeong Hospital, Seoul

value on privacy, peace, or quiet. Unless prior arrangements are made, patients usually share a room with a few others, and doctors or nurses will sometimes administer care in full view of whoever else happens to be there. Visitors and relatives are generally free to wander around at will, a natural result of the belief that it's family members as well as hospital staff who are responsible for watching over and attending to the patient. Those who are uncomfortable with this state of affairs would be better off visiting an international clinic.

INTERNATIONAL CLINICS

Several major hospitals in large cities such as Seoul, Busan, and Daegu have established international clinics for foreign residents and visitors, and more are opening as the medical tourism industry picks up. As local standards are already quite high, these don't necessarily offer better medical care, but they do tend to have higher quality of service. Doctors and nurses are usually fluent in English and in many cases Japanese or Chinese as well, and they are more accustomed to foreign patients' needs and expectations. Comfortable private rooms are available with Western meal services and entertainment. Of course all these extras come at a price, typically well above what you'd pay for identical treatment at a standard hospital, and people planning on visiting international clinics regularly would be advised to purchase additional coverage to supplement their government insurance.

Insurance

Health insurance is provided by South Korea's National Health Insurance Corporation (NHIC). It is mandatory for all foreign nationals working in the country and is also extended to any of their dependents. Foreigners who are not working but are resident here, such as students, can also opt for coverage for a monthly fee, typically around 50,000 won.

Foreign workers' premiums are calculated as a percentage of their monthly salary, with the current rate at around 6 percent. The employee pays half this amount, and the employer is responsible for the remainder. Contributions are typically deducted from monthly paychecks. Foreign employees should be enrolled in the system automatically when they start working and will receive an insurance card (currently more like a small booklet) from the NHIC. Foreign employees who doesn't receive the card or suspects insurance payments are not being made should raise the issue with their employer or the NHIC immediately, as technically they, or more likely their employer, are violating the law.

The NHIC is a "co-payment" program that covers the lion's share of most medical expenses but provides no assistance for optional or cosmetic treatment, such as plastic surgery, or in cases when the medical condition is a result of deliberate or criminal activity. How much of a medical bill is covered depends on where and how the patient has sought treatment. Generally for outpatient services, national insurance will cover 40-70 percent of the total costs, and for inpatient services—that is, after the patient has been admitted to a hospital or clinic—80 percent. The NHIC program also covers around 70 percent of the charges at dental or Asian medicine clinics and a similar portion of the costs of medications at pharmacies, when medication has been prescribed. These amounts—as with monthly contributions—are reevaluated by the NHIC each year. In most cases coverage is applied automatically, and the patients billed only for their portion of the co-payment.

Whether it's necessary to supplement government insurance with private coverage depends on the individual. For those who travel frequently, the answer is yes, as the NHIC program does not cover any medical costs incurred outside of South Korea. Likewise, those likely to be visiting international clinics or specialized hospitals regularly may want to purchase private insurance since their co-payments are likely to be fairly high. Treatment costs for chronic diseases such as cancer can also stack up quickly, even though they're at least partially covered by the national insurance scheme, and many locals purchase supplementary insurance for this reason. Additional insurance is available from local companies such as Samsung Life as well as international insurers like Bupa, who offer a range of plans catering to expatriates.

Pharmacies and Prescriptions

There are well-stocked pharmacies (*yakguk*) on virtually every South Korean street corner. Not long ago just about any medication would be handed out over the counter, but these days prescriptions are required for anything stronger than common cold remedies or painkillers. Many large hospitals have pharmacies on-site to fill prescriptions; every hospital will have a few in the immediate vicinity. Despite years of strident opposition by pharmacists, a few household drugs, including painkillers, antiseptic lotions, and fever remedies for kids, have started to appear in convenience stores, but many still don't stock them.

Pharmacists typically speak little or no English, but with a little miming will usually be able to recommend something for common gripes; well-known drug names such as Tylenol or aspirin are also widely understood. It's a good idea to hang on to the packaging for any medication you use regularly so you can simply bring it back to the pharmacy and ask for more.

Unfortunately, dosage information and instructions for local drugs usually appear in Korean only; if you are taking prescription medication, make sure your doctor briefs you on how much you should be taking and possible side effects.

AVAILABILITY OF PRESCRIPTION DRUGS

Drug manufacturers have a substantial presence in South Korea, and there are very few medications that aren't available here. Brand names may differ, however, and you may have to settle for a local equivalent, which any doctor should be able to recommend. If it's absolutely imperative that you stick to a medication from back home, it's probably safest to import it with you; remember to bring your prescription information along to avoid any hassle with customs officials.

MEDICAL RECORDS

After legal revisions that basically gave electronic records the same status as the paper versions, most South Korean hospitals have shifted to computer-based patient

HEALTH HAZARDS

Despite the national affection for insalubrious indulgences like alcohol and cigarettes, South Koreans on the whole are a health-conscious people, mindful of what they eat and regularly setting aside time for exercise. They've also amassed quite a list over the years of seemingly innocuous things that absolutely must be avoided as they're believed to be harmful or even fatal—much to the confusion and amusement of some expatriates.

The most prominent example of this is the dreaded "fan death." Leaving a fan on overnight in a room with no open doors or windows is generally considered to be potentially lethal. This is not your typical urban legend, but "common" medical knowledge perpetuated by some health authorities and the media, who, each summer, diligently report cases of people perishing of fan exposure.

Several theories have been advanced as to why the combination is so dangerous, the most popular being that the fan's motion creates a "vortex" that sucks oxygen from the air and leads to asphyxiation, or that sustained exposure to the wind created by the fan triggers hypothermia. Research, mainly done overseas, has yet to find any conclusive links between fans and these kinds of conditions, but that has done little to assuage the fears of South Koreans, who will sometimes argue they're uniquely susceptible to the fan threat. As a result, virtually all fans sold in South Korea come equipped with timers that people can set so they don't run all night.

This is far from the only new medical phenomenon foreign residents might come across. South Koreans are also very cautious about cold water, as many locals believe it will aggravate coughs or sore throats and is also problematic for digestion. Hence in many restaurants water or tea is served at room temperature or warm, even when the weather would seem to call for ice cubes. Eating unpeeled fruit, bathing soon after an injection, and drinking alcohol without some kind of food to accompany it are some of the other things said to pose health risks. You might do all these things without experiencing any ill effects, but some will argue that's just because you're not Korean.

information systems. Hospitals are obligated to provide patients with medical records or transfer them to other hospitals or doctors on request, but only international clinics will be able to provide records in languages other than Korean.

Preventive Measures

No vaccinations are required to enter South Korea, and the country has all but eliminated diseases such as malaria and typhoid, but hepatitis is still prevalent, and hepatitis A and B inoculations are recommended. There have been domestic outbreaks of avian influenza, but as of yet no human cases or casualties. The official rate of HIV infection is relatively low, with around 800 new cases reported each year. But some experts believe the real number is higher, and the standard precautions of avoiding unprotected sex or drug use should be taken. Technically any foreigner found to be HIV-positive can be deported immediately, though this practice has been challenged by South Korean courts.

Environmental Factors

AIR QUALITY

Thanks to innovations such as natural-gas bus fleets, the designation of greenbelts, and tighter restrictions on factories, South Korea's air quality has improved, especially in larger cities such as notoriously smoggy Seoul. Concentrations of substances such as particulate matter and carbon monoxide now remain within recommended limits most days of the year. That said, with so much traffic and industrial activity concentrated in a relatively small area, the Alps it's not. People used to more rural or pristine climes may experience some minor throat or lung irritations after moving here.

By far the biggest air-quality issue is not one of South Korea's making; every spring winds bring to the peninsula from neighboring China the dreaded *hwangsa,* or "yellow dust." This originates in China's expanding western deserts and picks up pollutants from cities on the heavily populated coast before continuing east to the Korean peninsula and Japan. The dust can cause respiratory problems, especially for the elderly and very young, and at its peak authorities usually call on people to stay indoors. Multiple television and radio stations and government websites offer regularly updated air-quality data.

WATER QUALITY

Water quality in South Korea is generally fair, though pollution, usually from industrial sources and the discharge of sewage, remains an issue in some rivers and coastal areas. The water supplied to homes is perfectly safe to use for bathing and apparently suitable for drinking, though most expatriates and locals stick to bottled water or install water filtration systems. The water served in restaurants is usually boiled or filtered.

SMOKING

While ads discourage the habit and nonsmoking zones are starting to pop up in places, in general it's open season for cigarette smokers in South Korea, which views tobacco with a permissiveness not seen in North America for decades. By some estimates close to half of all adult men are smokers. Cigarettes are dirt cheap and readily available everywhere, and a lot of restaurants and nightspots allow people to puff away wherever they like. Of course this leniency is extended only to men—South Koreans still view women smoking as strange, racy even, and while it's become more common to see girls lighting up on the street, many women will avoid doing so if they're not in or near a trendy café or nightspot.

The tide is slowly turning. Authorities have banned smoking in government facilities and large office complexes, for example, and the Seoul government plans to progressively roll out a smoking ban to all the city's restaurants by 2015. Nonsmoking bars have also emerged in areas like Seoul's cosmopolitan Itaewon district. However, for the time being, in many venues (bars in particular) nonsmokers have little choice but to grimace and bear it. Smokers, on the other hand, will have found their own little slice of heaven.

© JONATHAN HOPFNER

sign encouraging proper trash disposal

SANITATION

Sanitary conditions are generally quite good, and it's rare these days to come across a home or building in South Korea without access to modern plumbing, though in some areas squat-style toilets are still the norm. Restaurants, especially busy ones, are kept pretty spotless, and cases of food poisoning or contamination are fairly uncommon. Some caution needs to be exercised with street food, especially seafood, which is sometimes left sitting around without proper heating or refrigeration. Frequenting popular stalls where there's a high food turnover is the easiest way to avoid problems.

Disabled Access

It's readily apparent that South Korean society is generally not sensitive to the needs of people with disabilities in the lack of accessible facilities in most streets and public areas. Where there are sidewalks, they can be uneven and lack ramps, and many popular markets and shopping districts are constantly thronged with people, making getting around in a wheelchair difficult. Some, but far from all, buses have low floors and ramps for passengers with disabilities, and finding a public washroom with handrail-equipped toilets is a similar crapshoot. Newer office buildings and commercial complexes in Seoul usually have infrastructure in place for wheelchairs, but there are many more that don't. Those with disabilities usually find they need an able-bodied friend's help getting around the city.

People with disabilities do receive heavily discounted or free entry to many government facilities and tourist attractions, and the Seoul subway network has done a particularly commendable job of improving access with special sections for wheelchairs on trains, indicators in braille, and a comprehensive system of lifts, ramps, and stairclimbers to take people to and from street level.

Safety

The relative lack of street crime invariably tops some lists whenever expatriates discuss the main benefits of living here. Statistics vary, but most foreign residents *feel* a lot safer in South Korea than wherever they came from. People can and do roam around large cities like Seoul or Busan freely late at night without fear or incident. In part this is because these places really never do sleep; people, even young students, are out at all hours, and it's rare that you'll be walking utterly alone. But it also speaks to South Koreans' generally honest and orderly ways. Goods displayed unwatched outside of shops are left untouched; dropped wallets or lost mobile phones are regularly returned. Random attacks, and muggings in particular, are extremely rare.

That said, low crime doesn't mean no crime, and it's never advisable to throw all caution to the wind. Dark or abandoned areas are best avoided in the wee hours. Incidents of pickpocketing and bag-snatching, usually by young men on motorbikes, have been reported, as have break-ins, usually in smaller unguarded villas or apartment complexes. Don't get complacent, and lock doors and windows before you head out. Considering the country's hard-drinking ways, there's a remarkable shortage of alcohol-fueled violence in South Korea's streets, but it's wise to be a little cautious around packs of drunken men—foreign males, particularly if they're in the company of a young Korean woman, are very occasionally singled out for unwanted attention, as are foreign women, due to the unfortunate stereotype that they're more promiscuous than their South Korean counterparts.

For men: If you run into problems with the locals, keep your cool, and do your utmost to defuse the situation, even if that means swallowing your pride and walking away. In any altercation with a local it's safe to say the foreign male is automatically perceived to be at fault, and you may find yourself facing much worse odds than you anticipated when passersby jump in to defend their countryman (or men). The police, too, can be unsympathetic, and the enduring practice of "blood money" means you can expect to face a hefty medical bill from anyone who's suffered at your hands—even if they started it.

For women: Korean women tend to be very standoffish with men they don't know, and foreign women should exercise the same discretion when they're here—it's too easy for people to mistake what's meant to be friendliness as full-on flirtation in what is still a fairly reserved society. Be careful about accepting invitations from strangers to an event or coffee, as even this could be perceived as a "date." Men eyeing you up, initiating conversations for no reason, or seemingly tailing you can be warning signs, just as they are back home, and may be a cue to seek out the nearest place with a lot of people. Don't be afraid to call attention to yourself (or a man who's bothering you) if necessary—shame is a powerful inhibitor in South Korea and many locals will be happy to help you out. Local women often make sure they're with friends or conspicuously chatting on the phone to a "boyfriend" when they're out and about at night.

Large street demonstrations are a time-honored tradition in South Korea and are common in the summer months. These can look and sound pretty rowdy and usually attract an intimidating police response, with busloads of armored-up youngsters deployed to maintain order around protest sites. While tensions do boil over from time to time, they are for the most part highly ritualized affairs and no real cause for alarm, though it is obviously a good idea to steer clear of known trouble spots.

POLICE

South Korean police are generally honest and helpful, though perhaps less assertive than most Westerners expect. They're often visibly reluctant to get involved in low-level or domestic disputes, taking the view that the parties involved should sort things out. Some have posited that this is partly the result of a desire not to appear heavy-handed after decades in which the police force served as the chief agent of government repression.

While most police stations will be able to muster up an English speaker in emergency situations, most of the complaints foreign nationals have about the police are rooted in the language barrier. Aggrieved parties typically "argue" their case in front of police officers, who may issue an order or make an arrest based on this "testimony"; this puts non-Korean speakers at an automatic disadvantage, and it's vital that they secure the help of a local friend or legal representation as soon as possible. Regardless of the situation, remember this is still an authoritarian society, and keeping your cool and addressing police officers with respect pays massive dividends.

More often than not the police are lenient with foreign nationals. The clear exceptions to this are drug offenses or cases of assault against locals, which are pursued to the fullest extent of the law and almost invariably end with jail time or deportation (for drugs) or jail time and sizable compensation payments (for assault). Embassies are unlikely to be able to provide much assistance in these cases beyond recommending a lawyer.

DAILY LIFE

© JONATHAN HOPFNER

Buses carrying riot police are a fairly common sight in Seoul and other cities, especially in the strike-prone summer.

ACCIDENTS

South Korea's roads are by far the greatest hazard most residents will ever face here. The country has one of the highest traffic-accident fatality rates among developed countries, with about 14 traffic-related deaths for every 100,000 people each year—one of the worst rates in the OECD grouping of developed economies. Regardless of what you see the locals doing, when behind the wheel it's a good idea to drive defensively and to stick to the speed limits. Pedestrians should always use designated crosswalks or footbridges and avoid jaywalking.

House fires have become far less common since most homes shifted from charcoal to hot water as the primary *ondol* (under-floor heating) source, but check to make sure your residence is equipped with smoke detectors and an emergency call system, both fairly standard in newer apartment blocks.

NATURAL DISASTERS

The Korean peninsula is blessedly free of earthquakes when compared to neighboring Japan, but forest fires, typhoons, and flooding are almost annual occurrences. These are rarely serious enough to present a real threat or even disrupt the normal flow of business in places like Seoul, but it's best to keep an eye on weather conditions when planning any trips or activities, particularly in the tumultuous summer months.

CHILD SAFETY

South Koreans adore children and dote on them almost obsessively; indeed, the gravest peril a foreign child will probably face is an excess of spoiling by strangers. While incidences of kidnapping or abuse are certainly not unknown, they're generally less of a concern than in most Western nations. However, extra care must be taken not to lose a child in the country's ubiquitous fast-moving crowds, and some parents may find that for all their affection toward children, South Koreans seem to do little to protect them in some situations. Many young ones frolic in the streets unsupervised well after dark; quite a few taxis lack seat belts; and a lot of children's play areas look like they have seen better days.

MILITARY CONFLICT WITH NORTH KOREA

The possibility of another all-out conflict with North Korea has loomed since the Korean War ended in 1953 with no peace treaty and a very uneasy armistice. The bellicose rhetoric seems to ebb and flow with every change of government in the South, or the North's need to wheedle more aid out of the rest of the world. Unfortunately the last couple of years have seen tensions spike, with the sinking of a South Korean submarine and North Korea's first shelling of South Korean territory since the Korean War in 2010, and the death of former North Korean leader Kim Jong-il in 2011. Still, even these high-profile incidents have failed to stoke wider conflict, or to prevent the millions of people living in Seoul, just a few dozen miles south of the border, from going about their daily lives.

None of this is to discount the possibility of further conflict, but most analysts believe the North knows any move to mobilize its dilapidated military forces would be its last, and will remain content with issuing the odd dire threat. New arrivals soon discover the situation with the North has little bearing on their everyday lives, but they are of course advised to register with their embassies to be briefed on the appropriate course of action should war ever break out.

EMPLOYMENT

Not long ago, it seemed almost all the foreign nationals working in South Korea were soldiers, language teachers, or missionaries. What a difference a few years has made. While the English teaching industry is still a major employer (and the soldiers and missionaries are still around), with the country's prosperity on the rise and more local firms eager to spread their wings overseas, there's now a range of opportunities for non-Koreans in everything from acting to the food and beverage industry, finance, or consulting. Salaries are high by Asian standards, local labor laws afford employees a relatively high degree of protection, and the government is supportive of foreign talent, making for a broadly positive work environment.

Unfortunately, many of the lessons you learned in business school or past jobs may not apply when it comes to tackling the South Korean employment market. Some practices—the obsession with overtime or deference to seniority, for instance—can seem odd or counterproductive to someone weaned on Western management styles. But as is obvious from the country's rapid development, even with its handicaps South Korea's business sector is a highly successful one and has many elements worth learning from.

© RUFINA K.E. PARK

Teaching English

Teaching English is by far the most common occupation in South Korea for expatriates from most Western countries, simply because the local obsession with learning the language means there's a near-inexhaustible supply of jobs. There are around 25,000 foreign nationals in South Korea on language teaching visas, but the real number of teachers is probably higher since some work illegally.

If you're interested in teaching legitimately, there are a few options—universities, in-house corporate classes, public schools, and *hagwon* (private institutes), with the latter generally doing the most hiring. All carry on a substantial amount of recruitment abroad, and contracts typically include airfare to and from the teacher's country of origin and accommodations, as well as a salary of around 2 million won per month. As housing is taken care of, many teachers find it easy to save a good chunk of each pay packet.

The qualifications required for English teaching positions vary, but a bachelor's degree and a passport from a native English-speaking country are the bare minimum, and the best university and corporate positions often require master's degrees and years of experience. After a few well-publicized incidents of foreign instructors violating local laws, authorities have become more rigorous about background checks, and they now require most new hires to undergo health evaluations and to produce clean criminal records from their home countries. Any reputable employer should be familiar with current visa procedures (they change with alarming regularity) and be able to help you negotiate them.

Once you do get started, the average *hagwon* position will involve around 30 hours of teaching time per week, with a few additional hours for planning or administrative work. Some institutes run split shifts—early morning and late evening—to accommodate the typical student groups: schoolchildren and office workers. Class sizes are usually around a dozen students, and while almost all institutes employ Korean English teachers to instruct genuine beginners, foreign hires can expect to teach students of a wide range of English abilities largely on their own.

Co-teaching is more common in the university and public school environments, where class sizes are far larger and strict curricula often have to be followed. By far the greatest advantage of these positions for most is the substantial vacation time: Teachers often enjoy the same lengthy summer and winter breaks as their students. There are also fewer classroom hours than at private academies, especially in universities where some foreign professors teach only six or seven hours per week. Needless to say there's some heated competition for these posts.

Most foreign teachers enjoy their Korean experience, but some fall prey to bad employers, particularly in the *hagwon* industry, which is massive and virtually unregulated. Substandard housing, unpaid overtime, and the early termination of contracts, usually to avoid paying employees incentives agreed on when the contract was completed, are among the more common complaints.

Even if they're halfway around the world during the hiring process, the onus is on

INTERVIEW: ANDREW MONTEITH

© ANDREW MONTEITH

Andrew Monteith

Canadian Andrew Monteith arrived in Korea in 1996 to work as an English instructor in a *hagwon* and has been in the industry since, tackling everything from business English classes at some of the country's largest conglomerates to public schools and universities. He currently works for Seoul's Hongik University, one of the country's most renowned arts colleges.

Q: *You've been in the industry for some time—how have you seen things change since you began teaching?*

A: It's gotten a lot more difficult, especially if you're not qualified. There are more background checks, more hoops to jump

the teachers-to-be to check out any prospective employer as carefully as possible. If you're considering taking a job offer, ask to speak to current foreign teachers to sound them out about the school or institute and the standard of housing provided. Check any contract to make sure it's reasonably clear about the amount of hours you're expected to teach and what sort of tax and other deductions will be taken from your paycheck. Never surrender your passport to an employer, and remember there are government and legal agencies to turn to if your pay is being withheld or you're being mistreated. And at the end of the day, no matter what your boss might tell you, it *is* possible to simply leave if you're stuck in a dire situation.

The flip side of the coin is that a lot of "teachers" show up in South Korea thinking a stint in a *hagwon* will be a no-stress way to fund a vacation. Teaching is a job, and a pretty tough one at that, so count on instructing driven and demanding older learners or boisterous kids with demanding parents, and plan accordingly.

through, and private classes, which people could make a lot of money with before, are now almost nonexistent. There are just too many teachers here; since the economic downturn the market has been flooded. Even PhDs are applying for jobs. Being able to teach at a university with only a BA is a thing of the past. And despite the demand for qualifications getting higher, the money isn't getting better. There's also not much job security—you're always signing contracts, and you're not really guaranteed anything.

Q: *Given all those issues, why opt to teach here? What advice would you give someone contemplating the move?*

A: Korea's a safe place to work, and if you have credentials, it's a great place to work, especially in public schools. There are good *hagwon* around, but find out as much as you can about any *hagwon* job before you get here. The best thing to do would be to come here before you get a job and talk to people, get your own interviews.

Korea's not that expensive, transport is amazing, and there's a great expat community. Students are for the most part well behaved and motivated to learn. I've had a

great experience, but if you're looking to make a fortune, those days are over.

Q: *Any tips on dealing with Korean learners in the classroom?*

A: It's a cliché, but I try to make sure they have fun, to relate to them with personal experiences and use current references that they can understand. I try to teach a lot from outside the textbook and outside the country. University is enjoyable because the students are engaged, smart, and very respectful; they respond well when there's a teacher who's interested in the job and in helping them.

Q: *What about the administration side of things? How do you keep a good relationship with your employer?*

A: It's not that tough—follow the rules, be on time, and try to stay under the radar to a certain extent. Employers are mostly concerned about students and their evaluations, so as long as you keep the students happy, I don't see what could go wrong. Do your best, but most of all impress your students—be genuine with them and put yourself out there. If you engage your students, allow them to share their thoughts and ideas, it's a big deal for them, especially in a culture where that's often discouraged.

Self-Employment

Striking out on your own is a risky venture anywhere and seems even more so in South Korea, where signing up with the largest possible conglomerate and sticking with it for life remain the goal of a large part of the working population. But the country is beginning to foster an entrepreneurial culture in some areas, particularly in industries such as hospitality and the arts. The government is also steadily easing the rules governing foreign start-ups. Still, make no mistake—you'll almost inevitably need a lot of local help, or exceptional Korean language skills, and a lot of luck.

INTERVIEW: MICHAEL BREEN

© MICHAEL BREEN

Michael Breen

One of the expatriate community's more prominent figures, author and expert on the two Koreas Michael Breen first came to South Korea in the turbulent 1980s, covering the country for newspapers like *The Guardian* and the *Washington Times*. In addition to writing two well-received books about the peninsula—*The Koreans*, an examination of the Korean character, and *Kim Jong Il: North Korea's Dear Leader*—Breen worked extensively in the local communications industry and now heads his own public relations firm, Insight Communications Consultants, which helps clients such as Shell and the Bank of New York Mellon navigate the South Korean market.

Q: *For you, what are the biggest advantages and disadvantages of living here?*

A: I think South Korea presents a challenge, even for Koreans. There's a difficulty in understanding the place and operating here that goes beyond the language barrier. It's not completely transparent, and things aren't necessarily built for ease or efficiency. But there's absolutely a payoff for that. This is an incredibly engaging place; you find that even while people are criticizing it they're developing an affection for it. Other places don't seem to get into your heart the way South Korea does.

I think it's this combination of ethical idealism and earthy emotion that Koreans have. It's very nice, the idea that damaging the feelings of other people is a crime, the hospitality, but then they also get really worked up about things and sort of lose their rag [lose their temper] sometimes. For an Englishman who's used to being subdued, that's actually very liberating.

Q: *How has the living environment changed for expatriates since you arrived?*

A: There's far more familiarity with the outside world than there used to be. Young Korean couples are now honeymooning in places like Prague. There are far more non-Koreans living here. Foreign trade is no longer seen as a bad thing. Koreans have always been friendly, but you were always seen as an outsider before; not so much now. It's an ever-growing economy, and there has actually been a lifetime of growth in a couple of decades. So that has created a lot of opportunity.

Q: *What aspects of the living environment need improvement?*

A: The two biggest areas in the country that need addressing are the system of justice and the system of education. The prosecutors always win. Education is designed to produce little soldiers to work in the factories; it doesn't allow for individual creativity. These are two areas that need profound review or change. The best way to improve life for foreigners is to improve life for everyone.

Q: *What advice would you give an expatriate considering setting up a business here?*

A: Registration is the first of a range of complexities you'll have to deal with, and you need Koreans to help you with that. You've got to be good at the accounting, the legal issues, and the financing, or have colleagues who are.

Locals are very aware if the company they're dealing with is not Korean, but that's not only an issue in Korea. There's sometimes an assumption by Koreans that expatriates can teach English and hobnob with other expats, but not much beyond that. Whether you need a Korean face really depends on what your business is; in mine we do because we're an interface between companies and the media, so we need to be contacting and following up with the local press and dealing with their questions and issues. It can be challenging because the view of nationality here is still race-based and also tied to the language. But foreigners who speak fluent Korean can get over a lot of that.

It's a very hierarchical culture, especially for men. Korean companies all operate like the military. You can relate to someone in a different company or group by a title, and privates can't go around telling majors what to do. As a foreigner you can kind of get around all that. But one of the first things I've got to figure out [in meeting with a client] is how I'm going to present what I think in a way that's respectful.

[Developing contacts] comes down to the nature of the business and your personality. Despite what you hear, you can be an unsociable teetotaler and do well in business. Or you can be a gregarious drunk and do badly. That said, some embassies have their own bars—the British and Australian embassies in particular—and most countries have chambers of commerce, with the American chamber being the most active. If you went to university, you might want to see if there is an alumni association of its Korean graduates.

BUSINESS OPPORTUNITIES

As in any country, opportunities can be found just about anywhere you look, but with so many South Korean companies competing aggressively in most segments of the market, non-Korean entrepreneurs tend to stick to areas in which their language or culture gives them a head start.

Not surprisingly, given the number of foreign nationals that first come here as language instructors, many move on to open thriving language institutes or businesses recruiting teachers abroad to fill vacancies in South Korean schools. A number have also launched restaurants focusing on ethnic cuisine, which have grown immensely popular with an increasingly well-traveled local population. Others have concentrated on building links between South Korea and their home countries—helping South Korean firms source foreign executives, acting as a local agent for foreign firms or products, or breaking new international ground for South Korean goods.

While there are exceptions, most successful foreign business owners share a few traits: familiarity with their host market (meaning they've lived in South Korea for a few years before striking out on their own), at least rudimentary Korean language skills, and a solid local support network, whether family, old friends, or former colleagues. Contacts and personal relationships count for even more here than they do in the Western business world, and since banks and many firms will shy away from dealing with a start-up, having a few locals prepared to advocate on your behalf often proves crucial in getting a business off the ground. Established businesspeople therefore recommend entrepreneurs put in some legwork to meet and develop ties with South Korean professionals and companies in their chosen field. Chambers of commerce and industry associations serve as a good starting point for this sort of socializing, as do churches, alumni associations, and sports clubs.

STARTING A BUSINESS

There are relatively few restrictions on starting a business in South Korea, and foreign nationals are free to set up and fully own companies in all but a few restricted or semi-restricted sectors such as defense technology, agriculture, and publishing—provided they've got the cash.

After a couple of years of the government hiking minimums and closing loopholes, to set up a foreign-owned company, or a local branch of a foreign firm, now requires a minimum initial investment of 100 million won. This investment allows you to fast-track the company registration process through Invest Korea (www.investkorea.org), the government support agency for foreign investors, and should enable you to receive a visa to live and work in South Korea through your new corporation. The 100 million won doesn't have to sit in a bank account for a designated amount of time; you're free to make use of it as soon as the start-up process is complete, but you must provide documentation showing it was brought into the country from elsewhere. Foreign-invested companies and foreign employees of those companies are often eligible for significant tax and other perks, particularly if they're bringing in large amounts of capital, setting up in "disadvantaged" areas (i.e., outside of Seoul), or operating in industries the government is targeting for development, such as clean technology. Newly established companies can take the form of private businesses—basically one-person operations—or full corporations. The latter carry more paperwork and reporting requirements but have an easier time getting financing.

Foreign investment visas are reviewed on a regular basis and may be denied if the authorities see the firm as nonviable—consistently declaring losses or failing to pay taxes are among the things that will raise red flags. By contrast firms that are perceived to be contributing to the country, by for example employing large numbers of locals, can expect a very easy time of it.

If you can't or won't make the 100 million won investment needed to start up a firm the standard way, things get trickier and more ambiguous. Other possibilities include registering a company with a local partner. Foreigners with residency (i.e., "F"-class) visas are also free to set up businesses without any minimum capital requirements, but will have to brave the bureaucracy themselves. Locally established firms also face more restrictions on the amount of funds they can remit and receive from abroad.

The minimum capital requirements and rules for foreign nationals starting their own firms are a constant work in progress and adjusted regularly. It's not uncommon to get different stories from different officials, sometimes on the same day! It's therefore imperative to triple-check the latest regulations before making any concrete decisions. Invest Korea is probably the best source of information on these matters.

However you decide to open a business, unless you're fluent in Korean and have some very well-connected friends, turning to a specialist to guide you through the pitfalls and handle the paperwork should be considered mandatory. In addition to the free assistance offered by agencies like Invest Korea and the Seoul Global Center, there are many accounting and consulting firms that have substantial expertise in the start-up process and can negotiate around barriers you'd probably have trouble tackling on your own.

The Job Hunt

Expatriates working in South Korea can be divided into two main categories: executives sent or brought here from abroad, most commonly by a multinational corporation with operations here, but also increasingly by local conglomerates; and those who come here and pound the pavement to find something on their own. The former are treated to more benefits, such as relocation assistance, housing allowances, and international school fees, while the latter simply receive salaries, albeit salaries that tend to be higher than those paid to locals.

While migrant laborers from South and Southeast Asia are hired to work in South Korea's factories, the South Korean government prefers that companies import educated and skilled workers, and the visa system reflects this. Employment visas are divided into categories such as "technological guidance," "specially designated activities," and "professional"—basically all implying the holder is an expert in one area or another—and when your employer applies for a visa, the immigration authorities will expect you to be able to provide degrees, certification, or at the very least experience that confirms your status. For this reason, South Korea can be a tough job market for those without higher education or who are at an early stage in their careers.

WHERE TO LOOK

As in most countries, building on personal connections and contacts is usually the best way to find an opportunity in your field, or at least to be the first to know when one becomes available. While multinationals frequently advertise positions via websites or recruiting agencies, outside their annual intake of graduates, South Korean firms still rely a great deal on word of mouth.

There are several major recruiters in Seoul that foreign nationals in search of executive or management positions can deposit their résumés with. Jobs for expatriates are also advertised sometimes in the local English-language newspapers and via online job search engines such as JobsDB.com and Jobpot.com. Checking with or joining the various chambers of commerce in Seoul is also a good idea for job-hunters, as many maintain directories of foreign-invested enterprises active in the country and receive early notification of job openings.

WHAT EMPLOYERS WANT

While the picture shifts regularly, overall both local and multinational companies here look to foreign nationals to fill a function that can't be taken on easily by a local—imparting knowledge or processes from the multinational's head office, for example, or leading a local company's sales negotiations with foreign clients. Skills or a solid education in areas like marketing or consulting are therefore in demand, as is financial-industry experience as more South Korean banks and brokers seek to expand alliances or build their businesses abroad. Many engineering and energy executives have found work in South Korea's burgeoning automotive, shipbuilding, steel, and refinery industries. Professional sports—both on the coaching and the playing side—and the media—including TV, radio, and voice acting—are other niches that foreign nationals have penetrated with some success. Those with information-technology backgrounds

DRESSING THE PART

It'll be immediately apparent to anyone who witnesses Seoul's rivers of dark suits during rush hours that office attire is more conservative—and homogenous—than is typical in the West. While non-Koreans may get slightly more leeway, suits (and ties), preferably in neutral colors such as gray, black, and navy, are virtually mandatory for any male working in an office environment. For women, pantsuits or blouses with skirts (of a conservative length) are equally acceptable. High heels are by no means required, but most Korean women wear them while commuting or to meetings then promptly switch to flats when they're in the office. Men, meanwhile, will often trade their shoes for a pair of slippers when at or around their desks.

The "casual Friday" concept has reached Korea, and many offices allow their employees to dress down on that day. However, it's far from universally applied, so take your cue from your coworkers—especially your boss.

tend to face more difficulty as South Korean IT graduates are highly skilled and obviously far more in tune with the norms and needs of the local market.

Strictly speaking, Korean language skills are neither needed nor expected for most positions offered to expatriates, but they do go a long way in the workplace and will certainly give any job applicant an immediate edge over other candidates.

Times are changing, but much of the equal-opportunity philosophy that suffuses Western workplaces has yet to seep into South Korean companies. It's not at all uncommon for prospective employers to specify the desired gender, age, and even appearance of candidates when they advertise a job position, and a photo must accompany virtually every job application. Some local firms will be uncomfortable hiring a woman or a youngish person for a senior management position or an older candidate for a mid-level post, out of fear this could disrupt workplace harmony. Many middle-aged local executives would be confused or angered by the prospect of taking orders from a woman in her 30s, no matter how educated or competent she happened to be.

THE HIRING PROCESS

Except for the photos with the applications mentioned above, the hiring process here isn't likely to produce too many surprises for anyone who's undergone job interviews back home. Companies will usually call a large pool of candidates for a brief initial interview and then conduct follow-up interviews with more promising candidates, often with several senior executives present.

As in other countries, most of the questions will focus on a candidate's background, what they feel they can bring to the company, and in the case of a foreign national, their reasons for being in South Korea or wanting to come here. The line of questioning sometimes takes a more personal bent than it would in North America; don't be taken aback, as this is usually just an attempt to establish a rapport. It's uncommon, but certainly not unheard of, for a local company to fly a candidate in from another country exclusively to conduct an interview.

After a hiring decision is made, the company will typically offer the successful candidate a contract, which can usually be negotiated slightly before a final deal is reached. Bear in mind that in South Korea contracts are seen more as a starting point or a guideline than the ironclad documents they are in the West. Make sure all the big bases—pay, hours, dismissal procedures, and so on—are covered, but don't expect it to touch on everything. Also count on some obligations or expectations arising independently of it.

SALARIES AND BENEFITS

Expatriates dispatched here from their home countries can often count on a "package" that includes a salary, usually paid in a mix of local and home currencies, housing, schooling for dependents, insurance, and so on. Local hires, on the other hand, will almost exclusively consist of a salary paid in won. When it comes to expatriate salaries, the sky's the limit.

Locally, pay packets are highly dependent on the company's circumstances and the candidate's history and negotiation skills, but to put it in perspective, fresh graduates typically make 2-3 million won per month and senior managers 4-7 million won per month. Some companies pay an annual bonus of around one month's salary, but it's not as widespread a practice as it used to be. Small bonuses for the Lunar New Year and Harvest Festival holidays, however, are still standard. Many, but by no means all, firms provide perks such as health insurance (on top of the standard government variety), assistance with education, housing, and vehicle purchases, or use of company condominiums during holidays—perhaps because all these things often come from the same company or its affiliates!

The Work Environment

The office is one of the arenas in which South Korea's Confucian traditions are most readily apparent. Many companies have adopted Western-style structures or management initiatives in name only, and these are often halfheartedly implemented. A lot of South Korean firms remain authoritarian and hierarchical, with a reluctance to adopt new ideas or change rapidly. The impressive performance of these companies on the global stage proves the local way of doing business isn't always the wrong one, but expatriates are bound to find some practices very different with some adjustment required.

EMPLOYER EXPECTATIONS

As a foreign national you'll be somewhat off the hook, but it's safe to say South Korean firms expect more devotion to the company than your average Western corporation, and they are much less reluctant to intrude on your private life by pleading with you to work on a weekend, for example. Employees are expected to work "until something is done" rather than adhering to a strict schedule, and indeed you'll soon find out many South Koreans are reluctant to leave the office until the boss has done the same. The payback for this, such as it is, is the high degree of loyalty most South Korean firms display toward their workers; layoffs, for example, are still a fairly rare occurrence.

Your supervisors are likely to put a great deal of emphasis on developing a personal relationship with you, and many office parties, lunches, and sometimes even weekend trips will be devoted to this cause. While they may be open to feedback, the word of higher-ups prevails and is not to be questioned excessively, particularly in front of an audience. Of course the standard workplace rules about punctuality and dressing well apply.

EMPLOYEE CULTURE

Every worker is a member of a team, but that really hits home in South Korea. Employees, or at least employees of individual departments or divisions, are expected to work together, play together, attend each other's weddings...you get the idea. A great deal of emphasis is placed on group harmony, to which everyone contributes by exhibiting a certain amount of deference toward their seniors, looking out for the interests of their juniors, and picking up any slack with a minimum of complaint. Mistakes or problems with individual coworkers are usually raised as discreetly as possible and left to senior managers to sort out. Although it sometimes happens, bawling someone out in front of all and sundry is a loss of face for all involved and is seen as catastrophically bad form. The downside of this, of course, is that issues are often not raised until they're simply to big too ignore.

Labor Laws

The government's need to secure the cooperation of labor in the nation's development, and the strength of the unions in many industries, mean South Korean employment laws afford a decent amount of protection to the worker. If you suspect your employer is breaching the law or treating you unfairly, there are several possible avenues of recourse you can pursue.

CONDITIONS AND LIMITATIONS OF WORK VISAS

With the exception of residency visas, which allow the holders to seek jobs and hop from employer to employer freely, most visas in South Korea are tied to a specific employer and have to be renewed each year. Moonlighting for other employers is not generally permitted, but more than a few people do it anyway.

In the event that you do decide to change jobs in South Korea, you'll need a letter acknowledging and accepting your resignation from your original employer (your new bosses may be able to help you get this) and for your new paymasters to apply for another visa on your behalf, at which point the old one will be canceled and a new one will replace it. This sometimes involves a trip to a Korean consulate abroad to secure the new visa there. If you resign from a position, your employer will usually cancel your visa, and you'll have only a couple of weeks to leave the country.

WORKERS' RIGHTS

Foreign workers are entitled to the same rights and protections as their South Korean counterparts, which should be outlined in any contract with an employer. These include maternity leave (90 days), child-rearing leave (30 days), and severance pay of about one month's salary for every year worked, issued on leaving the company. The law also stipulates that an employee should be paid at least once a month without fail and that employers must enroll their workers in the national pension, health insurance, unemployment insurance, and industrial accident schemes, the costs of which are shared by both parties. Taxes should also be deducted from your pay packet on a monthly basis, and a tax return filed around the beginning of each year.

Any problems with overdue wages, wrongful dismissal, or simple questions can be directed to the Ministry of Employment and Labor, which runs hotlines in English and several other major languages, or the Seoul Bar Association, which provides free legal consultation for foreign workers and can also assist with action if needed.

Workplace discrimination is an issue that South Korea has yet to tackle as zealously as other countries, though some change is afoot—age discrimination in hiring has been banned, for example, though enforcement is another matter. In cases of serious discrimination or harassment, the National Human Rights Commission is generally viewed as the best agency to contact.

DAILY LIFE

FINANCE

South Korea can be a puzzling mix of the punishingly expensive (rents in Seoul and imported goods, for example) and extraordinary bargains (local food and transport), but most expatriates find it a pretty effective place to make and save money. Even at local firms, salaries are reasonably high and assistance is often provided with things like housing and medical expenses. Taxes are low, at least by the standards of many Western countries, and tipping virtually nonexistent.

The country has a modern banking system with a number of international lenders, and it has steadily been dropping controls on what non-South Koreans can and can't do with the money they earn here. But strangely, what should be one of the more straightforward elements of life in South Korea—managing your earnings—often proves to be one of the most puzzling and controversial. This is both because of the sometimes volatile financial environment—the currency, and the stock market, seem to take turns being the region's best- and worst-performing—and the apparent reluctance of local lenders to provide the full range of banking services to foreign nationals. Arm yourself with persistence and a bit of knowledge, however, and more than a few apparent barriers will quickly vanish.

Cost of Living

"How much does it cost to live in South Korea?" is one of those questions like "How long is a piece of string?"—the answer is, it depends. Try to replicate the suburban North American or British life here, living in a stand-alone house with a good-sized yard and shopping for things like steaks and cheese every day, and your expenses will be astronomical, since all these things will cost two or three times what they would back home. At the other extreme, live in a small apartment in a provincial city, get by on public transport, and stick mainly to Korean food, and this can be a very cheap place indeed.

Location is another important factor in working out a monthly budget. People tend to burn through cash more quickly in larger cities such as Seoul and Busan not only because rents are higher but because the array of restaurants, events, and department stores is a constant source of temptation to spend.

TYPICAL MONTHLY EXPENSES

Accommodations are by far the biggest expense expatriates have to deal with, assuming they are not taken care of by an employer—which, given the unique challenges of the South Korean real estate market, they often are. In Seoul, if you're not prepared to put down a sizable *jeonse* deposit, you should budget around 1 million won per month for a studio or one-bedroom apartment in a convenient location, and twice that for a place capable of housing a family. Rents will be about two-thirds to half of these levels in Busan or major provincial cities. Many apartments, particularly those in newer, larger complexes, also have a monthly maintenance or management fee that sometimes has to be paid separately by the tenant. These fees can vary greatly (be sure to ask!) but are usually around 100,000 won per month.

In almost every town, the university districts have an abundance of cheap, often dormitory-style accommodations that may suit a young student or single person; they typically cost around 300,000 won per month.

Utility costs are fairy consistent throughout the country. In a midsize dwelling, plan on spending around 70,000 won per month on electricity and/or gas (many apartments use a mix of both for heating and cooking). This can rise substantially in the peak winter and summer months when heating or air-conditioning is used. Water costs are often bundled into maintenance fees but, if broken out separately, will be about 10,000 won per month. Utility charges, especially in newer apartment blocks, are sometimes combined into a single monthly management fee based on the size of a dwelling—look into these before signing any rental contracts as they're typically charged at above the standard government rates and can turn a place that sounded like a bargain into something unaffordable.

Unlimited broadband Internet services, which are about the only type on offer for most South Korean homes, cost about 30,000 won per month, and cable with a limited selection of international channels is around the same amount. Phone bills—fixed and mobile lines—start in the 25,000-30,000 per month range.

Groceries are a bit of a mixed bag. Basically, if it's something produced locally, it's probably cheaper than it would be in your home country—things like tofu, vegetables,

A SAVER'S GUIDE

South Korea can be a pricey place to live, but as is true anywhere, a bit of planning can trim your monthly expenses substantially. Here are a few ideas worth considering to save more of your hard-earned won.

- Housing is usually the biggest single expense expatriates have. If at all possible, consider adhering to the South Korean style and putting down a large deposit (*jeonse*) on any house you move into, which will bring rental costs down substantially. Depending on your visa status, employer, and salary, you may be able to secure a fairly low-interest loan (usually called *jeonse daechul*) from a local bank for this purpose.

- If you don't mind a more local living environment, steer clear of expat-heavy areas such as Seoul's Hannam-dong and Seongbuk-dong, where housing, restaurants, and even groceries all come at a premium. As the name of a neighborhood can factor heavily into rental and other prices, often moving to a less-renowned area just a short bus ride or walk away will allow you to enjoy most of the perks of a posh part of town without the eye-watering bills.

- Buy your fresh produce at local wet markets or street vendors. The selection is seasonal and often more limited than at department stores or grocery stores, but also fresher and much, much cheaper.

- Avoid traveling on long weekends and peak holiday periods such as the months of July and August, when nearly everyone in the country is on their way somewhere. Airlines, hotels, and guesthouse operators are all pretty shameless about jacking up prices when demand peaks, but also offer some real bargains in the off-season.

- If you have to send money back to your home country regularly or are worried about fluctuations in the exchange rate, consider opening a foreign-currency account with a local bank. These usually require minimum deposits but afford the holder some protection against exchange rate variations and, at some banks, offer more favorable interest rates and reduced remittance charges.

- If your city or area offers one—and most do—buy a contactless smart card (called T-money in Seoul, Mybi in Busan, etc.) to pay subway and bus fares. These offer an automatic discount on the fare every time they're used, frequently allow you to transfer services within a certain time frame without paying twice, and sometimes even result in the odd discount at smart card-ready shops.

- If you can't survive without a regular intake of cheese, granola, frozen pizza, and other Western delights, consider a membership in retailer Costco, which has branches in major cities throughout South Korea. This warehouse-style superstore imports much of its selection from its parent firm in the United States, and as such, it is one of the best, and cheapest, sources of imported delicacies like bagels, sausages, and coffee. In fact many of the foreign food stores in places like Seoul simply buy their goods from Costco and mark them up for unwitting consumers. Better to go to the source.

market in Jeollanamdo

pork, chicken, and seafood are all relative steals. But there are several exceptions to this rule—some fruit, such as locally grown pears and melons, are very pricey, especially out of season, and South Korean beef commands a hefty premium over that imported from the United States or Australia. Local wet markets have the best bargains on produce but can be tough to navigate without Korean language skills. Most expatriates end up doing their food shopping at the nearest branch of a megastore chain like E-mart, which has a wide selection and fair (if not especially low) prices. Supermarkets specifically geared toward foreigners are usually more expensive. A grocery budget of 100,000 won per week should be enough to keep the average expatriate in plenty of food with a limited number of non-Korean luxuries such as cheese or wine; double or triple that figure for a family or those who need to consume a lot of imported comforts.

Entertainment and travel costs also have to be factored into a budget but aren't massive unless you're a loyal patron of the hottest high-end nightclubs and top hotels. Plenty of meals can be had for less than 10,000 won, and a good night out at a local pub will rarely run more than 30,000 won or so, as long as you're prepared to stick to domestic beers or spirits. Domestic transport and accommodations tariffs are very low by Western standards—Seoul-Jeju, one of the most expensive flights in the country, is around 80,000 won, for example. However, while a few budget carriers have emerged, the era of low-cost international travel has yet to truly arrive in South Korea, so plan on spending 400,000 won or more on plane tickets even to the countries next door. Day-to-day medical expenses, especially if you're enrolled in the national insurance scheme, are also nothing to worry about—a typical consultation at a hospital or clinic, including medication fees, will cost 10,000-20,000 won. However, prices can be higher at international clinics and may also snowball quickly if long-term care is required.

TIPPING POINTS

As in other countries in Northeast Asia, tipping is generally not practiced in South Korea, due to the long-held and pervasive view that good service is a right rather than a favor or bonus. Years of exposure to Western culture haven't altered this mind-set, and in most restaurants and bars efforts to leave a gratuity would do nothing but confuse the proprietor. If you'd like to express appreciation, a simple *sugo haseyo* (roughly "thank you for you hard work") will suffice.

There are a few situations and places in which tipping is possible and may sometimes be expected, though it's certainly not a requirement. These include:

- Taxis: It's good form to let drivers keep the small change from a fare if they've been nice (the same goes the other way–drivers will often round down fares for passengers!)

- Higher-end and expat-centric bars

and restaurants: Some fancier restaurants, especially in hotels, will tack a 10 percent service charge onto the bill, though there's no need to tip on top of this. The staff at bars and restaurants frequented by a lot of foreigners sometimes gets used to tipping because a good chunk of the clientele does it, but again–not mandatory.

- Security guards: Many apartment blocks in Korea have security guards, and some residents will make a habit of bringing them fruit or boxes of juice, soft drinks or (if they're splurging) alcohol from time to time. This isn't a tip per se but a way to ensure a prompt response if assistance is required in the future– and it works like a charm. The same also works as a "thank you" gesture for helpful workers, officials, and so on.

SHOPPING

Shopping is one of South Korea's favorite pursuits, and the retail scene is so diverse and highly developed that people flock from all over Asia to explore it. There was a time when high tariffs, lackluster demand, and perhaps some lingering nationalism conspired to limit the presence of foreign goods, but more appear on the shelves each year. It's now possible to find a lot of the branded goods from back home, or at least passable local replacements. There's also a wealth of products produced domestically—everything from handicrafts to funky clothing, stationery, electronics, and rice wine—that warrant some intensive exploration.

South Korea's shopping landscape can be divided into a few tiers. At the higher end you've got department stores such as Shinsegae and Lotte, which, contrary to the dowdy image the term evokes in some other countries, are generally high-class complexes with floor after floor of designer clothing, household goods, and well-stocked grocery stores. Slightly further down the retail chain are superstores such as E-mart and Lotte Mart, which usually have a wider array of furniture, clothing, and food at slightly lower prices, but less in the way of luxury goods. Almost every major town in South Korea has at least one department store and a superstore branch or two, and larger cities, like Seoul or Busan, literally have dozens.

The low end is taken up by traditional markets, which are either at permanent locations or convene every few days. Particularly for those with limited Korean skills, a stress-free shopping experience they're not—they can be crowded, full of

shopping complex, Seoul

© RUFINA K.E. PARK

unfamiliar sights and smells, and haggling is sometimes required—but they can't be beat for bargains on produce, meat, and sometimes clothing and household items as well. There are also convenience stores or *supa* (miniature supermarkets) on nearly every urban street corner that sell a limited variety of fruit, vegetables, rice, noodles, and other daily necessities.

Larger cities will usually also have a few "foreign" supermarkets catering to non-Koreans with tempting displays of wine, spices, cheeses, and other goodies, but they're expensive and should never be frequented for everyday purchases. There are also a handful of branches of U.S. wholesaler Costco in South Korea, and they are a good source of imported food provided you're not adverse to coughing up the membership fee and buying in bulk.

Foreign residents will soon discover that independent retailers tend to congregate in certain areas that are basically wholly dedicated to specific products—Seoul, for example, has several fashion districts crammed with boutiques and cosmetic shops (Apgujeong, Myeong-dong, and Samcheong-dong) an electronics area (Yongsan), a furniture town (Nonhyeon), and even a motorcycle street. The practice might seem counterintuitive—why set up shop in a place where there's a bunch of people already doing the same thing?—but because competition is so fierce in these neighborhoods, inevitably it works in favor of the consumer. Check with local friends or colleagues before making a major purchase to see if there's a district renowned for whatever it is you want to buy.

Banking

For expatriates, banking is in some ways the quintessential South Korean experience. Banks are nearly everywhere, there's plenty of choice available to the customer, and service is generally courteous and efficient. Much use is made of the latest technology, with ATM, telephone, and Internet banking and bill payment all likely to be as sophisticated or even more so than they are wherever you come from.

But scratch the surface by making some more complex demands—to wire a bunch of money back home, for example, or for a mortgage—and some pretty antiquated practices can come to the fore. South Korea used to control rigorously the amount of money that could leave the country to clamp down on currency speculation, and some tellers will act like the bad old rules are still in place (which they aren't). You may be

© JONATHAN HOPFNER

a branch of Woori Bank, one of Korea's largest lenders

told flat-out that it's against the rules to lend a foreign national money or issue a foreign customer a credit card (which it isn't).

Too often these sorts of refusals are issued as the easy way out if a bank official can't be bothered tackling the paperwork or isn't comfortable explaining the matter to a customer in English. All banks (and sometimes even different branches of the same bank) have different requirements, of course, but don't hesitate to question any decisions or policies that seem odd to you—at first with the institution's management, and if that doesn't work, with a helpful agency like the Seoul Global Center. Also consider banking with a company that has set up service desks or products specifically for foreign residents—Korea Exchange Bank (KEB) and Shinhan Bank are probably the best examples—or with a local branch of an international bank such as Citibank.

CURRENCY

The South Korean currency is the won, which is divided into coin denominations of 10, 50, 100, and 500 and bills of 1,000, 5,000, 10,000, and 50,000. Coins of 1- and 5-won denominations still make the odd appearance. Preprinted checks (*supyo*) in units of 100,000 and sometimes 1,000,000 are also commonly used and can even be requested at bank machines. These basically function like cash but have to be signed in front of merchants, and smaller shops or restaurants may sometimes be hesitant to take them.

The won is generally seen to be a stable currency, but it tends to take a beating whenever there's a significant regional or global economic crisis. From late 2008 to early 2009, for example, it shed around 40 percent of its value against the U.S. dollar before beginning a slow recovery. It's currently hovering around the 1,100 per dollar level, roughly in line with economist surveys that suggest its "true" level is in the 900-1,100 per dollar range. Foreign exchange authorities are not above intervening in the market to strengthen the won when they feel it's under attack or to keep the currency relatively cheap to help out the country's exporters. There's little you can do to shield

FAMOUS FACES

The faces that adorn South Korea's currency are a good insight into the country's values. Rather than contemporary figures, philosophers and scholars drawn from the mists of history take precedence over presidents or warlords.

- 1,000 won: Yi Hwang (1501-1570), prominent Confucian scholar who established the Dosan Seowon, a private academy that still exists today.
- 5,000 won: Yi I (1536-1584), another

Confucian scholar renowned as a politician and social reformer.

- 10,000 won: Sejong the Great (1397-1450), Korea's most celebrated ruler and inventor of the hangul alphabet.
- 50,000 won: Shim Saimdang (1504-1551), an artist, writer, and calligrapher who is viewed as a model of Confucian ideals and was also the mother of Yi I.

1,000 won: Yi Hwang

10,000 won: Sejong the Great

5,000 won: Yi I

50,000 won: Shim Saimdang

Korean banknotes

COURTESY OF BANK OF KOREA

DAILY LIFE

yourself totally from exchange rate fluctuations, but some expatriates request a mixed won-home currency salary for this reason or open up a foreign-currency account with a bank like KEB.

OPENING AN ACCOUNT

Opening an account with a South Korean bank is the easy part. Simply bring your alien registration card, the chief piece of local ID, to any bank branch, and you'll be issued a bankbook in a matter of minutes. Some banks will also allow foreign nationals to open a bank account with only a passport, but this has become less common and, even if permitted, services will be limited. There's little distinction between savings and checking accounts in South Korea, and savings accounts are the default, though interest rates tend to be very low. Fixed-deposit, foreign-currency, and other varieties of accounts are also available at most banks.

Bank passbooks function much like bank cards and can be used to make deposits, withdrawals, and perform other functions at bank machines. If you also want a bank card or a "cash card"—the local version of the debit card—you'll have to ask for it and will usually be charged a nominal fee. Note that none of these cards will be equipped for overseas use; international ATM cards have to be specifically requested and involve some more paperwork. This is one of those privileges that are sometimes arbitrarily denied to non-South Koreans; there's absolutely no law preventing it, so be prepared to push your case, or if all else fails, to take your business elsewhere.

CREDIT CARDS

After many years in which they were starved of local plastic, it's now increasingly common for foreign nationals to hold credit cards issued in South Korea, but your safest and most hassle-free bet will probably still be to bring one from home. Relatively open-minded companies like KEB and Shinhan will grant credit cards to anyone they decide meets their "criteria," which can be a little arbitrary but usually includes working for a "respectable" employer and residing in South Korea for a certain period. Other banks can often be persuaded to do the same by a Korean colleague or spouse who's willing to "sponsor" you or if you put down a deposit. In nearly all cases, limits are quite low and balances have to be paid off in their entirety every month unless otherwise specified. The "Visa" logo doesn't mean you can shop internationally with your card either; KEB, for example, requires that you notify them before your card can be activated for use abroad.

The good news is that if you do have a card issued here or overseas, you'll find it's accepted almost everywhere, provided it's a Visa or MasterCard. It's also common in South Korea to use cards even for miniscule purchases, such as a packet of gum at the convenience store.

LOANS

While there are no hard-and-fast rules against providing unsecured loans to foreign residents, or foreign-owned companies, most banks are reluctant to do so in all but the most ironclad cases. Even foreigners on hefty pay packets won't have access to anywhere near the levels of financing that they could probably get in their home countries—or, for that matter, what a local of similar means would be offered. That reality aside, decisions on loans usually come down to the individual bank or bank officer, and there's no harm in asking. Having a steady (and lucrative) job, a local spouse and a residency ("F"-class) visa, or local assets, particularly real estate, are some of the factors that can tip the balance in the applicant's favor.

ATM AND INTERNET BANKING

ATMs in South Korea function much the way they do anywhere else but are commonly found in bank branches themselves rather than on the street and in shopping malls, and they operate only during designated hours, usually from 8am to just before midnight. Most (but not all) will have a button to switch from Korean to English, Chinese, or Japanese, and a few—usually one per branch of a major bank—will be equipped to take foreign cards, usually identified with a "Global ATM" sticker or the Maestro,

Plus, and Cirrus logos. If in serious doubt, try to find the nearest branch of an international bank like Citibank, which will inevitably have ATMs that take foreign cards.

International withdrawals don't usually incur charges on the South Korean end, but your bank back home is bound to bill you US$5 or so per transaction. Domestically, small charges, typically 1,000 won or so, apply for conducting ATM transactions outside business hours or using a card from a different bank at a bank machine. Withdrawals or fund transfers are also subject to limits usually agreed on with your bank when you establish an account.

Internet banking is a mixed bag. The range of services available in Korean is spectacular, and virtually all major banks now have websites built in English and other major languages that allow you to check balances, pay bills, transfer funds, or even remit money overseas. However, many have a tendency to revert to Korean when things go awry. Security, while well-intentioned, is also a hassle—in addition to dongles or onetime password cards you'll need a digital security certificate downloaded from the bank that you're supposed to use for all online banking (and e-government) transactions. To top it all off, many banks require the installation of complex firewalls and ActiveX controls—which, of course, function properly only in Microsoft's Internet Explorer. The security gauntlet has caused more than a few expats to give up on Internet banking altogether. If you dare, KEB and Shinhan (again) probably have the most foreign-friendly sites.

REMITTANCES

Remittances abroad by South Koreans and expatriates alike used to attract a fair amount of scrutiny from banks and the authorities but are now common transactions. Legally speaking, foreign nationals are free to send up to US$50,000 per year out of the country with few or no questions asked, and more than that if they can prove the funds were legitimately earned in South Korea. Remittances can be done through your bank—some can even set up automatic or online remittances for you—or through companies like Western Union, although the fees will be higher. South Korean banks typically charge around 20,000 won for a wire transfer that will arrive in the recipient's account in one or two business days. Fees tend to be lower for online remittances or accounts specifically set up for the purpose.

Foreign nationals are required to nominate a "primary" foreign exchange bank for any remittances abroad—this will by default be the first bank you wire funds overseas from. Remitting money from another branch of the same bank is fine, but if you want to send funds home from another bank altogether, you'll have to fill out a form to "switch" your designated foreign exchange institution—not a massive inconvenience, but another layer of paperwork.

Rules and restrictions on remittances can vary widely among banks, branches, and tellers. If you're dealing with a bank that insists on tight limits or wants to stamp your passport every time you send funds overseas (not unheard of), it's time to follow up with the bank's customer service center or seek out a more amenable place.

There are few restrictions on receiving money wired from abroad, but banks must report any remittances worth over US$10,000 to the tax authorities, and will sometimes require you to contact your branch before releasing funds.

Taxes

SOUTH KOREAN TAXES

As in most countries, South Korea's tax system is a complex, shifting beast, but it's also highly modernized and fair, and some efforts have been made to unravel its mysteries for expatriates. Residents of South Korea—generally defined as anyone who works here or who has lived in the country for a year or more—are subject to tax on income they earn locally, as well as most international income that happens to be reported to the tax authorities (a process that more than a few foreign taxpayers avoid for obvious reasons).

South Korea has a progressive tax rate that begins at 6 percent for annual earnings of 12 million won or less and tops out at 38 percent on earnings of 300 million won per year or more, plus a 10 percent surcharge on total tax liability. This is complemented with a rather generous array of deductions and exclusions for everything from credit card spending (which the government wants to encourage because it makes purchases and hence sales tax easier to track) to transportation, charitable, educational, and medical expenses. Foreign nationals will usually be given the option of forgoing all deductions in exchange for their income being taxed at a preferential flat rate of 15 percent, which can represent a better deal for those with limited spending or no dependents.

Taxes should be deducted from your salary at the standard rate each month by your employer, and employers also generally assist with the completion of an annual return due early each year that will result in an additional payment being requested or, if you're lucky, a refund. If you're not able to count on outside help, the required forms can be obtained in English from the National Tax Service, and the agency also runs a multilingual tax counseling service that can guide you through the filing process, answer tax-related inquiries, and look into cases where taxes are being improperly applied or withheld by an employer.

U.S. INCOME TAXES

U.S. citizens working in South Korea are still subject to taxes in the United States, but under an income tax convention agreed on by the two governments, in theory they are able to deduct any tax paid in South Korea against their U.S. tax bills. If you spend at least one tax year in South Korea in which you don't return to the United States for more than 35 days, you're likely to qualify for the Internal Revenue Service's Foreign Earned Income Exclusion, which exempts the first US$95,100 (as of 2012) earned by a U.S. national resident abroad from U.S. income tax. There have been rumblings for some time about this exclusion being revoked—check with the IRS or U.S. Embassy locally for current tax information and advice on how to file your U.S. returns.

OTHER COUNTRIES' INCOME TAXES

South Korea has avoidance of double taxation treaties with a number of countries, including Canada, Australia, Ireland, the United Kingdom, South Africa, and New Zealand, that allow nationals of these countries to set any taxes paid in South Korea against their home tax obligations. Most countries also allow citizens fulfilling certain requirements to declare nonresidency for tax purposes, which usually exempts them from tax on (or even having to report) income made elsewhere. These requirements vary from country to country and are adjusted regularly but generally involve having minimal attachments (like income-generating property) back home or spending a certain amount of time abroad each year. As declaring nonresidency can make a return back home more complicated, it's usually recommended only for people spending a protracted amount of time abroad. Make sure to get the latest from your tax authorities or a tax planner before making any hasty decisions, and don't forget that being outside of the country doesn't automatically exempt you from having to complete annual tax returns.

Pensions

Most foreign nationals working in South Korea are automatically enrolled in the mandatory national pension system, which is overseen by the National Pension Service (NPS). The contribution rate to an employee's pension is currently set at 9 percent of monthly salary, split evenly between employee and employer, up to a maximum 3,750,000 won. Pension payments should be deducted automatically during each pay cycle, and the NPS usually sends the employee an annual statement showing the balance of their pension account.

When the worker can enjoy these pension spoils depends on where that worker is from. Nationals of South Africa, Singapore, and a handful of other countries can opt out of paying into the pension system altogether, since their respective governments allow South Koreans to do the same. Nationals of a few other countries, including Canada, Australia, and the United States, are eligible to claim their total pension payments as a lump-sum refund when they cease working and depart South Korea, again because their governments afford South Koreans similar privileges. Anyone else, including Brits, will have to wait until they're 60, when (if they're still in South Korea) the government will start returning their contributions in the form of regular old-age pension payments.

Investing

The standard "buyer beware" rules apply, but there's no doubt the South Korean economy holds a lot of promise for investors. It has had the odd rocky year, but overall the trend seems to be consistent strong growth. Some domestic firms are already global industry leaders, and others are steadily becoming more competitive. South Korean stocks tend to trade at a discount to Asian peers (in no small part due to the threat, however remote, of conflict with North Korea) and are seen by many regional analysts as relatively undervalued. Compared to places like China, South Korea's equities, bond, and foreign exchange markets are also liquid and well-regulated.

Bear in mind however that South Korea is still an emerging market (just), and as the rewards are often greater, so are the risks. Ignorance about the machinations of the South Korean business and legal environment, and the export-dependent country's inherent vulnerability to global financial storms, means nasty surprises are always a possibility. By all means, seize the opportunity, but don't get carried away.

© JONATHAN HOPFNER

Seoul Finance Center

MARKETS AND HOW TO INVEST

South Korea's main stock exchange is the Korea Composite Stock Price Index (KOSPI), which consists almost exclusively of domestic companies led by heavyweights like Samsung Electronics, POSCO, and Hyundai Motor. There's also a secondary market, the KOSDAQ, which was set up to highlight smaller, mainly technology-based start-ups, and specialized markets for instruments like derivatives and commodities futures. All markets are operated by the Korea Exchange, which is generally perceived as a sophisticated, tech-savvy outfit. It is not, however, geared toward foreign investors: Many listed companies make materially important announcements in Korean only, for example.

There are few restrictions on foreign investment in local markets or repatriation of stock gains. For residents, the easiest way to begin investing in the local market is to open an account with a local brokerage such as Daewoo Securities or Samsung Securities, quite a few of which can provide English-language investment advice and online trading platforms. It's also possible for nonresidents to open accounts with local securities firms, although it requires some more paperwork.

Another option is to invest in KOSPI-focused funds through an international bank or broker. Mirae Asset, for example, runs a Hong Kong-based KOSPI-tracking exchange traded fund or ETF, while HSBC is among the banking giants offering "capital secured" growth funds that guarantee a certain level of protection to investors while spreading their money throughout the KOSPI and other regional exchanges. Individuals are generally exempt from capital gains tax on share sale proceeds provided they hold a 3 percent or less stake in the relevant firm; however if this threshold is exceeded, gains can be taxed at up to 33 percent.

COMMUNICATIONS

Communications is an area in which South Korea excels, and even the most disillusioned resident would find it difficult to complain about the state of the country's networking. This is especially true when it comes to the Internet—South Korea regularly tops regional and global broadband penetration tables, and in most homes connection speeds range from fast to positively blistering. This is partly a function of demographics—a highly concentrated, mainly apartment-dwelling population has made it easy to wire up most cities—but also a function of a culture that has rarely failed to embrace technology with a vengeance, and has since moved on to wholeheartedly adopt newer advances like next-generation wireless standards and streaming television to mobile devices. A demanding customer base and keen competition among Internet, mobile phone, and fixed-line providers has kept the quality of services high and prices fairly low.

But foreign residents will also face some speed bumps on South Korea's information superhighway. Unique technical standards limit the presence of non-South Korean manufacturers in the domestic cellular market, and some find their preferred models are unavailable here. Mobile phone companies are only grudgingly easing the requirements for foreign nationals seeking standard payment plans or contracts, which basically seemed designed to preclude anyone who wasn't local from getting their

hands on a handset. And few South Korean government agencies or retailers seem to keep the foreign population in mind when designing the authentication and payment systems for their websites, hampering access to the country's otherwise admirable e-commerce sector.

Telephone Service

Phone services are widely available and generally excellent, though as in other countries the public's increasing reliance on mobile phones has led to the scaling back of public fixed-line phone services in some areas. Many homes, shops, and restaurants are also doing away with landlines altogether, and mobile phones now outnumber standard phones nationwide by around three to one. Both fixed-line and mobile phone charges are usually billed monthly and can be deducted directly from a bank account or paid via the Internet or at banks, branches of service providers, or convenience stores.

LANDLINES

Korea Telecom (KT) is the country's dominant fixed-line provider, with SK Broadband a very distant second. The phone company residents end up with can come down to the area they live in rather than personal choice. Installing a landline is quick and easy, although you'll probably need the help of a Korean speaker. You can lodge a connection request with either provider online or by dialing their service hotlines—www.kt.com or 100 for KT, and www.skbroadband.com or 108 for SK Broadband. You'll need to give the phone company a copy of your passport and alien registration card. Fees for installation, which will usually take place within a day or two, are around 30,000 won, and the basic monthly charge for a phone line is just over 5,000 won. Customers can sometimes save on installation and call charges by opting for the Internet-based (VoIP) phone lines offered by cable companies such as C&M as part of a bundled package of services, but voice and connection quality can be an issue.

Rates for domestic calls via landlines are quite reasonable; around 10 won per minute within the same city or province and 20-30 won per minute for calls to other areas. Calls to mobile phones are more expensive at around 80 won per minute. Most providers offer slight discounts for calls made at off-peak (nighttime) hours.

Standard international calls on the most commonly used services (KT 001 and LG U+ 002) cost around 300 won per minute to the United States, 1,000 won a minute to East Asian, Canadian, and European cities, and 1,500 won per minute to destinations in South Asia, South America, or the Middle East. As with local calls, very slight discounts usually apply on holidays and from midnight to 6am local time. Several budget operators, such as SK Telink, offer significantly cheaper rates for calls to popular international destinations and special discount packages or prepaid cards for frequent overseas callers.

CELLULAR PHONES

Even the newest of new arrivals soon works out that in South Korea, without a cellular phone, you simply don't exist. By most accounts there's a phone in the country for every man, woman, and child, and many people have different handsets for personal, office, and family use. The latest models can be used to watch live TV broadcasts, conduct banking, pay bus fares—you name it. Getting by without a mobile phone in South Korea is certainly possible, but it will raise a few eyebrows, and given the generally low cost, near countrywide coverage, and wide range of services available, few foreign residents consider it.

There are a few pitfalls to watch out for, however. South Korea uses the CDMA network standard also popular in the United States, but not in the rest of Asia or Europe, where GSM dominates. Regardless, any mobile phone brought here from overseas probably won't work out of the box, as few foreign brands meet the country's unique technological specifications. These have been eased in recent years, and foreign entrants like the iPhone have a decent foothold in the market, but it's still firmly ruled by Samsung and LG. If you have a 3G handset and a roaming deal with your home provider, you'll be able to access 3G networks here, but airtime will be expensive, so this can't be advocated as a long-term solution. Some mobile devices purchased abroad, such as iPhones and iPads, can be used on a local contract, but will first have to be "unlocked" by a local mobile provider.

Until very recently, phone companies were reluctant to offer foreign nationals anything but prepaid cellular services out of fear they'd flee the country and renege on contracts. This has changed, but prospective foreign customers may still find some outlets hesitate or refuse to sign them up to long-term mobile service plans. Provided you work in South Korea, there's no real justification for this, and a call to the phone company's customer service hotline or expatriate support agencies like the Seoul Global Center will usually result in any barriers mysteriously vanishing.

SK Telecom, KT, and LG U+ are the three main mobile carriers, and all offer fairly similar voice and data service packages that should be available to any resident with a work visa, local bank account, and identification. Virtually all the new cellular phones on offer in South Korea are smartphones, and it can be a struggle to find a plain-vanilla mobile.

Signing a mobile phone contract usually entitles the new customer to a free handset or heavy discounts on flashier models that can be paid for in installments on the phone bill. Standard smartphone service plans range from around 30,000-90,000 won a month, with the more expensive plans including more free talk time and text messages and hefty data allowances. Beyond those local calls are billed at about 120 won per minute, data charges run around 50 won per megabyte, and international tariffs are similar to those on landlines. Receiving calls is always free. Prepaid phones, for which the customer can buy and replenish talk (or web browsing) time by purchasing cards, are also widely available and sometimes easier to source for foreign nationals, but on a per-use basis they work out to be far more expensive than standard contracts.

PUBLIC PHONES

While their numbers have dwindled in recent years as the mobile phone renders them obsolete, public phones are still fairly common in South Korea, especially along major streets and in subway stations. They're divided into three kinds: those that take coins, those that take phone cards, and those that take both. Phone cards are usually available at any convenience store or newsstand and come in denominations between 2,000 and

10,000 won. Local calls are billed at around 20 won per minute. International calls can be made via public phones that accept phone and credit cards.

To save on international call charges, many foreign residents use Internet telephony services such as Skype, which allow people to make calls with a computer, Internet connection, and headset for little or no cost. Prepaid phone cards with steeply reduced per-minute rates for international calls are also widely available at convenience stores and other retailers, although the quality of service can vary.

Internet

About the only fault one could find with South Korean Internet services, if it is a fault at all, is that it's nearly impossible to get a dial-up connection. Broadband is so stable and ubiquitous that few are prepared to settle for anything else. Ten megabit-per-second (Mbps) connections—twice as fast as the typical DSL links seen in the United States—are standard, and speeds in newer apartment complexes equipped with what are known as *kwang* (light) broadband networks top out above 100 Mbps. Services of up to 1 gigabit per second (Gbps) are also being rolled out countrywide. Fixed-line broadband is augmented with the country's homegrown wireless technology, known as WiBro, which blankets much of Seoul and is being extended to other cities, and independent wireless networks in many retail spaces, coffee shops, and offices. Near-constant lightning-quick connectivity and the good things associated with it—streaming video, Internet phone calls, online shopping, media downloads—are a source of great pleasure for foreign residents and have made South Korea a recognized authority in Internet-based industries such as online gaming. Also, to the chagrin of movie and music studios, such resources make it a hotbed for pirated content.

ONLINE SOCIALIZING

With high-speed Internet access and smartphones so ubiquitous, it's no surprise social networking is a major pastime—and big business—in South Korea. The country has an enthusiastic population of Twitter users—more than three million by most counts—and Facebook is also popular. However, both are recent entrants to the scene and have to compete for users with some heavyweight local incumbents.

The granddaddy of domestic social networks is Cyworld, operated by SK Communications. It allows users to interact and cultivate friendships through mini-avatars, and the avatars and their surroundings can be dressed up by spending virtual currency on clothing and accessories. At its peak more than a quarter of the population had an active Cyworld account. A series of embarrassing, high-profile data leaks and rising competition have eaten into that user base, and many analysts now reckon Facebook has a wider reach in South Korea.

Other popular local services include me2day, a microblogging service similar to Twitter, and instant messaging applications NateOn and KakaoTalk. The latter is arguably the most popular Android smartphone app in the country, and many foreign residents soon find they have to jump on board if they're to have any hope of keeping in touch with local friends.

HOW THE INTERNET ALMOST BROUGHT DOWN A PRESIDENT

WIKIMEDIA COMMONS/COURTESY OF HENRIK HANSSON GLOBAL JUGGLER

Former President Lee Myung-bak addresses a conference in 2008.

Plenty of people were aware the Internet was playing a larger and larger role in the lives of young South Koreans—most of them bank, shop, date, forge friendships, and form opinions online—but few foresaw just how powerful a tool it had become.

In the summer of 2008, thousands of locals, many only high-school age, began taking to the streets of central Seoul to voice their discontent with the administration of then-President Lee Myung-bak, who had stoked anger by failing to consult the public on a series of controversial decisions, including one to reopen the South Korean market to U.S. beef imports. Outraged citizens had flooded the message boards of popular Internet portals such as Naver, forming makeshift activist groups and discussing ways to push Lee from power.

In just a few weeks, scattershot protests had turned into massive nightly candlelit vigils that effectively shut down the city center and continued for weeks on end. While there were a few scuffles, the campaign was relatively free of the large-scale violence that had accompanied student-led protests in the not-so-distant past. It were also notable for drawing in many ordinary working families, including their children, which often gave the whole event the tone of a festival.

The most remarkable thing about the demonstrations was the way technology supported them from start to finish. Websites regularly updated the public on Lee's alleged transgressions. Mobile-phone text messages advised people on where to rally; reporters and camera operators from blogs and online newspapers documented the entire movement and, many argued, helped keep the police in check by providing a 24/7 view of events on the ground. And though the president stuck to his guns and the protests eventually fizzled out, the broader campaign was apparently successful enough to worry the authorities. In the wake of the protests politicians enacted regulations that made online defamation a criminal offense and also moved to limit the ability of citizens to publish anonymous comments or opinions online. Activists have decried the moves as a crackdown on free speech, and in 2011 press freedom advocacy group Reporters Without Borders placed South Korea on its list of countries where the Internet is "under surveillance."

DAILY LIFE

KT, LG, and SK Broadband are the main home Internet providers and will usually be able to complete an installation just a day or two after it's requested. Installation fees are typically 30,000 won, and while the company will supply all the necessary equipment, it may charge a monthly rental of 7,000-10,000 won for a modem and other peripherals. Installation and rental fees are almost always waived if a user signs a 12-month or longer service contract. Monthly tariffs for standard broadband service with unlimited data usage average around 30,000 won. Unlike their foreign counterparts, most South Korean Internet providers typically don't provide subscribers with email addresses, so you'll want to make sure you sign up for a web-based service such as Gmail or Hotmail to keep in touch with people here and back home.

Those without a home connection can head for the nearest PC *bang* (room), the South Korean version of the Internet café, which are found on every street corner. These range from cramped smoky hovels populated by adolescent gamers to plush outlets with ergonomic chairs and top-end printing equipment frequented by professional types, but they are inevitably cheap—typically 1,000-2,000 won per hour—and reliable. Wireless connections are also found all over the place, but there are fewer free or open wireless connections than there are in your average Western city center; even coffee shops where you're a customer will present log-in requests.

The failings of South Korea's IT infrastructure are mainly on the software side. Many important government, bank, and retail sites are in Korean only and often require users to input a South Korean ID number before they can proceed with the convenient online transactions that so many agencies promise, effectively cutting foreign nationals out of the e-commerce loop. The government has promised to bridge the gap by persuading more sites to accept alien registration numbers, but a lot of work remains to be done in this regard. Firefox, Safari, and Google Chrome users will also feel like something of a persecuted minority—virtually all South Korean websites are optimized for Microsoft's Internet Explorer, and many require the installation of small security programs or ActiveX scripts that work properly only on Windows systems.

Postal Service

The national postal service, government-run Korea Post, is inexpensive, reliable, and efficient, with standard mail taking just a day (sometimes even less) to reach anywhere in the country, and rarely more than a week or two to arrive at overseas destinations—if there is a delay, it's probably on the receiving end. Letters or parcels shipped to South Korea likewise seem to have little trouble finding their way to the intended recipient, no matter how mangled the English version of the local address.

Standard letters or postcards can simply be dropped into mailboxes if you've got the appropriate postage; otherwise you'll have to make a trip to the post office (*uchaeguk*). Each city district will have at least one, and they vary from small branch outlets to towering beehives in busy places like central Seoul. They offer the full range of standard postal services, as well as courier options, stationery sales, and even postal savings accounts. Most offices will have separate counters for domestic and international services—in smaller places you'll have to line up, and in others you can take a number at the appropriate place and wait until it's called.

Domestic postage rates range from 220-340 won for most standard items; plan on around four or five times more for air mail to major overseas destinations. Korea Post runs its own courier (Express Mail Service), and rapid deliveries are also available through local "quick service" companies and international logistics firms like DHL,

post office

UPS, and FedEx. It costs only 10,000 won or so to send a 30-kilogram box just about anywhere in the country via EMS, but fees to ship things overseas quickly are far higher—most couriers charge 25,000-50,000 won for two- or three-day delivery of documents to North American or European cities.

Media

The days when South Korea's press was staid and state-controlled are well and truly over, and there's now a thriving and competitive—some would say crowded—domestic media scene that covers all forms of media and sectors of the political spectrum. Many foreign residents are somewhat taken aback by the power of the Internet journalists, bloggers, and debaters collectively known as "netizens," whose speculations on government or corporate malfeasance have been known to provoke full-scale protests. Web zines and forums have replaced the role of traditional media outlets for many South Koreans, particularly the young.

NEWSPAPERS AND MAGAZINES

The granddaddies of South Korean print journalism are the *Chosun Ilbo, Dong-a Ilbo,* and *Joongang Ilbo,* all with fairly long histories and conservative slants. The *Chosun* and *Dong-a* have English Internet editions that reproduce a limited number of stories from the print versions, whereas the *Joongang* publishes its own English-language paper—the *Joongang Daily,* distributed with the *International Herald Tribune.* At the other end of the spectrum are newer, typically more left-wing publications such as the *Hankyoreh,* businesses dailies serving the stock-trading set, and commuter papers full of light news and entertainment for subway passengers. Unfortunately very little content is made available in other languages, so non-Korean speakers miss out on a great deal of the scope of South Korean debate.

Beyond the *Joongang Daily,* the English-language press is confined to the *Korea Herald* and *Korea Times* newspapers, as well as a few event-oriented magazines like *Seoul, Groove,* and *10.* All are inoffensive enough reads and a good source of information on expatriate-oriented events and businesses, but they are unlikely to win any reporting prizes and rarely tackle the controversial political and social developments that cram local headlines. Recent years have seen the welcome addition of a handful of regional English-language publications targeted at the chronically underserved areas outside the capital, including *Busan Haps* and *Jeju Weekly.*

TELEVISION AND RADIO

South Korea's biggest TV and radio broadcaster is the government-backed Korea Broadcasting System (KBS), which runs multiple channels and stations dominated by news programs and soap operas. Its challengers include MBC and SBS, which are known for dramas, variety shows, and harder-hitting documentaries. None have any foreign-language programming of note.

Locally, the only major foreign-language broadcaster is Arirang, a government-sponsored TV and radio station with a focus on promoting South Korea to the outside world. Many foreign residents find its language and cultural programs informative, but its constant trumpeting of all things Korean is hard for others to digest. Some international channels (BBC, CNN, CNBC, etc.) are available from cable providers like Skylife for a monthly fee.

Cable television is widely available and, as it's increasingly based on Internet protocol TV (IPTV) technology, is often included in "bundled" service packages that lump it with discounted broadband Internet and telephone services. Standard cable packages include hundreds of channels, but only a dozen or so with regular foreign-language programming, usually news, movies, and Chinese and Japanese state broadcasters. The Korean Cable TV Association maintains an up-to-date list of the providers serving neighborhoods throughout the country. Charges are usually 15,000-30,000 won per month plus equipment and installation fees, the latter often waived if the customer signs up for a year or more.

Those who crave more television variety may want to try satellite TV service such as Skylife, which has the largest range of foreign-language channels legitimately available. Monthly fees aren't far off those for regular cable, but installation and equipment charges are significantly higher, in the 200,000-300,000 won range.

Seoul, Busan, and Gwangju have launched government-supported English-language radio stations with local news, traffic, and weather information, and other cities have similar plans.

TRAVEL AND TRANSPORTATION

South Korea is not a massive country; truly far-flung communities are rare, so perhaps linking its towns and cities and moving people from one place to another was never going to be a overwhelming problem. Nonetheless, over the past few decades the government has tackled the issue of transportation with diligence, foresight, and a flurry of funding befitting a far larger and less manageable place.

The results are obvious and largely commendable. Whatever complaints foreign residents have, few of them involve getting around. The country's main international airport has been lauded as one of the world's best. Almost every major city has an enviable rapid transit system. Intercity buses are frequent, plush, and cheap, and sleek high-speed trains or commuter flights are an option if the bus isn't quick enough. Across all forms of transport, fares are generally low, delays uncommon, and full-scale breakdowns virtually unheard of.

If South Korea does have a weak spot in transport terms, it's probably the roads—while they're almost universally modern and well-maintained, heavy traffic, particularly in the Seoul area, the often aggressive local style of motoring, and poor signage can make driving in South Korea a trying experience at times.

© RUFINA K.E. PARK

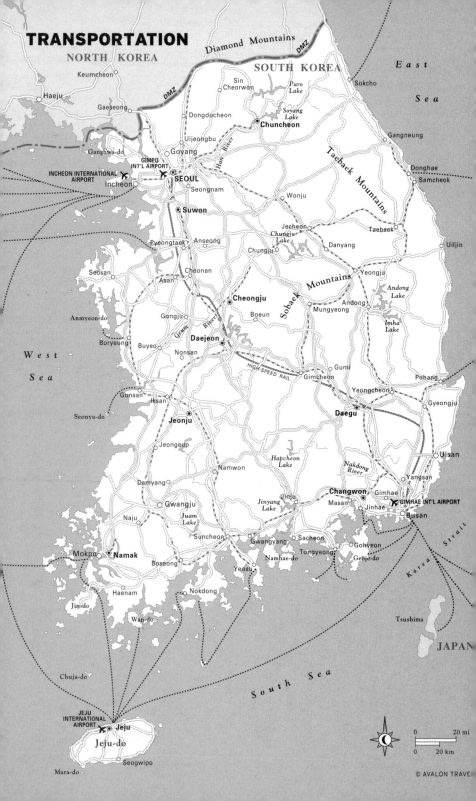

By Air

South Korea's closed border with the reclusive North makes overland travel to the country impossible for most visitors, so the vast majority arrive by air. Incheon International Airport, which opened in 2001 on a massive patch of reclaimed land off the coast, 43 kilometers (26 miles) west of Seoul, is the country's main gateway. The airy glass-and-steel structure, one of the busiest transport hubs in the region, regularly notches up awards for its efficiency, comfort, and services, which include the standard duty-free and foreign exchange outlets as well as a few exceptional touches like an on-site health spa.

Around 80 airlines serve Incheon, including the country's flagship carriers, Korean Air and Asiana Airlines. There are regular direct connections to major cities in Asia, Europe, and a few destinations in North America, including Vancouver, Toronto, Los Angeles, Atlanta, and New York, with many other cities accessible via code-share arrangements. Round-trip flights from the West Coast of the United States to Seoul start at about US$1,000 in off-peak seasons; children up to 12 are usually entitled to fare reductions of 20 percent or so and infants about 80 percent.

Gimpo International Airport, on Seoul's western outskirts and the country's main airport before Incheon relegated it to second-tier status, and Busan's Gimhae International Airport also have some international traffic, mainly commuter flights to cities in neighboring Japan and China and a few services to popular Southeast Asian vacation destinations like Bangkok and Cebu.

Domestically, Korean Air, Asiana, and upstarts like Jeju Air run dozens of flights per day connecting Seoul with Busan, Daegu, Ulsan, Jeju Island, and other sizable cities. These are a quick and relatively inexpensive way to get around—the country's longest flight, Seoul to Jeju, takes only about an hour and costs about 80,000 won. As airports are often located some distance from city centers, however, many travelers find buses or trains a more convenient way to move around the mainland.

The domestic heavyweights ensured they were locked out for years, but a handful of budget carriers, including Jeju Air, Jin Air, Malaysia's Air Asia, Japan's Peach and Cebu Pacific Air from the Philippines now serve South Korea with regular flights to other Asian destinations. Ticket prices are usually slightly cheaper than those offered by the standard carriers, but the rock-bottom rates found on similar outfits in Europe are rare. On the plus side, there are fewer problems with service and hidden surcharges.

While airlines the world over boost prices during times of peak demand such as holidays, in South Korea they've got it down to an art, and the peak periods tend to last longer—virtually the entire summer (July-September) and winter (December-February) school vacation periods, with a few others in between. Even with the high fares, tickets disappear quickly, so it pays to plan and book any vacations early.

DAILY LIFE

By Train

South Korea has a well-developed rail network that has expanded rapidly since the first train lines linked Seoul with the port of Incheon more than a century ago. The government-owned Korea Railroad Corporation (Korail) runs all the country's long-distance rail services as well as some commuter lines that feed into the Seoul metropolitan subway network. Two major lines, the Honam and Gyeongbu, connect Seoul with the southwestern port of Mokpo and Busan, respectively, with branch lines extending to virtually all sizable towns nationwide.

Trains are punctual and comfortable, but—with the glaring exception of the high-speed Korea Train Express (KTX) service—often slower than express buses, particularly when highway traffic is relatively light. That said, many prefer the more relaxed pace of rail travel, as well as the amenities offered on longer train routes—washrooms, dining cars, and even wireless Internet access.

TYPES OF TRAINS

Long-distance trains in South Korea are divided into three classes (*ho*); four if the KTX bullet train is included. *Tonggeun,* previously known as *Tongil* or "unification" class trains, are short no-frills commuter services usually linking a few small towns to larger hubs. They typically have no assigned seating and a layout that's only a few steps up from the average subway car.

Mugunghwa trains, named after South Korea's hardy national flower, are a substantial step up, with air-conditioned cars, individual reclining seats, and usually dining and first-class sections. These are the workhorses of South Korean rail travel, stopping most frequently along longer routes. *Saemaul* or "new village" trains are the highest class and fastest of standard train services; they have larger, more comfortable seats than their *Mugunghwa* counterparts and make fewer stops, completing the Seoul to Busan journey—one of the nation's longest—in under five hours.

Prices vary according to train type, class, and distance. A *Saemaul* ticket from Seoul to Busan, for example, costs around 43,000 won; for another 6,000 won you can bump yourself up to first class. The same trip on a slower *Mugunghwa* train costs under 30,000 won.

Standing head and shoulders above the other services is the KTX high-speed train, based on France's TGV technology and launched with much fanfare in 2004. The KTX connects Seoul with Daejeon, Daegu, and Busan via the Gyeongbu Line and Gwangju and Mokpo via the Honam Line, reaching speeds of around 300 kilometers per hour (180 mph) on a special high-speed track that is still in the process of being extended. The KTX has slashed the travel time from Seoul to Busan to just over two and a half hours, making it a legitimate alternative to flying—in fact, the introduction of the service has proved a substantial headache for airlines now facing dwindling passenger numbers on important domestic routes. The trains are sleek, quiet, comfortable, and equipped with washrooms and some facilities for the disabled. While there are no dining cars, vendors regularly make the rounds selling light snacks, coffee, soft drinks, and beer.

TRAVEL TIMES

Here's a short list of key destinations with approximate travel times to and from Seoul by common modes of transportation.

- Busan: Train (KTX) 2 hours 40 minutes, bus 5 hours
- Chuncheon: Train (ITX) 1 hour 10 minutes
- Sokcho: Bus 3 hours
- Daejeon: Train (KTX) 1 hour, bus 2 hours
- Daegu: Train (KTX) 2 hours, bus 3 hours 30 minutes
- Gyeongju: Train (KTX) 2 hours, bus 4 hours
- Andong: Train 4 hours, bus 3 hours
- Jeonju: Train (KTX) 2 hours, bus 2 hours 45 minutes
- Yeosu: Train (KTX) 3 hours 40 minutes, bus 4 hours

Like other trains, the KTX has standard first-class (*tukshil*) seating. Standard class is perfectly adequate for most, but larger passengers may find it somewhat cramped and want to spring for special class, which has far roomier seating and nice perks such as free newspapers and mineral water. KTX speed and service come at a reasonable premium: A one-way Seoul-Busan journey typically costs about 60,000 won, or around 80,000 won for first class.

BUYING TICKETS

Purchasing tickets for all classes of train travel is a straightforward affair. Given the frequency of most services, reservations are not absolutely necessary except for travel on weekends and important holidays such as Lunar New Year, when millions of Koreans make their way back to their hometowns.

Train tickets can be booked through travel agents such as Hana Tour, at Korea Tourism Organization information centers, or purchased directly, up to two months in advance, at train station ticket counters or automatic ticketing machines. Major stations such as Seoul and Busan have special counters staffed with foreign-language speakers for overseas visitors, but in smaller towns you'll be on your own. Korail also runs an on-again, off-again English-language Internet booking system, though tickets reserved this way still have to be picked up at the station of departure.

Korail offers discounts on fares of up to 75 percent for children, seniors, and student passengers, as well as smaller reductions for passengers purchasing tickets early, using automatic ticketing machines, or changing trains. These are generally applied automatically at the time of purchase. Foreign nationals can also take advantage of the "KR Pass," which is similar to European rail passes and allows unlimited travel on the rail network for periods of three to ten days for a cut-rate flat fee, but these have to be purchased overseas at designated travel agents.

By Bus

Bus travel may suffer from an image problem in most parts of North America, but in South Korea it's by and large a delight, rivaled only by the train in terms of comfort and very often the fastest way between points A and B. Buses connect almost every point in the country and travel in designated lanes on many roads and highways to help them avoid the traffic snarls that plague so many car drivers. Best of all, they run frequently and are a very good value, with fares rarely exceeding 30,000 won even for the longest trips.

EXPRESS BUSES

While intercity (*jikhaeng*) buses dominate the back roads between some smaller towns, express (*goseok*) buses, which ply the nation's highways, account for the vast majority of bus travel. These are usually large roomy coaches with spacious reclining seats and storage racks or undercarriage compartments for luggage. Onboard washrooms are a rarity, but buses will usually stop every two or three hours at highway rest areas with bathrooms, shops, and food stalls.

As express buses run frequently—as often as every 10 or 15 minutes for major routes—reservations are not usually necessary, and tickets are bought on the spot at bus stations, although advance booking is a must prior to major holidays. Larger stations will have some schedule information displayed in English, but this is a rarity at smaller ones, where the timetable may be nothing more than a few characters scrawled on a board.

Larger cities will typically have multiple express bus stations serving different directions or routes—in Seoul, for example, most buses depart from the Express Bus Terminal in Gangnam, but the Dong (Eastern) Seoul Terminal serves several major cities in the eastern provinces, and the Nambu Terminal serves many towns in the central and southern regions. Unfortunately it's all too easy to get these places mixed up; bus travelers should double-check where they'll be departing and arriving.

By Boat

While it's rarely anyone's first choice, there are a few places in and around South Korea that can be reached by ferry as well as by car or plane, and some very picturesque getaways that are accessible only by boat. Ferries are usually large and extremely seaworthy vessels, with some of the bigger ones equipped with private cabins, restaurants, and even karaoke bars and casinos.

Within South Korea the most popular routes include Incheon, Mokpo, and Busan to Jeju Island, as well as Pohang to the rocky green island of Ulleongdo in the East Sea. Smaller vessels ply the waters between ports such as Incheon and Yeosu and dozens of outlying islands popular in the summer months with fishing enthusiasts and day-trippers.

It's a little-known fact that South Korea has more international sea connections than just about anywhere else in the region. Scheduled ferry services link Incheon with a dozen cities on China's east coast, including Dalian, Tianjin, and Qingdao. Busan on the east coast is an obvious jumping-off point for Japan, with a rapid hydrofoil to Fukuoka and slower services to Hiroshima and Osaka. There are also services between the northeastern city of Sokcho and Russia's far east port of Vladivostok.

Standard-class ferry tickets are usually slightly cheaper than air tickets for the same route, but shelling out for luxuries like private cabins can make a boat trip cost substantially more.

By Bicycle

South Korea's cycling culture is still very much a work in progress. Cyclists have taken heart from some remarkable improvements in recent years, especially in major cities, such as the development of a 40-kilometer (24-mile) cycling trail along Seoul's Han River and even the emergence of the nation's first "cycling capital" in the otherwise undistinguished town of Sangju, North Gyeongsang Province. There's also a thriving community of mountain biking enthusiasts who take to a diverse network of trails on the outskirts of cities like Busan and Daegu.

That said, biking is still very much a form of recreation rather than transport—bike routes in the middle of major cities are limited or nonexistent, and urban cyclists braving the traffic in places like Seoul are a fairly rare sight, mainly because local drivers have little regard for cyclists or their safety. While committed cyclists will be able to find some spots to practice their craft, cycling can't be recommended as a viable form of commuting anywhere but in South Korea's very smallest cities.

bikes for rent along Seoul's Han River

DAILY LIFE

© CRAIG D.C. LEWIS

Public Transportation

South Koreans may love their cars, but most city-dwellers still rely on public transit to get around on a daily basis. It's therefore of a very good standard—and extremely affordable—in most urban areas.

SUBWAY

The majority of South Korea's largest metropolises, including Seoul, Busan, Incheon, Daegu, Daejeon, and Gwangju, have subway systems, although outside of Seoul and Busan's mazelike networks they're generally limited to a line or two.

While there's some variance between cities, subways are usually the most foreigner-friendly form of transport, with plenty of clear color-coded maps, bilingual ticketing machines, and signs and announcements in Korean and English (and sometimes in Chinese and Japanese). Trains typically run from around 5am to just after midnight, with fares based on distance and ranging 1,000-1,800 won or so. Fares can be paid in cash at automatic ticketing machines or staffed counters, and in some cities, like Seoul and Busan, with electronic stored-value cards that are also designed to work with other forms of transportation. Tickets or cards are used twice—once when you enter the train platform and again when you leave, so hang on to them.

While they can be crowded, anyone used to the well-worn undergrounds of some Western capitals will find South Korea's subways a relief; the trains are usually squeaky-clean and appear every few minutes like clockwork. Delays and service outages are rare enough that they make the news. The subway systems are also remarkably safe, even late at night, although pickpockets sometimes try to take advantage of packed cars to part people from their wallets, and groping of female passengers is certainly not unknown.

© SUNG KUK KIM/123RF.COM

Seoul's subway is one of the most heavily used underground rail systems in the world.

© JONATHAN HOPFNER

commuter bus

CITY BUSES

Urban buses supplement the subway networks in some cities and are the only form of public transit in others. Routes are usually identified by numbers with the bus's point of origin and final destination prominently displayed on the front and rear windows. Other major stops are sometimes listed on the side of the vehicle, and detailed route maps are usually displayed inside. Outside major tourist routes in Seoul and Busan, these signs will be in Korean script only, but some cities, Seoul in particular, have limited English-language signage as well as reasonably complete route information available in English and other languages online. Buses are also often color-coded to indicate the type of route they serve: within a neighborhood or from a suburb to the city center, for example. Fares, usually around 1,000 won, are paid when boarding; if a stored-value card is used, it has to be touched to a scanner again when disembarking.

Like the subway, buses are usually frequent and fast, skirting traffic with special bus-only lanes. If anything, they're sometimes a bit too quick—South Korean bus drivers seem to be constantly striving to beat the clock, barreling through yellow lights, careening around corners, and giving passengers only a few seconds to board or step off. The often manic driving, coupled with crowds and cramped seating, means inner-city buses are not the most comfortable way to get around, particularly during rush hours.

TAXIS

Taxis are one of South Korea's great conveniences; they're inexpensive, reliable, and readily available enough that residents rarely have to think twice about hailing one. While their design varies from place to place and they come in different sizes—sedans, minivans, even SUVs—they're easily identified by plastic signs mounted on the roof and a display mounted in the front windshield that, somewhat counterintuitively to Westerners, is lit red if a cab is available. Yellow or green lights or characters tend to mean the taxi is on call or reserved; no lights indicate that it's occupied or otherwise unavailable.

Taxi meters are nearly universal, and there's very little variation in fares nationwide, with the initial fare usually set at 2,400 won and rising in 100 or 200 won increments based on distance traveled. Tipping is far from universal or expected, but allowing drivers to keep the small change from a fare is a nice gesture if they've been helpful.

Some cities also have *mobum,* or deluxe, taxis, identified by their jet-black bodies and gold accents. Compared to normal cabs, these offer more spacious seating, more room for luggage, and accept more modes of payment, usually including credit cards (though more and more standard cabs now do that too). They also offer, at least in theory, a higher standard of service from drivers. While they're a good backup option when run-of-the-mill cabs aren't available, most passengers find they're not really worth the substantial premium—they cost around twice as much—for most trips, especially since newer cabs rival them for amenities and comfort.

Cabs can usually be found at taxi stands, which are strategically located in the vicinity of major bus or subway stops; in front of major hotels and shopping complexes; or simply flagged down on the street. You can also call a taxi, usually for a small surcharge. Very few drivers speak any amount of English, so it's helpful to have your destination written down in Korean, as well as a few nearby landmarks, since in the absence of a logical address system for most South Korean cities, landmarks are used to navigate. Many cabs claim to offer translation help via mobile phone interpretation services, but you shouldn't count on these always working, or the driver even knowing they're available.

While not unheard of, rigged meters and instances of drivers taking lengthy detours or otherwise trying to bump up fares are rare. A far more common gripe is the bizarre system that takes hold when demand for cabs outweighs supply, such as Friday nights after the subway closes. When this happens, obviously unoccupied cabs will often inch their way along the roads taking their pick of passengers who shout destinations into open taxi windows in the hopes they'll appeal to a suddenly awfully picky bunch of drivers. Some entrepreneurial drivers will even stuff their vehicles with a bunch of strangers going to the same area (or in the same direction), a lucrative practice, since by some distortion of justice everyone usually ends up having to pay the full fare. Unfortunately there's not a lot anyone can do in these situations except battle it out with the rest of the crowds, or wait out the rush.

Driving

South Korea has one of the world's largest automotive industries and the infrastructure to match, so driving is certainly a possibility for any foreign resident determined to have their own set of wheels. Whether it's worth investing in a car or not depends to a large extent on where you'll be located and your tolerance for South Korea's sometimes difficult road conditions, which have less to do with the streets themselves than the occasionally hair-raising local style of driving.

In larger cities with good transport networks, such as Seoul or Busan, a car is certainly not a necessity, and in fact it may be more trouble than it's worth, since traffic and finding parking are near-constant headaches. Vehicles are very handy, though, in places where public transportation is more limited, and for residents determined to explore the country—some of South Korea's more interesting nooks and crannies are difficult to reach by train or bus. Many expats with large families, even in Seoul, also find having their own car makes it a lot easier to ferry young children around and do large grocery runs.

BUYING OR RENTING A CAR

Cars are relatively inexpensive in South Korea, especially by Asian standards, making buying the most sensible option for residents considering anything but a short-term stay. However, this applies only to domestic models—imported cars are prohibitively expensive and sell for far more than they do in their country of origin, partly because of the tariffs the government maintains to protect local automakers. Popular sedans like the Hyundai Avante or Renault Samsung SM3 with the standard range of options go for around 16 million won including taxes; add 1 million won or so for goodies like leather seats, parking sensors, or GPS navigation. Gas-sipping minicars like the Kia Morning cost about half as much and receive special discounts on parking and road tolls. Expatriates are also free to buy used cars, provided the original owner issues them the vehicle registration and a transfer contract; these can be a real bargain as the value of vehicles tends to depreciate quickly and there's a steady supply from foreigners returning to their home countries.

Getting a new vehicle ready for the road is a fairly painless process. Dealers are required to assist car buyers with the registration of new purchases for no extra charge, and they will take care of everything if you provide them with the necessary paperwork, which includes copies of your alien registration card and passport. New vehicles will be given a temporary tag that allows them to be driven for around 10 days before it must be exchanged for permanent registration sticker and license plate at the closest district office. Insurance is mandatory for any vehicle with an engine size of over 50 cc, and new cars are also subject to government inspections every two years. Most cars are also subject to automobile taxes, usually paid on a quarterly basis, that vary according to make and age.

Potential car owners should also take parking into consideration—most sizable villas or apartment complexes will assign a parking space to tenants automatically, but if your home doesn't, you'll have to either pay for parking at a lot nearby or jostle for a place on the street, and the latter is a regular source of ugly disputes among neighbors.

Many companies also offer car rental services. While renting works out to be considerably more expensive than buying over the long term, it also means the rental firm will take care of any bureaucracy, and insurance and roadside assistance are usually included in the fees, making it a good stopgap option. Medium-class sedans can be rented for around 1 million won per month. Many rental firms can also arrange drivers, although this ups the bill substantially, typically by 100,000-160,000 won per day.

DRIVER'S LICENSES

International licenses from most countries can be used in South Korea until they expire, after which a foreign resident has to obtain a local license to drive in the country. If you've already got a driver's license from your country of origin, it can be exchanged for a local license at the Seoul Global Center or branches of the national Driver's License Examination Office. Applicants must also provide three photos and copies of their passports and alien registration certificates, and are subject to a quick physical examination, as well as possibly a short written exam depending on where their license was issued. Your old license will be retained until the next time you leave South Korea, when you can get it back by turning in your local license and providing proof of your departure, such as a plane ticket.

If you don't have a license and want to apply for one in South Korea (and are over 18), you'll have to provide the agency with your passport, alien registration card, three photos, and about 50,000 won to cover the costs of the application, education, and testing. Would-be drivers have to complete an hour-long traffic safety course at one of 26 government-run testing locations nationwide. They also have to pass a multiple-choice exam (available in English and a few other languages) and course and on-road driving tests that cover things like parallel parking, sudden stops, and gear changes.

A standard driver's license also entitles the bearer to drive scooters or motorcycles with engine sizes of up to 125 cc; for anything bigger than that, a separate class of license is needed.

RULES OF THE ROAD

On the surface, South Korea's roads will look reassuringly familiar, especially to North Americans—people drive on the right, traffic signals and lanes generally work in the same way, and road signs and symbols (apart from the regular absence of English) are nearly identical to those back home. Anyone driving here for the first time, however, quickly learns that the unwritten rules of the road are very different. While things are improving, local drivers are still somewhat notorious for their aggressive and occasionally dangerous ways. People regularly ignore speed limits and honk to berate those who don't, cut into other lanes without signaling or a second thought, run red lights and stop in the middle of intersections, park (and sometimes drive!) on sidewalks, and engage in mini-games of chicken on narrow roads (the bigger vehicle usually wins). Foreigners soon find they have to drive substantially more aggressively and be a lot less polite to survive local rush hours.

Driving laws are similar to those in other countries, if somewhat more loosely applied, with prohibitions on illegal parking, violating speed limits, driving under the influence of alcohol, or using mobile phones behind the wheel. The rules are enforced by police patrols and cameras in some areas, and violations are punished with tickets that usually include a fine and demerit points—earn enough and you'll lose your license. For more serious infractions, such as drunk driving, offenders will be criminally prosecuted.

© CRAIG D.C. LEWIS

Many road signs in South Korea are bilingual.

While the traffic rules aren't likely to shock new arrivals, the South Korean way of dealing with accidents might. According to local convention, any driver involved in an accident is partially responsible, simply by virtue of the fact that they happened to be there at the time, even in incidents where the blame clearly lies with one party (a rear-ending, for example). This means both parties involved in an accident are expected to compensate each other at least to some extent, though the driver perceived to be more at fault will usually pay more.

In minor fender benders, settlements are generally agreed on by both parties on the spot without the involvement of insurance companies or (if possible) the police, but for bigger incidents both will have to be called in. While insurers will typically cover all compensation claims, how much each party has to pay depends to a large extent to how successfully they can plead their case with the police, so if you're not a fluent Korean speaker, it's vital to have the contact numbers for your insurer or a Korean friend or colleague close at hand, and to get them involved as soon as possible. Make sure receipts are issued for any compensation payments issued to another driver.

PRIME LIVING
LOCATIONS

OVERVIEW

The majority of people moving to South Korea—particularly if they're relocated there by an employer—end up settling in the capital, Seoul, simply because it has the greatest range of business and job opportunities on offer. But for those who are free to choose their new home, or who are more concerned with lifestyle than earning potential, South Korea crams a surprising array of options into its 40,000-odd square miles. Whether you prefer bustling cities or more bucolic towns, cooler weather and a quick ride to the ski slopes in the winter or a subtropical climate with beaches nearby in the summer, there's a place in the country that can accommodate.

The following chapters cover the main areas of the country where expatriates are most likely to congregate and that offer the most to foreign residents in terms of services, infrastructure, and general livability—not necessarily the places that are the most picturesque or appealing to tourists. They cover Seoul, surrounding Gyeonggi Province, the western region (Chungcheong and Jeolla Provinces), the eastern region (Gyeongsang Provinces), the north (Gangwon Province) and Jeju Island.

SEASONAL HIGHLIGHTS

The changing seasons are one of nicer things about living in South Korea—though it might not feel that way in the depths of another sweltering summer or frigid winter. Following are some key annual events that can help visitors get the most out of the time of year. As exact dates vary from year to year check with the Korea Tourism Organization for the latest.

- Spring (March-April), **Jinhae Cherry Blossom Festival:** The streets and mountain paths of this pretty southern town are lined with cherry trees that explode into delicate pink blossoms as the weather warms.

- Summer (August), **Busan Sea Festival:** Busan makes the most of its coastal location with this summer extravaganza, which is staged across several beaches, including the perennially popular Haeundae, and includes outdoor concerts, art performances, and water sports programs.

- Fall (October), **Fall foliage at Seoraksan:** One of Korea's most striking mountain ranges is even more impressive at this time of year, when the slopes are ablaze with autumnal yellows and reds. Be prepared to share the splendor with thousands of other trekkers however—this is a popular spot.

- Winter (January), **Taebaeksan Snow Festival:** Brave the chilly temperatures in this high-altitude northern community and be rewarded with pristine white landscapes, ice sculptures, sledding, and other frosty activities.

SEOUL

For millions of South Koreans—and a lot of the country's foreign residents—there is, quite simply, no other address. Seoul and its environs account for almost half of South Korea's population and dominate the country's political and business sphere in a way few other capitals can match. For the expatriate the sheer scope and relentless pace of the place can be daunting, but there's also plenty of room for comfort—whether it's Western housing, designer labels, or decent pizza, there's more of the familiar here than just about anywhere else in the country.

The capital's high-density urban sprawl contains something for just about everyone. Businesspeople will appreciate the networking opportunities, and parents and students will enjoy the quality of international-standard education on offer. The artistically and culturally inclined will have hundreds of galleries, museums, and historical sites to explore; night owls will have little difficulty finding places to dance until the crack of dawn. Throw in an excellent public transportation network, safe streets, and a good variety of accommodation options, and it's easy to understand why some expatriates never make it beyond the city limits.

Of course, Seoul also has its shortcomings. The city's northern location means it often has harsh winters. Air quality, while it has improved markedly in recent years, can be poor, especially in the spring when winds bring in dust from China. Major streets are constantly thronged with cars and crowds. Space constraints mean housing is frequently expensive and cramped, at least by North American standards. And

© JONATHAN HOPFNER

Seoul city center

while the government has tried to introduce more green space into the city, there's still a shortage of places to soak up some fresh air or to stroll. How well new arrivals take to Seoul seems to depend on where they came from; city-dwellers tend to feel right at home, while people with suburban or rural backgrounds may find they need some time to adjust.

GYEONGGI-DO

Long seen as little more than Seoul's backyard, Gyeonggi-do, which encircles the capital, has started coming into its own. A small but diverse province that includes everything from busy suburbs to coastal mudflats and the nearly deserted badlands near the inter-Korean border, it is home to some of the country's fastest-growing "new towns," modern and meticulously planned communities such as Songdo and Bundang that offer easy access to Seoul and newer, more spacious apartment complexes, without the traffic snarls and cramped conditions of the capital. Many expatriates find these areas a good compromise between Seoul's nonstop hustle and the more sustainable pace of smaller-town life.

Its proximity to the Demilitarized Zone separating the two Koreas means Gyeonggi Province is also home to a substantial number of U.S. military and support staff, particularly in towns like Uijeongbu and Dongducheon, though the atmosphere in these places is more family-oriented than frontline. Gyeonggi-do's largest cities are the industrial centers of Suwon, the provincial capital, and Incheon, an independently administered Yellow Sea port where South Korea's main international airport is located. The development of Songdo, a futuristic city taking shape on reclaimed land along the Incheon waterfront that the government is determined to groom into a major regional finance center, looks set to lure more foreign nationals to the province.

a country home in Gyeonggi-do

THE WEST (CHUNGCHEONG AND JEOLLA PROVINCES)

A scenic place of rolling hills, verdant fields, and dramatic coastlines, the west of the country has long been South Korea's breadbasket, with its emerald rice paddies and fish-rich bays providing much of the national food supply. With its fresh produce and generous portions, the region has developed a well-deserved reputation for offering the country's finest indigenous cuisine. On a less positive note, its formerly largely poor rural population caused many leaders throughout the country's history to dismiss it as a backwater and concentrate their development efforts elsewhere, giving rise to distinctions and resentments that persist to this day.

The west has long since outgrown those stereotypes, however, and its expanding centers are building altogether different reputations and attracting more expatriates in the process—often people who prefer easygoing ways to excitement or who have a serious interest in traditional culture. Gwangju has gained renown as a center for the arts as well as the photonics and high-tech materials industries, while Daejeon has focused on building one of the country's most successful science and technology clusters. Jeonju is a smaller city that is an important educational center and boasts some of the country's best-preserved traditional architecture.

THE EAST (GYEONGSANG PROVINCES)

The mountainous east of the country is where South Korea's postwar industrial revolution began—which in many ways is still ongoing. The country's largest and most powerful conglomerates have their roots in the Gyeongsang Provinces, and many of the foreign engineers and experts they hire consequently end up in the region.

Most of the major cities here dot the coast, including Pohang, a significant steel industry center, and Ulsan, little more than a fishing village a few decades ago but now a thriving hub of the shipbuilding, automobile, and petrochemical industries. Busan,

South Korea's main port and second-largest city, was one of the first places in the country to host a sizable foreign population, and with its multiple international ferry links and a renowned film festival, it maintains a cosmopolitan flavor. It also enjoys some of the mildest weather on the peninsula. Farther inland, Daegu, the third-largest city in the country, sits at the heart of South Korea's transportation network and does a bustling trade in textiles, fashion, and Asian medicine. It'd be wrong to assume the region is all smokestacks and smelters. It is home to several national parks, and with the open-air museums of Gyeongju and Andong, is also South Korea's beating historical heart.

GANGWON-DO

Located in South Korea's far northwest, Gangwon is the highest province in the country in terms of latitude and altitude. A dramatic region of rocky slopes, old forests, and isolated fishing villages, it's the least densely populated part of South Korea, making it an ideal destination for peace-seekers or outdoors buffs. The breathtaking scenery of areas like Seoraksan National Park and steadily improving transport links with major cities like Seoul and Busan have made tourism Gangwon's main industry, with a particular focus on winter sports—but its geography also means winters can be harsh, with vast amounts of snowfall. Major centers with expatriate populations include Sokcho, a harbor town famous for hot springs and seafood; Gangneung; and Chuncheon, the province's capital and largest city.

JEJU ISLAND

An oval island about 100 kilometers (60 miles) south of the peninsula, Jeju has been dubbed Korea's Hawaii, and though the comparison is a bit of a stretch, it does share comparatively warmer weather and people who view themselves as distinct from their mainland cousins. The country's only autonomous province, Jeju is unmistakably Korean, yet retains a culture of its own, with locals who pride themselves on their

© ANNE HILTY

port on Jeju Island

laid-back ways and speak a distinct dialect that can be all but unintelligible to outsiders. The island also possesses some unique and striking geographical features, including the country's highest mountain, vast networks of volcanic caves, and beautiful white-sand beaches.

Domestic tourism has been the mainstay of Jeju's economy, but the island is seeing more international visitors as well as foreign residents who come to work in areas like hospitality or education, or simply to soak up the good life. The provincial government has made a strong push in recent years to attract more expatriates and overseas investment, reserving plots of land for international schools and apartment complexes and easing regulations on taxation and foreign home ownership.

SEOUL 서울

It's a travelers' cliché that you have to get outside of the big cities to really experience a country, but in South Korea, arguably, that doesn't apply. For most intents and purposes, Seoul *is* South Korea. It has been the capital for almost seven centuries, and the metropolitan area houses almost half of the nation's population. It has shrugged off multiple government attempts to distribute the country's spoils more equitably, and stubbornly dominates the national economic and political scene in a way few other world capitals can match. The president's residence and the seat of government are here, as are virtually all corporate headquarters, the most prestigious schools, the vast majority of the country's wealth, and the largest museums and concert halls. It's South Korea's chief international gateway, main engine of commerce, and top reservoir of artistic talent. While other cities' fortunes ebb and flow, over the past few decades Seoul has only gotten bigger and (bar the odd hiccup) more prosperous, spilling well beyond its historical borders as locals and overseas visitors alike pour in to seize the opportunities it presents.

With so many things concentrated here, Seoul has clear advantages for foreign residents. It has by far the largest expatriate population in the country, so it's relatively easy to meet up with like-minded people or tap into support networks. The city's

government and a good many citizens are accustomed to dealing with non-Koreans, so services such as English-language education, banking, and medical care are better developed and more readily available than elsewhere. Seoul boasts a greater breadth of cuisine and a more varied—and hedonistic—nightlife than any other city in South Korea. The infrastructure—particularly public transportation and communications—has been tweaked to near-perfection.

And in a metropolis this big, one rarely if ever runs out of new corners to poke around or things to do. A surprising amount of history—temples, markets, colonial architecture—has managed not only to survive the capital's tumultuous past but to remain very much alive. Elaborate ceremonies and lively festivals are a monthly occurrence, celebrating Korea's Confucian heritage, the passage of the seasons, and even contemporary dance music.

Of course all this comes with a catch. Precisely because it's such a desirable place to reside, space in Seoul is constantly at a premium. There are well over 10 million people here (more than double that if you include the surrounding satellite towns), and at peak times you'll feel as if you're sharing the sidewalks, subway, and department stores with nearly all of them. The surrounding mountains and broad Han River give the city a striking physical setting and a much-needed touch of nature. But unfortunately, much of Seoul's beauty has been paved over to make way for roads and drab apartment blocks, and despite the seemingly constant building spree, traffic remains a headache and real estate prices are still by far the highest in the country. The size and sheer density of a single district—never mind the whole place—can be downright intimidating. As foreign-friendly as the city has become, the language barrier still rears its head daily for those who don't speak Korean. Those not keen on the pungent and sometimes fiery flavors of the local cuisine may struggle at times, since international dishes aren't available on every corner, and even if they are, they may have been heavily doctored to suit local tastes.

And what about the people? It's difficult to generalize about Seoulites, since a large proportion of them are originally from elsewhere, but there's some truth to the widely held view (mainly outside the capital) that they're sophisticated but cool and emotionally distant, focused largely on their own goals and rarely inclined to lend time or a helping hand to strangers. Of course, the same could be said for city-dwellers just about everywhere, and considering the scope and highly competitive nature of the place, Seoul can be surprisingly unpretentious and kindhearted. People tend to look gruff or rushed but will almost always respond promptly and politely to requests for assistance—sometimes even when they're not asked. Scams of the type that pervade some other Asian cities—pickpockets, rigged taxi meters, and the like—are uncommon, and violent crime is generally not a concern. In smaller family-run shops and restaurants, service is often as cordial as in any country town, especially if you're a repeat visitor.

There are easier places to come to grips with, but Seoul possesses an energy and air of possibility that rarely fail to intoxicate, and for most the benefits of residing in the city far outweigh the disadvantages. More than a few people even learn to call it home permanently.

PRIME LIVING LOCATIONS

A PLACE WITH POWER

Seoul is miles from the coast, ringed by mountains that an ever-expanding population has to work its way around, buffeted by icy winter weather, and at least for the last 60 years, within striking range of an often hostile neighbor. It's natural to wonder why anyone would pick such a spot for the country's bustling capital.

In fact, when judged according to the principles of *pungsu*—the Korean pronunciation for the Chinese art of geomancy, feng shui—Seoul's location couldn't be better. Legend has it that in the 14th century, when Joseon Dynasty founder King Taejo was scouting out a place for his new capital, a renowned Buddhist monk and geomantic expert who served as the king's adviser, Muhak, urged him to select the place that basically remains the center of Seoul today.

Muhak's view had much to do with the mountains that surround Gyeongbokung Palace and the presidential residence of the Blue House. In *pungsu* mountains are known to channel vital energy (*ki*) and also have a protective function. Seoul's original palaces were bordered by four:

Bukhansan to the north, Namsan to the south, and the city's two main guardians—the "blue dragon" of Naksan to the east and the "white tiger" of Inwangsan to the west. This made it all but certain that the royals inhabiting them would enjoy long lives and that their enemies would find them difficult to vanquish.

The area's geomantic quality was reinforced further by the fact that structures could be built with Bukhansan at their back to face the Cheonggyecheon stream and, farther south, the Han River. *Pungsu* basics state that water can retain vital energy that would otherwise be scattered; thus the positive energy carried by Seoul's mountains is effectively fenced in, at least north of the river.

The upheavals that Seoul has faced in the centuries since it was founded would seem to suggest that the geomantically auspicious site hasn't done it much good at all, but the city (and its mountains) have managed to endure. At the very least, there was an underlying order to the seemingly random development of the capital.

The Lay of the Land

Seoul proper sprawls over 600 square kilometers (230 square miles) and is mostly a dense conglomeration of high-rises and smaller apartment blocks interspersed with the odd hill or patch of greenery. The city contains 25 (*gu*) or districts, which are subdivided into over 500 (*dong*) or neighborhoods. It is neatly divided by the Han River and ringed by mountain ranges, which form a lovely backdrop when skyscrapers aren't crowding them out.

The Han River is not only a physical boundary but a psychological one; Gangbuk, the area north of the waterway, is the "old" Seoul and contains most of the city's ancient palaces, gates, and other historic assets. The granite slopes of the Bukhan mountain range mark the old city's northern boundary and loom over the current presidential office or Blue House and, just below it, the pavilions of Gyeongbokgung, the largest of Seoul's palaces. Seoul's vaguely Gothic-looking City Hall and bustling Namdaemun Market are not far to the south; many embassies and corporations are based near here, along with Cheonggyecheon, a pleasant restored waterway that eventually empties into the Yellow Sea. Just south of City Hall are the fashionable Myeong-dong shopping

Many residents of Seoul are originally from elsewhere.

district and Namsan (South Mountain), a hill that once served as Seoul's southern boundary but is now better known for the needlelike Seoul Tower and one of the city's most frequently trammeled parks.

Spilling from Namsan's southern slopes down to the Han River is the still crowded but mainly residential Yongsan district, which houses a major U.S. Army base and is the epicenter of Seoul's foreign community. Other districts of note north of the river include Mapo in western Seoul, where several notable universities and the lively Hongdae and Sinchon club districts are located.

The area south of the river, Gangnam—now a household name worldwide thanks to rapper Psy's YouTube hit "Gangnam Style"—could be considered Seoul's more modern face. The buildings tend to be newer and taller here and the streets wider and adorned with pedestrian-friendly touches like broad sidewalks and shady trees. Gangnam is a major hub for the finance and information technology industries, and a mass of trendy shopping and entertainment zones have sprung up to cater to the young professionals that these businesses employ, including the vast COEX shopping complex and ritzy Apgujeong, Seoul's answer to Rodeo Drive. West of Gangnam is Yeouido, a large island jutting into the Han River dominated by the blue-domed National Assembly and the de facto national headquarters for many of the country's investment banks and broadcasters.

CLIMATE

Seoul shares the humid continental climate of most of the Korean Peninsula, with pleasant but short springs (late March-May), muggy and frequently wet summers (June-September), and crisp, clear autumns (October-November). Winters (December-March) are among the coldest in the country due to the city's northern location, with temperatures in January and February averaging around -5°C.

TRANQUIL TEAHOUSES

If you need a respite from the relentless energy of Seoul's streets, which is all too likely, consider heading to one of the city's old-style teahouses (*chatjip*). These are in danger of being crowded out by chain coffee shops in some neighborhoods but continue to thrive in areas that Seoulites visit for a bit of tradition, like Insa-dong and Bukchon.

From the moment you enter a teahouse it's clear they're carefully designed to put the customer at ease. The lighting is soft and the colors muted. The decor consists of carefully placed ceramics or scrolls of graceful calligraphy. Seating is usually on cushions on the floor or wooden benches, with nooks and cubbyholes affording patrons privacy. The soundtrack may be the plaintive strains of old music, running water, or even live birds.

The typical *chatjip* has a dizzying range of beverages, from relatively common concoctions like green and roasted corn tea to more exotic blends said to be good for a variety of ailments. These include *ssanghwa-cha*, a slightly bitter concoction of medicinal herbs said to warm the body and ward off colds, and *daechu-cha*, a tea made of jujubes that apparently relieves coughs and muscle pain. Teas are usually served with *ddeok* (rice cakes) or Korean sweets, and customers are encouraged to linger, making tea shops an ideal hangout for writers, artists, or the simply contemplative.

While you'll spot teahouses all over the city, the back alleys of Insa-dong, where they're at their more atmospheric, is a good place to start looking. The esoterically named "Moon Bird Thinks only of the Moon," with its garden-like interior, and *Yetchatjip*, which is home to about a dozen free-flying birds and prides itself on its fruit teas, are two of the more renowned.

CULTURE

Unsurprisingly, many of South Korea's cultural treasures old and new are concentrated in Seoul. While decades of war and rapid development have taken a toll, the city has managed to retain some of its historical assets, including a handful of palaces, gates, and royal shrines where ancient ceremonies are frequently reenacted. The country's most extensive collection of artifacts is housed at the massive National Museum of Korea in the Yongsan district, and dozens of smaller museums throughout the city offer collections of everything from folk culture to chicken figurines. The previously rather anemic art scene has taken a marked turn for the better in recent years with the addition of the Leeum Samsung Museum of Art, which boasts an exceptional selection of contemporary work, and the profusion of cutting-edge galleries in the Hongdae, Samcheong-dong, and Sinsa-dong areas, long haunts of South Korea's up-and-coming painters, musicians, and designers.

Seoul has multiple live music and performance venues, including the Sejong Center for the Performing Arts in the old city center, the home base of the metropolitan philharmonic, opera, and dance companies, and the Seoul Arts Center, which frequently hosts musicals and imported classical acts. The city is now a regular stop on tours by international rock and pop acts, and there's also plenty of capable local talent on display most nights in the live music bars of Hongdae and Itaewon. The global dance culture has taken firm root here, with big-name DJs making regular appearances in the megaclubs of Itaewon and Gangnam.

Daily Life

Seoul's expatriate population is fairly large—there are nearly 400,000 non-South Korean nationals living in the city—and it is rapidly expanding and increasingly diverse, which means most new arrivals have little trouble finding like-minded people to socialize with or organizations that cater to their interests. As the city is still somewhat off Asia's beaten expat path, foreign nationals in Seoul tend to bond quickly and are highly supportive of each other, although the transient nature of expatriate life means you may see a lot of friends come and go. The local government maintains an excellent—and entirely free—help center service for foreign residents that can assist new arrivals with issues like housing, securing utilities, and banking; it's headquartered near City Hall and has branches in expat-heavy areas like Yongsan and Gangnam.

Much of the expatriate social scene revolves around the restaurants and (especially) the pubs of Itaewon, but even teetotalers can find plenty to keep them busy. Clubs such as the Royal Asiatic Society and Korea Foundation offer tours and lectures for culture buffs, while the more athletically inclined can join football, hiking, or even Ultimate Frisbee associations. Support groups exist for everyone from vegetarians to pregnant women, and the city also hosts several very active international chambers of commerce. Services for all major religions are freely available, though Christians and Buddhists may find themselves better served than Muslims due to South Korea's limited Muslim population.

MEDIA

Seoul has three English-language newspapers—the *Korea Herald, Korea Times,* and the *Joongang Daily,* which is distributed with the *International Herald Tribune.* All are of limited journalistic merit and aren't in the habit of providing insightful political commentary or scathing exposés—the local-language press does a far better job of that—but they have classified and listings sections that are a good source of information on expatriate-oriented goods and services. An ever-changing cast of free (or nearly free) magazines such as *Seoul, Groove,* and *10* cover the Seoul scene in exhaustive detail, with a particular focus on culture, events, and nightlife. Most of these titles can be picked up in bars and restaurants in Itaewon and Hongdae. The city also has an English-language radio station, TBS eFM, which broadcasts local news and traffic information.

HEALTH

Health care is good throughout South Korea, but Seoul boasts the best medical services in the country. In smaller neighborhood clinics, most support staff and more than a few doctors can't speak any English, but the city has five major hospitals where 24-hour English services are available. These include Yonsei University's Severance Hospital, which opened in 1885 and was the country's first Western-style medical institution, and the Samsung Medical Center in southern Seoul, which has highly skilled specialists in areas like physical rehabilitation and pediatrics. Costs can be high for services or treatments not covered by national or private insurance, so be sure to ask. The Itaewon area also has several outlets such as the International Clinic where English-speaking doctors can be consulted on minor health issues.

INTERVIEW: YAERI SONG

© YAERI SONG

Yaeri Song

A Seoul native but raised in the United States, Yaeri Song returned to the city of her birth in search of opportunity and has found no shortage of the same, taking on roles in fields such as entertainment, communications, and public relations. In 2011 she founded what's quickly become one of the key go-to sources of information for residents and visitors keen to seek out the less trammeled corners of the city's cre-

ative and recreational scenes—online publication Seoulist (http://seoulistmag.com).

Q: *Can you explain your background—how long you were in Korea, when you went to the States, and why you elected to return to and stay in Seoul?*

A: I was born in Seoul and moved to the United States when I was in first grade. Aside from the fact that I had relatives here, I wasn't too interested in Korea until I became interested in Korean film. I had studied filmmaking in college, and I decided to come back to work in Korea's entertainment industry.

Q: *How would you say the returnee's experience differs from that of the typical expat? What advice would you give someone of Korean descent considering the same move?*

A: The returnee's experience is twofold: It can be easy to be a returnee; we often have family or relatives living here, and anyone of a certain Korean heritage can easily obtain a visa that gives them similar working and health care rights as any Korean citizen. On the flip side, if you have Korean blood but can't speak or act Korean, the locals will give you a much harder time. A lot of older Korean adults can't wrap their heads around the fact that someone may look Korean, but can't speak the language.

Advice for anyone coming to Korea, especially if they're planning to live and work in Korea for over a year: Make the effort to learn the Korean language because the ability to observe, communicate with, and understand those around you can either

SCHOOLS

In Seoul proper the main international schools are the Seoul Foreign School, which was founded in 1912 in the northwestern part of the city and offers both U.S. and British curricula, and the far younger Yongsan International School, which is just east of Itaewon and models itself on the U.S. system. Both are certified, accept students from kindergarten through high school, and boast expansive well-equipped campuses. Though they are nominally Christian institutions, most parents don't find religion excessively emphasized, and students of all faiths are welcomed. Newer additions to the international school scene include Dwight School, which has an International Baccalaureate program, and Dulwich College, which follows the British curriculum.

make or break your experience here. Also, it's easy for most English speakers to fit in with the *gyopo* (overseas Koreans)/expat community, but seek out opportunities to be among Korean natives. It's from them that I have learned countless nuggets of local wisdom, from current memes and expressions to the best *makgeolli* (rice wine) bars. If I had stayed in my comfort zone, I don't think I would've had the insights or information to start and sustain Seoulist.

Q: *Can you talk a bit about Seoulist—when you started it up what were your primary motivations?*

A: Before I landed in Seoul, I was working in New York City where there's a wealth of weekly city publications. When I came to Seoul, there were really no go-to resource on the city culture and lifestyle, aside from a handful of expat magazines and blogs which I found to be very Itaewon-centric and limiting. So with the help of some very talented friends, friends of friends, and contributors, we soft-launched Seoulist in February 2011.

Q: *What sort of advice would you have for a non-Korean contemplating a business venture in Seoul, in terms of forging connections and making it a success?*

A: The city government offers generous support to foreign investment. The Seoul Global Center offers free consulting and classes for the budding entrepreneur as well. And like anywhere else in the world, it's also important that you get out and meet people. Surround yourself with veterans and long-term expats who are part of the scene. These people have chosen to stick around for a good reason, and that kind of optimism and energy never hurts.

Q: *What are your favorite things about Seoul—and what do you think could be improved, especially as regards facilities for visitors or expats?*

A: I have a love/hate relationship with the changing faces of Seoul. On one hand, there's constant stimulation because I never return to the same neighborhood to find it just as I left it. On the other, there's some wistfulness when a brand-new shop replaces your old favorite café. I like that Seoul is always changing, but it's not a city that allows for much nostalgia.

As for improvement, getting a smartphone for visitors is really tough and expensive, and I feel like having GPS and instant access to information is really integral to tourism 2.0. And although there is more English and foreign-language signage now than ever, language accessibility is also spotty unless you're in a big attraction or touristy neighborhood like Myeong-dong or Insa-dong.

Looking ahead, I think the government could reconsider what it is about Seoul that draws visitors. Oftentimes it's just Seoul's palaces and beautiful palace food that are carefully packaged and presented to the rest of the world, but most visitors I know who fall in love with Seoul can't get enough of the impossible alleys, the gritty street food, and other urban scenes and scenery the government doesn't think to advertise.

Seoul International School is also well-regarded, but it is located outside the city in neighboring Gyeonggi Province.

The limited number of institutions and keen competition for places conspire to keep prices high. Most schools have a tuition structure that includes local currency and U.S.-dollar fees to guard against exchange rate fluctuations, as well as extra charges for things like buses and extracurricular activities. All told, parents can expect to spend around 18-25 million per year to send a child to one of the major international schools.

Most of the major international schools also run preschool and kindergarten programs. Independent institutions for young learners include the Early Childhood Learning Center and the Franciscan School, which are in the Yongsan district and take students up to five or six years of age. Seoul also has French, German, Japanese, and Chinese schools that follow the curricula of those countries.

SHOPPING

Shopping is one area where Seoulites are spoiled for choice. There are small super-markets, gadget shops, and clothing outlets on virtually every corner, but the serious consumer will inevitably head for certain neighborhoods that tend to specialize in one product or another. These include Yongsan (computers, electronics, and pirated DVDs), Myeong-dong (cosmetics and youth fashion), Insa-dong (art and antiques), Itaewon (imported clothes and food), and Gangnam and Apgujeong (boutiques and designer goods).

While there are many well-equipped malls and department stores, such as the opu-lent Galleria in Apgujeong, COEX in Gangnam, and Migliore in Myeong-dong, the real deals (and more interesting finds) tend to be at street level. Few places demonstrate this better than Seoul's largest markets—Namdaemun and Dongdaemun, both in the old city center. Both are sprawling, crowded warrens of shops and stalls that offer some of the best clothing and textile bargains in the country, assuming your negotiat-ing skills are up to par.

Where to Live

Seoul may be a massive place, but the city's expatriates have traditionally confined themselves to just a handful of neighborhoods. Yongsan, with its heavy diplomatic and military presence, is the unofficial headquarters for foreign residents, but quite a few also choose to live close to their offices in the Jung-gu and Gangnam business districts. Mapo-gu is popular with young singles due to its large numbers of students, who have lent the district a rollicking nightlife and bohemian flair.

JUNG-GU AND JONGNO-GU 중구/종로구

These districts north of the Han River and Namsan formed Seoul's original down-town and are still home to a large number of embassies and office complexes, as well as major cultural and tourist draws like Changdeokgung Palace and Insa-dong, an arty street lined with craft shops and traditional teahouses. While it has a few sedate pockets, by and large this is a bustling built-up area, crammed with towering build-ings, neon signs, and round-the-clock traffic snarls.

Jung-gu and Jongno-gu are well connected to the rest of the city, with the down-town core served by no fewer than four subway lines, but the range of shopping and dining options available in buzzing neighborhoods like Jonggak and Myeong-dong mean there's little call to leave. Many expatriates live here because they work in the city center and prefer not to commute, or because they like the feeling of being in the middle of it all. But the area's crowds and relative lack of green space make it a tougher sell for large families or those in search of the quiet life.

Most of the accommodations here cater to executives and are in large apartment blocks. There are a number of serviced residences, including the Fraser Suites in

Insa-dong and the Vabien complexes near Seodaemun subway station, that cater to executives with fully furnished apartments and suites and facilities like in-house restaurants and fitness centers. While these are well-appointed and centrally located, they don't come cheap, with rates for one-bedroom 80-square-meter units starting at around 3 million won per month and rising to over three times that for more spacious three- or four-bedroom units.

A slightly more cost-effective option are the district's many "officetels," a term for buildings usually strategically located in central areas that combine a few low floors of retail or office space with apartment units farther up. Designed for young working professionals, officetels are usually new and clean, but also tend to be spartan and somewhat cramped due to their high-density layout, resulting in some fairly reasonable prices. Large officetels like the We've Pavilion, just east of the Sejong-daero thoroughfare and about equidistant from three subway lines, and Brownstone, west of City Hall near the Chungjeongno subway station, have studio to three-bedroom apartments ranging from around 80 to 150 square meters that start at about 1 million won per month with a 10 million won deposit; they cost from around 450 million won to buy outright.

Those in the market for a more local experience might want to look in the Bukchon district, a cluster of beautifully preserved *hanok,* or traditional Korean homes, north of City Hall between Gyeongbokgung and Changdeokgung Palaces. Once the preferred address for Korean nobility, this is a quaint area of winding alleys and low snug houses, most topped with old-style flared tile roofs and set in gated courtyards. The area has undergone something of a renaissance of late, with many cafés, restaurants, and galleries springing up to serve a growing community of artistic and literary types. While a few of the old houses show their age, many have been restored and given modern touches like air-conditioning and underground parking. Some are occasionally available for rent or sale, with those that have undergone minimal refurbishment similar in size and price to two-bedroom apartments in the area.

SEONGBUK-GU 성북구

Overlooking Seoul's old downtown from the lower slopes of the Bukhan mountain range, Seongbuk district is a prosperous area known for its somewhat bucolic feel, with winding streets lined by large, stately homes, many of them embassies and diplomatic residences. In addition to its abundance of stand-alone houses, the chief attractions of the area are its relative tranquility, views, and swift access to hiking and recreational activities. The main downside is the lack of transport options compared to other neighborhoods—though close to the city center in terms of distance, subway stations are few and far between, and the area's steep roads can make walking or taking one of its tiny "village buses" a daunting prospect in icy winter conditions.

Most expatriates cluster in the Seongbuk-dong area, which has wide range of homes available in everything from modified Korean to English country manor to sleek, modernist styles. What most do have in common is a hefty price tag—rents start at around 3 million won per month for homes of around 200 square meters, with a two- to three-month deposit, and the more opulent houses can go for ten times that.

YONGSAN-GU 용산구

Yongsan (Dragon Mountain) district, which stretches from Namsan to the northern shores of the Han River, has been at the heart of Seoul's international community since the United States set up its main base here during the Korean War. Yongsan Garrison is perpetually due to be relocated, but given the district's heavy concentration of embassies, international schools, and expat-friendly stops and eateries, most of the foreign residents will no doubt remain. Arguably Yongsan's star attraction is Itaewon, an east-west artery a short distance from U.S. Army headquarters packed with clothing and souvenir shops, restaurants, and nightspots. The street once had a decidedly seedy character but has spruced itself up remarkably and is now better known for continental cuisine and sleek lounges than bad behavior and girly bars. The opening of a subway line for the area in 2001 boosted its convenience and has drawn more visitors from other parts of the city.

Many foreign nationals choose to live in Yongsan because it is quite simply the only place they feel at home. More English is spoken here than in other parts of Seoul, businesses and landlords are more accustomed to non-Koreans' wants and expectations, and most expat-oriented clubs and activities meet or take place in the area. Grocery stores carry imported delicacies like tortilla chips and pesto, and everything from dim sum to foie gras is a short walk or cab ride away. It's a fun and colorful part of town, home to a staggering variety of nationalities and religions that all seem to get along just fine.

Unfortunately, because of the abundance of well-paid expatriates in the area, there's a lot of upward pressure on rents. Haebangchon, an enclave to the north of Itaewon served by Noksapyeong subway station, is generally viewed as the cheapest option in the district. Most of the apartments here are villas, the South Korean term for small four- to five-story apartment blocks, or former homes divided into apartment units. Diminutive (50-square-meter) studio or one-bedroom apartments can be had for 300,000 won per month and up, usually with a deposit of 1-5 million won. Prices rise as apartments approach the main Itaewon strip.

Just south of Itaewon is the Hannam-dong area, long the domain of ambassadors, U.S. military officers, and the old Seoul elite. This area is also dominated by villas, although there are a few larger apartment complexes and stand-alone homes. Rents here start at around two million won for an 80-square-meter two-bedroom unit.

Selling prices for these villas vary greatly depending on size and the age of the building, but as it's perceived as a good location, you'd have a hard time finding anything serviceable under 400 million won.

Hannam-dong runs into Dongbinggo-dong to the west and the UN Village to the east, two of the only areas in Seoul, along with Seongbuk-dong to the north, where large stand-alone homes with yards are commonplace. These are generally well-built and spacious (over 300 square meters) and come with some furniture and standard appliances; however, rents are nothing short of stratospheric, with little available below five million won per month. Buying outright would probably set you back one billion won or more.

West of Hannam-dong and closer to the river, Ichon-dong is dominated by freshly built apartment complexes and is known as Seoul's "Little Tokyo" due to its popularity with Japanese residents. A number of other nationalities have flocked to the area as well, lured by its new homes and proximity to the Yongsan Family and Han Riverside

© CRAIG D.C. LEWIS

Yongsan-gu

Parks. Complexes such as the Asterium and City Park offer plush high-rise living from around four million won per month for three-bedroom 180-square-meter units, without a substantial deposit. Prices even for standard units in the area's modern developments average around 750 million won.

MAPO-GU 마포구

Mapo-gu, a district in northwestern Seoul, is famous for a couple of things: the striking kite-shaped World Cup Stadium and higher education. At the heart of the district stand venerable Yonsei University, one of Seoul's top schools, and Hongik University, the generator of some of the country's top art and design talent. Generations of students have imbued the district with a youthful energy and a vast profusion of offbeat boutiques, coffee shops, and nightclubs. The narrow streets around Hongik's main gate and Sinchon Rotary, to the south of the Yonsei campus, are packed with revelers nearly every night of the week.

Tucked away from the main roads are hundreds of *goshiwon* (dormitories) and older villa-type apartments catering to the relatively impoverished student demographic. The area is far from ideal for families but represents one of the best propositions in Seoul for the young and cash-strapped: good eating, nonstop nightlife, and a short subway ride to the city center, all for fairly low prices. Rents start at around 400,000 won for a no-frills studio apartment with a minimal deposit. Shared accommodations are common in this area as well. Purchase prices for villa and standard apartment units in this district are usually in the 300-500 million won range.

While not technically part of Mapo-gu, Yeonhui-dong is a quiet residential neighborhood close to Yonsei University and home to a number of expatriate families that move there for the nearby Seoul Foreign School. It is a relatively expensive area, with 120-square-meter three-bedroom apartments on offer for three million won per month, and stand-alone four-bedroom houses going for twice that. As elsewhere in the city, selling prices for quality stand-alone homes will start in the one billion won range.

GANGNAM 강남

The ritzy Gangnam district lies just south of the Han River and has evolved into a downtown to rival Jung-gu and Jongno-gu in the north. With its grid-like streets, posh department stores, offices, and five-star hotels, it has a more futuristic—some would say superficial—feel than other parts of Seoul. The first major landmark after crossing the river from the north is the shopping mecca of Apgujeong, which rivals any Western fashion center in terms of upscale brands per square foot. Below Apgujeong are the huge COEX shopping and convention complex and, just across the street, the rather incongruously located Bongeunsa Buddhist Temple. Two of Seoul's main intercity bus terminals and the Seoul Arts Center are located in the southern stretches of the district.

Gangnam has a reasonable expatriate presence, including many executives for the finance and information-technology companies headquartered in the skyscrapers clustered around Samseong and Yeoksam subway stations. The district is rivaled only by Yongsan in terms of its range of dining and nightlife options. The area has traditionally been seen as most desirable by upwardly mobile locals, however, who have created vast property price bubbles in wealthy outposts like Apgujeong. Gangnam's expatriate residents also complain sometimes of feeling cut off from their counterparts north of the river, especially after the subway shuts down or if they drive—evening and weekend traffic on the bridges crossing the Han can be a sight to behold.

Gangnam's dense vertical cityscape means officetels and large apartment blocks are the main varieties of accommodations on offer. The M Chereville near Gangnam Station and Oakwood next to the COEX complex offer serviced residences starting at around three million won per month for a studio. Major officetels in the area such as the Lotte Gold Rose start at around 1.5 million won per month for a 56-square-meter

Bongeunsa Buddhist Temple in the Gangnam district

© SEAN PAVONE/123RF.COM

studio with a deposit of four months' rent, while newish one- or two-bedroom apartments average 2-4 million won per month. Rental rates at complexes in Seolleung to the west or Yangjae in the south tend to be lower.

The Gangnam area is South Korea's most desirable address, and purchase prices reflect this; the average apartment price hovers around 750 million won.

Getting Around

Seoul has developed one of the world's most extensive and efficient public transportation networks, which makes bypassing the city's hair-raising traffic a breeze. Consequently many expatriate residents never see the need to buy a car, though they can still come in handy for large families or longer journeys.

BY SUBWAY

Launched in the 1970s and still being extended as you read, Seoul's vast subway network consists of over a dozen lines that span nearly 1,000 kilometers (180 miles) and ferry some eight million people each day. While some of the stations, particularly major transfer points like Jongo 3-ga or Sindorim, can be crowded and confusing, by and large it's a very user-friendly system, with all signs and major announcements in Korean and English (and often Chinese). Stations are about two minutes apart and cover nearly every corner of the city, as well as neighboring Incheon and parts of Gyeonggi Province. Delays or breakdowns are extremely rare, but many lines do shut shortly after midnight. Fares start at 1,000 won. Passengers can also purchase electronic stored-value cards that offer a discount of about 10 percent on regular fares and can also be used on buses and even in some taxis and shops.

BY BUS

Given the city's notoriously unpredictable traffic, the subway is often a better option than buses, but they do link some destinations, particularly within neighborhoods or on the outskirts of Seoul, that the train tends to underserve. Some—but by no means all—buses have bilingual English and Korean signs and stop announcements, and route information is available in English online. Smaller green buses are usually limited to routes in a single neighborhood, while blue buses ply longer routes between neighborhoods and major city centers. Fares start from around 1,000 won. Red buses, which connect far-flung suburbs with central Seoul, cost more.

BY TAXI

Taxis are abundant and scandalously cheap compared to other world capitals, with the meter starting at 2,200 won and fares rarely exceeding 10,000 won for standard hops. *Mobum* or deluxe, taxis, distinguished by their black and gold design, offer a more luxurious ride than the average cab; they're usually larger sedans with more leg and luggage room and, it's claimed, especially knowledgeable and courteous drivers. However, they're about twice as expensive as standard cabs, and most long-term residents see them as necessary only if no regular taxis are available.

Taxi drivers are generally a pleasant and honest enough bunch, although as in any city, you do get a few bad apples. Few speak any amount of English, so it's always helpful to have your destination or a major landmark nearby written in Korean to show the driver. With most cabs now boasting mobile handsets and onboard GPS navigation systems, the days of endlessly circling an area in a fruitless search for a destination are now basically over. Tipping is not expected, although offers to let the driver keep small amounts of change from a fare are always appreciated.

The only problems you're likely to experience with cabs will be late at night in major entertainment districts, when a lot of customers are struggling to make their way home and demand for cabs regularly exceeds supply. This sometimes brings out mercenary behavior on the part of drivers, who may want to charge passengers inflated flat fares or refuse services altogether to people who aren't going somewhere particularly convenient or lucrative. There's not a lot you can do in these situations except practice patience and wait for the next cab to come along.

GYEONGGI-DO 경기도

For centuries the northwestern province of Gyeonggi-do has been bound to the city it completely encircles, Seoul, in terms of geography, economy, and spirituality—indeed, the province's name can be roughly translated as "the area surrounding the capital." But it would be a mistake to view it as nothing more than an extension of South Korea's main metropolis. For one thing, it bumps up against several other important places, like the eerily tranquil Demilitarized Zone (DMZ) to the north that divides the two Koreas, and the trade routes of the Yellow Sea to the west. And it houses a number of vital assets of its own, including the country's main international airport, several bustling ports, a major central government administrative center, United Nations-recognized heritage sites—the list goes on. Relatively small in area, it packs in sleepy national parks and fishing villages as well as humming industrial complexes. Gyeonggi-do is the most populous province in the country, and its newer cities are among South Korea's richest and fastest-growing, testament to the high level of quality of life on offer.

Although it has been a strategically important region since the Joseon Dynasty, Gyeonggi-do only really came into its own in the 1960s, when the completion of highways to Seoul made even its outer reaches viable production and housing bases for the capital. Previously largely agricultural, it has quickly taken on a more high-tech

© JONATHAN HOPFNER

character and is now a center for the production of goods like microchips and hybrid car batteries.

For foreign residents, Gyeonggi-do can be an attractive proposition. Many areas offer quick and easy access to Seoul, with direct connections to the capital via subway or express bus lines, and without, or at least with less of, some of Seoul's chief downsides—overcrowding, pricey real estate, and pollution. Because many cities in Gyeonggi-do developed relatively recently, they tend to be better laid-out, better appointed, and have more green space than Seoul's older high-density districts. The province's relatively young, upwardly mobile population has encouraged the development of a range of dining, nightlife, and retail districts that are almost as broad as those found in the capital proper, as well as highly-ranked educational, cultural, and medical facilities.

It could be said that Gyeonggi-do lacks a character of its own, but the flip side of that—diversity, at least by South Korean standards—is Gyeonggi-do's defining and perhaps most attractive trait. It draws not only families who commute to schools or offices in Seoul but also workers and experts from throughout the country—and beyond—who serve the province's varied industrial base. And it offers new arrivals an unrivaled assortment of living options, from long-established commercial centers like Suwon and Incheon to ultramodern "new towns" such as Seongnam, as well as quieter communities in less-sculpted natural settings. Authorities are adding some of the region's most ambitious infrastructure projects to the mix, including Songdo, an expanding "international business district" on a patch of reclaimed land along the west coast that the government and developers hope to groom into one of Asia's preeminent economic hubs. It looks like Gyeonggi-do will soon be able to say—if it can't already—that it has something for everyone.

The Lay of the Land

Occupying the northwestern corner of South Korea, Gyeonggi-do has a total area of around 11,000 square kilometers (4,250 square miles) and borders mountainous Gangwon-do to the east and the Chungcheong provinces to the south. Much of the province consists of flat broad plains that once made it an ideal spot for the cultivation of rice and other crops, but farms have given way to housing estates and factories in most areas. In the north and east of the province the terrain grows more mountainous, and there are several national parks and ski resorts that serve as a much-needed recreational outlet for stressed Seoulites. Gyeonggi-do's western extreme is a muddy segment of coastline dotted with small islets and pierced by several bays that sometimes shelter fishing fleets but were never deep enough to serve as natural ports.

At the heart of the province, much like the center of a doughnut, is the separately administered Seoul metropolitan area. Incheon, a coastal city just east of Seoul that serves as the capital's main port, is also self-governing but is included in this chapter due to its location and tight links with other parts of the province. Gyeonggi-do's capital and most populous city, Suwon, as well as popular Seoul bedroom communities such as Seongnam and Anyang, are located along an arc running just 20-30 kilometers (12-18 miles) south of Seoul proper.

The stretch of Gyeonggi-do lying just north of the capital, against the inter-Korean border, was left largely undeveloped for years over worries it would be the first place to be hit in the event of a North Korean attack, and was home only to a few fearless farmers and U.S. and South Korean military installations. But as those concerns have subsided, the region has undergone a period of rapid growth, with more families and young professionals piling into conveniently located communities that were once almost exclusively military towns, such as Uijeongbu and Dongducheon.

CLIMATE

Gyeonggi-do's climate is virtually identical to Seoul's, although higher elevations tend to receive and retain more snow than the capital in the winter (December-March)— an important trait for the many skiing enthusiasts who take to the province's slopes.

CULTURE

Most residents of Gyeonggi-do will of course have the option of traveling to Seoul regularly to get a cultural fix, but the province has more than a few assets of its own. Interestingly, while Incheon and Suwon host a few reasonable galleries and museums, a lot of Gyeonggi-do's biggest cultural jewels are outside major cities. They include the Nam June Paik Art Center in Yongin, south of Seoul, established by the envelope-pushing multimedia artist himself near Gyeonggi's excellent provincial museum. Yongin is also home to the stunning Ho-Am Art Museum, which boasts an unrivaled collection of mainly Buddhist work amassed by the founder of the Samsung group, and the Korean Folk Village, a reasonably authentic approximation of traditional agricultural life. The Bucheon Philharmonic Orchestra, based in an undistinguished Seoul satellite town of the same name, is widely viewed as the country's finest. Each summer Bucheon also stages PIFAN, a festival of fantasy and science-fiction films that draws enthusiasts from the world over. Gyeonggi also includes entire communities dedicated to the arts (Hyeri Artists' Village) and literature (Paju Book City).

Several important historical sites are found in the province, including the island of Ganghwa-do, a former royal retreat littered with temples, tombs, and palace ruins, and Suwon's Hwaseong Fortress, an impressive network of gates, walls, and parapets that's been declared a UNESCO World Heritage Site. Icheon and the neighboring county of Yeoju, southeast of Seoul, have been renowned for centuries for the quality of their ceramic arts. Though somewhat more troubling, a tour of the Demilitarized Zone dividing the two Koreas is a good way to gain a better understanding of the conflict still gripping the peninsula.

DEMILITARIZED DAY-TRIPPING

The 248-kilometer (154-mile) Demilitarized Zone (DMZ) separating North and South Korea may be bristling with land mines, tank bunkers, and well-armed soldiers, but that hasn't stopped it from turning into one of South Korea's top attractions. Each year thousands of visitors, most of them local, make their way to the Zone for an up-close look at one of the region's perennial flash points. With its steady stream of tour buses, tongue-in-cheek signage, gift shops hawking conflict-themed merchandise, even a nearby amusement park, many are surprised to find the DMZ is less trip wire than tourist trap, but it's still a one-of-a-kind experience that military history enthusiasts or anyone with even a passing interest in geopolitics won't want to miss.

There are a few ways to see the DMZ. The truce village of Panmunjeom and the Joint Security Area, where the armistice ending the Korean War was signed and still one of the only sites for North-South exchanges, can be visited only by travelers on a group tour. The general consensus is that the tour offered by Koridoor (www.koridoor.co.kr), endorsed by the

U.S. military-affiliated United Service Organizations (USO), is the best, as it's partially run by military personnel and takes visitors places some other tours can't, such as one of the infiltration tunnels dug under the zone by North Korean soldiers. Guests must agree to be on their best behavior and stick to a dress code that forbids tank tops, sandals, or excessively baggy clothing, among other things. Most tours leave Seoul in the early morning and return the same day, in the evening.

If that sounds like too much hassle, it's possible to visit other sites close to the DMZ on your own. Imjingak, a park set up near the city of Paju to explore the theme of unification and equipped with monuments, historical exhibits, and an observatory, is one of the more popular.

There are hopes the tourist dollars will continue to flow long after the border opens. The thin human presence in the DMZ has made it a treasure trove of rare plant and animal life, including endangered species that some officials are betting will prove a great lure for nature enthusiasts when the Zone itself is no longer needed.

Daily Life

Next to Seoul, Gyeonggi-do has the largest foreign population in the country, with around 300,000 foreign residents. A significant proportion are migrant workers, usually from South or Southeast Asia, who work in Gyeonggi-do's many factories, but they also includes executives, teachers, and military personnel. Expatriates are spread throughout the province, with higher numbers in larger cities such as Incheon and Suwon and popular Seoul satellite towns such as Seongnam.

Most city halls have at least some English-language information on housing, garbage disposal, and other daily life issues available either online or on-site to help new arrivals settle in. Because of Gyeonggi-do's proximity to Seoul, much of the socializing among expatriates tends to take place in the capital, and residents will probably also need to head to Seoul to participate in clubs or associations geared toward specific interests. While there are a few religious institutions in Gyeonggi-do that offer English-language services—Incheon's Jooan Methodist Church and Suwon's Nations International Church are two examples—Seoul has a far wider range. Residents also need to depend on newspapers and broadcasts from Seoul for English-language news and entertainment. All that said, most sizable cities in Gyeonggi-do have dining and entertainment districts of their own where expatriates tend to congregate, such as Bupyeong in Incheon and Yeongtong-dong in Suwon.

HEALTH

The provincial government runs a 24-hour emergency medical information hotline (1339) and has designated several recommended hospitals for foreign residents where multilingual treatment is available. These include Ajou University Medical Center in Suwon and St. Mary's Hospital in Uijeongbu. Standards of care are very high, and the hospitals run some specialist clinics in areas such as neurology and family medicine.

SCHOOLS

Gyeonggi-do has several international schools that draw in students from the province and Seoul proper, some with more expansive campuses than their counterparts in the big city since land tends to be cheaper and more abundant. Seoul International School (SIS) and Korea International School (KIS), both in Seongnam, and the Gyeonggi Suwon International School in Suwon are among the best known and best equipped. There's also an International Christian School in Uijeongbu, and a branch of the California-based Chadwick School has opened in the Songdo International Business District. All accept students from prekindergarten through high school and are accredited by agencies such as the U.S.-based Western Association of Schools and Colleges.

Tuition rates at all these institutions are high, with a mix of local and U.S. currency fees that typically adds up to over 20 million won per year for elementary school and rises as students get older. U.S. citizens are sometimes permitted to send their children to schools on U.S. military posts in Dongducheon and Uijeongbu if spaces are available.

SHOPPING

Residents of Gyeonggi-do will have little trouble finding any of the necessities or common consumer goods they could want on local shopping excursions, but more exotic imported items might require a quick jaunt to Seoul. Major high-end department store chains, including Hyundai and Lotte, have multiple branches in Suwon, Incheon, and Seongnam, as do discount "hypermarkets" like E-mart and Home Plus, which sell clothing, appliances, and a generally healthy range of Western groceries. The Lafesta and Western Dom shopping and entertainment complexes, in Goyang's upmarket Ilsan district, are probably the most diverse conglomerations of youth-oriented boutiques and restaurants in the province, with multiple shops and eateries offering foreign delicacies, bars, and cinemas.

A more traditional—and economical—retail experience can be had at Gyeonggi-do's traditional markets, a concession to the region's agricultural traditions, which generally run every five days or so. These have excellent bargains on local grains, crafts, and produce, but also some sights and smells that may put off the less adventurous visitor. Moran Market in Seongnam and Osan Market in Osan, which has operated for nearly three centuries, are the most active.

Where to Live

Decisions on where to live in Gyeonggi-do tend to be based on proximity to work and budget, since a reasonable lifestyle can be had in any one of the province's major centers. Expatriates who earn their money in Seoul but prefer to reside somewhere slightly more sedate have flocked to the well-designed newer districts of bedroom communities like Songdo, Goyang, and Seongnam, while those whose workplaces are in Incheon or Suwon often prefer living in those cities rather than "reverse commuting" from Seoul, where housing tends to be far more expensive—especially as city authorities gear up to create more international business zones and expatriate-friendly facilities. While much of the foreign population of Uijeongbu and Dongducheon isn't there by choice—the two communities represent one of the linchpins of the U.S. military presence in South Korea—they have attracted a number of civilian residents who appreciate their relatively diverse populations and closeness to countryside.

INCHEON 인천

A heaving harbor town of nearly three million, Incheon is South Korea's third-largest city. Its metropolitan city status means it's administered independently from surrounding Gyeonggi-do, although in practice it's still very much a part of the province and the greater Seoul area. Its prime position on the Yellow Sea coast means it's been an important port for centuries, and it quickly became home to some of Korea's earliest foreign settlements when the country emerged from a long spell of isolation in the late 19th century.

Its position as an international gateway was restored by the opening of the country's main airport here in 2001, and should be burnished further by a purpose-built international leisure and business zone taking shape on the city's waterfront.

The districts nearest the harbor—Jung-gu, Dong-gu, and Yeonsu-gu—form the heart of old Incheon, a lively but crowded tangle of relatively low-rise buildings that extend from the coast to the hilltop enclave of Jayu Park. The city's old Chinatown and foreign quarter, which contains several noteworthy turn-of-the-20th-century buildings, are also located near the waterfront and lend the area some historic ambience, but most expatriates live in the more affluent eastern Bupyeong-gu. Strategically located at the intersection of the Seoul and Incheon subway lines, Bupyeong is a relatively new and rapidly developing area of wide roads and orderly apartment blocks, prized for its convenience and abundance of facilities, which include the city's largest gym, a lively nightlife district, and a massive underground shopping complex connected to Bupyeong subway station. Rents in relatively new apartment projects in the area, such as Hyundai's The Loft, start at around 500,000 won for a studio, with deposits of around 10 million won. Selling prices average around 250 million won.

An emerging alternative to Bupyeong is Songdo, a massive business and residential venture that's taken shape on a 1,500-hectare patch of reclaimed land just southwest of central Incheon. While much of the city's infrastructure, including spanking-new apartments, meticulously groomed parks, international schools and subway lines, is already in place, it's still very much a work in progress. The government and developers are proud of Songdo's environmental credentials and hope to transform it into a

© RUFINA K.E. PARK

Songdo development, southwest of Incheon

hub to rival places like Singapore and Dubai. That's some way off, and it still feels a tad sterile and sparsely populated, but development is continuing at a fast clip, and the area looks set to attract a number of international organizations and businesses in the coming years, including the offices of a new United Nations-operated climate fund. New, nicely equipped two-bedroom apartments in complexes such as the Sharp Central Park are currently trading hands for around 330 million won. Rents are fairly high at around 1-1.5 million won for two- to three-bedroom units, with deposits of 10-20 million won.

SUWON 수원

Gyeonggi-do's provincial capital, Suwon, is a pleasant city of just over one million only 30 kilometers (18 miles) south of Seoul. Like most South Korean metropolises, much of Suwon is a relatively uninspiring mass of high-rise buildings and busy streets, but it does have the distinction of being the only walled city left in the country. Its downtown core is completely encircled by the over 200-year-old Hwaseong Fortress, and the structure's magnificent towers and pavilions, as well as the green finger of Paldal Mountain near the city center, make for some inspiring vistas.

Suwon is a major center for South Korea's electronics industry and one of the main production bases for tech giant Samsung, meaning it has a sizable population of foreign software developers and engineers, as well as language teachers, laborers, and military personnel. The Yeongtong-gu area just to the east of the city center tends to lure the most expatriates.

An affluent, largely residential district of relatively new high-rise apartment blocks, Yeongtong is well laid out and well served by public transit, and it offers close proximity to the central Paldal-gu area, which Yeongtong was actually part of until relatively recently. Paldal-gu is home to Suwon's central train station as well as AK Plaza, a major retail complex, and government offices. Rents at newer apartments in Yeongtong-gu start at around 600,000 won for a one-bedroom unit, with deposits of 10 million won. Apartment prices in Suwon are manageable by South Korean standards, with modern one- to two-bedroom units in the range of 250 million won.

SEONGNAM 성남

The city of Seongnam, just south of Seoul's ritzy Gangnam district, has witnessed exponential growth over the last decade as Gangnam's affluent professionals have pushed their way into the neighboring jurisdiction in search of more space. Nearly all of them have flocked to the Bundang area, an impressive amalgamation of green space and towering high-end condominiums. With its expansive congestion-free roads and abundance of parks, Bundang is one of South Korea's closest approximations to the suburbs found outside major North American cities.

Bundang's expatriate community is also expanding quickly. Apartments here are generally priced similarly to comparable accommodations in Seoul—around 1-2 million won per month for one- or two-bedroom units in refined complexes such as the SK Park View—but are often better designed and offer more space and amenities (shops, restaurants, fitness centers, playgrounds) than those in the capital. Fairly large (70 square meters and up) units can be purchased for as little as 150 million won in older developments but will cost five or six times as much in newer or well-located ones.

The city itself is also a very nice place to live; it's connected to the Seoul subway system, and there's excellent shopping and dining available at upmarket complexes like the AK Plaza. The 42-hectare Central Park and tree-lined banks of the Tancheon, a stream that runs through the heart of Bundang, offer an abundance of recreational opportunities. Small wonder some Seoulites now take time out to visit Bundang rather than the other way around.

PRIME LIVING LOCATIONS

© RUFINA K.E. PARK

Bundang is similar to a typical North American suburb.

GOYANG 고양

Much like Seongnam to the south, Goyang, a few kilometers northwest of Seoul, is an affluent bedroom community purpose-built for families working in the capital. And like Seongnam, it's been around for centuries but is now best-known for a single, prosperous, and very new area in Goyang's case, Ilsan. This enclave, consisting of two districts in western Goyang, is barely over a decade old but has already won over a large number of residents with its state-of-the-art housing and meticulously planned public areas.

Ilsan is a place of superlatives. Among other things it boasts the largest artificial lake in South Korea, at the heart of an expansive park crisscrossed with biking and jogging trails, and one of the biggest concert venues outside the capital, the Goyang Aram Nuri Arts Center. As well as the standard department stories it has the atypical Lafesta and Western Dom complexes, semi-outdoor shopping and entertainment plazas that serve as Goyang's de facto downtown and reverberate every night with the sounds of revelry from dozens of hip bars and restaurants.

Ilsan is also almost unique in offering a sizable number of Western-style detached two- and three-story homes, most only around one or two years old and clustered near Jeongbalsan Mountain just northeast of the Lake Park. Designed in a variety of styles, these offer a sizable amount of space and usually private yards to putter around in, but when the neighborhood is likened to the Beverly Hills of South Korea, you know they're not going to come cheap. Prices for houses in this area hover at around 1 billion won, with rents starting at 3 million won per month with deposits of 20 million won or more for nicer units.

Compared to this, upscale apartment developments such as the We City Ilsan Chai look like a bargain, with purchase prices starting at around 750 million won and rents averaging around 1.5 million won for a two-bedroom unit in the 70-square-meter range, usually with a minimum deposit of 10 million won.

UIJEONGBU AND DONGDUCHEON 의정부/동두천

These cities, just north of Seoul on the metropolitan rail line and not far apart, are two of the final sizable settlements before the inter-Korean border and represent one of South Korea's first lines of defense against the North, a situation that's emphasized by the heavy local and U.S. military presence in the area. In decades past this meant they were known largely for Cold War-style armed tension and the raunchy nightlife that seems to accompany legions of enlisted men around the world, but as the threat of imminent conflict between the two Koreas has subsided, more Koreans and non-military foreign nationals have moved in, with the population of the area nearly doubling over the past decade.

While physically unremarkable, residents like these towns because they're of a manageable size—Uijeongbu has a population of around 400,000, and Dongducheon just a quarter of that—and because they're just an hour outside of Seoul but far closer to nature. Dongducheon is bordered on the north by Soyo-san, a magnificent range of craggy peaks and waterfalls that delights hikers year-round. And outside the cramped areas surrounding the train and bus stations—it's a major transport hub—Uijeongbu has some very sedate neighborhoods surrounded by mountains and bisected by streams.

The two communities' long-standing foreign presence means there's also plenty of infrastructure and amenities available, like international schools, U.S.-brand clothing outlets, and Mexican restaurants, that are limited to nonexistent in other South Korean towns of similar size. Not all of this will be desirable to everyone—Dongducheon still has a fairly saucy bar district serving largely military traffic, but the less salubrious bits are easy enough to avoid.

The area's rapid growth and the generous rents paid by military personnel living off base mean housing costs in Dongducheon and Uijeongbu are fairly high. Newer two-bedroom apartments of around 80 square meters in larger complexes will typically rent for around 1-1.5 million won per month in both towns, and sell for 200 million won and up.

Getting Around

Major cities in Gyeonggi-do have extremely well-developed transportation services—in fact, that's one of the main selling points for commuters who relocate into the province from Seoul and often find it faster and easier to get from a neighboring city to central Seoul than to cross Seoul itself. Roads in many areas are relatively new and are therefore more sensibly laid out with better signage than those in the capital, although traffic can still be a problem on the major highways surrounding Seoul, particularly on the weekends.

BY SUBWAY

All the locations mentioned in this chapter are connected to the Seoul subway system to at least some extent, and more lines and stations are constantly under development in areas where train services are limited, such as the outskirts of Bundang and Uijeongbu. Travel times to central Seoul average around one hour and fares are typically 1,200-1,500 won.

BY BUS

In addition to train lines, Incheon, Suwon, Seongnam, and Goyang have fairly extensive inner-city bus services that link major landmarks or districts and allow residents to get around quite easily without a private vehicle, though some residents might feel a car is necessary in Uijeongbu and Dongducheon. Most important for commuters are the express buses, typically red or orange, that connect outlying cities—usually via bus stations, train stations, or major shopping complexes—with key destinations in Seoul. These run frequently, are very affordable—tickets are typically 3,000-5,000 won—and are also comfortable, with seats on many routes guaranteed. The buses travel in special lanes that help them bypass traffic jams, and many commuters find them a more pleasant option than a cramped, standing-room-only subway journey.

BY TAXI

Taxis are readily available throughout the province, and as in Seoul fares usually start at about 2,200 won and stay under 10,000 won for journeys within a city. Residents of Gyeonggi-do can run into trouble after the subway shuts down at night, when many are forced to take Seoul cabs to their far-off places of residence. This is rarely a problem—in fact many drivers are all too happy with the fat fares—but can quickly get expensive by South Korean standards, with tariffs to most provincial cities from Seoul at around 30,000 won. Some drivers will want a slightly higher flat fee or "tip" to cover the cost of traveling back to Seoul with an empty cab; fast or aggressive driving on longer trips (usually so the driver can return to Seoul and pick up another fare as soon as possible) is another common complaint.

Many of these issues can be avoided by making contact with a cab company based in your city and asking for numbers or specific drivers you can contact for trips between Seoul and your home when necessary. Many firms run special commuter services or offer discounts for regular customers, and there are far fewer chances for problems when you're with a driver who's returning to his home base.

THE EAST

South Korea's geographically varied and culturally rich eastern region has been at the forefront of the country's development since its earliest days as a nation, when it was the power base of the Silla kingdom that took the first major steps toward unifying the peninsula. This legacy is still visible in the area's abundance of historic sites; it is a land littered with the tombs of former rulers, ancient observatories, and some of the nation's finest examples of Buddhist temple architecture.

But this has always been a place that has looked forward as well as back. Few other parts of the country have played a greater role in its meteoric rise from postwar poverty to export powerhouse. South Korea's early leaders—most from the east themselves—capitalized on the region's abundant resources and deep coastal bays to transform it into a major engine of prosperity, overseeing a rapid proliferation of plants, refineries, shipyards, and smelters and transforming ramshackle fishing villages into full-blown cities that are the stomping grounds of some of South Korea's largest companies. The region's coastal ports have also made it a nexus for seaborne trade with neighboring Japan, Russia, and beyond.

Its recent manufacturing success has created a number of employment opportunities in the area and attracted a sizable population of expatriates that runs the gamut from engineers and shipping professionals to teachers and restaurant owners. Many foreign

© RUFINA K.E. PARK

nationals as well as South Koreans are drawn here initially for work reasons and dismiss the place as a sort of industrial theme park, which it certainly looks like in parts. But they soon discover eastern South Korea offers more than just smokestacks and jobs.

With industry and commerce heavily concentrated in a handful of cities, the region has a nature- and culture-crammed hinterland to explore that includes the "open-air museums" of Gyeongju and Andong, the snow-dusted cliffs and plunging waterfalls of Seoraksan National Park, and sandy coastal beaches. Even the cities themselves tend to be smaller and far more manageable than the sprawling Seoul agglomeration, with tighter-knit foreign communities and, some would say, fewer stressed-out locals. And while they can't match the capital area for sheer variety, major eastern towns all have a decent assortment of restaurants and watering holes, plenty of sporting opportunities, and good medical and educational facilities. Transport links to Seoul are also myriad and excellent, and many expatriates find they need to use them a lot less than they originally anticipated.

The Lay of the Land

The eastern region is divided into three provinces. Gyeongsangnam-do (South Gyeongsang Province), which occupies the southeastern corner of the country, is the most populous by a large margin and also contains two of the region's largest cities—Busan and Ulsan—although both are administered independently. With most of its residents on or within a few miles of the coast, this is a place that moves to the rhythm of the sea, heavily dependent on its ports, fishing, and shipbuilding. Not surprisingly, the province is treasured by South Koreans for its beaches and fresh seafood.

Gyeongsangnam-do's northern neighbor, Gyeongsangbuk-do, is less populated, made up largely of broad river-crossed plains abutted by a scenic coastline, and neatly encircled by mountain ranges. Its major settlements include Pohang, an important port and center for the domestic steel industry, and, farther inland, Daegu, South Korea's fourth-largest city.

North of Gyeongsangnam-do is Gangwon-do, where the lengthy north-south Taebaek mountain range crests in a series of deep valleys and craggy peaks. The province's limited amount of arable land and rugged terrain contained its growth, and to this day it remains the most thinly populated part of the country. The upside to this is that it has become a refuge for nature lovers, adventure seekers, and just about anyone else looking to escape South Korea's urban sprawl, provided they can tolerate a scarcity of foreign amenities and goods. Gangwon-do's expansive national parks, ski slopes, rushing rivers, and dramatic coastline—well, at least the bits that aren't fenced off and rigorously patrolled due to the province's proximity to North Korea—offer an array of alpine scenery, tranquil hideaways, and outdoor activities that can be tapped into year-round.

CLIMATE

Like the rest of South Korea, the east enjoys a temperate climate with four distinct seasons, but there are some regional variations. The southeast of the peninsula, including major coastal cities like Ulsan and Busan, offers some of the mildest weather in the country next to Jeju Island. The summer humidity is moderated by sea breezes, and temperatures rarely dip below freezing in the winter, making snow a very rare sight. Conversely Daegu, which lies inland in a mountain basin, has some of the hottest summers in the nation as warm sticky air is trapped there by the surrounding hills. In the winter months, Gangwon Province, particularly areas at higher elevations or near the Demilitarized Zone, is noticeably colder (typically 4-5°C) than the southeast and receives more snowfall than anywhere else in the country.

Where to Live

BUSAN 부산

South Korea's second-largest city, Busan, is a thriving oceanside metropolis of around four million people that manages to feel like a couple of different places at once. The old downtown is very much an extension of the harbor, a massive forest of cranes and containers facing the East Sea that is the biggest in the country and among the five busiest in the world. But Busan's up-and-coming districts have less to do with the sea trade than culture and leisure, and if we're making port-town comparisons, are more Miami Beach than Marseilles. The city is dense and sprawling, but its seaside perch and forested hilltops give it a certain visual flair. It's busy but still manages to maintain a laid-back feel, and thanks to its abundance of seafaring types and international festivals, it is fairly cosmopolitan. Throw in the beaches, a solid arts scene, and the low cost of living, and it's obvious why Busan is beginning to present some strong competition to Seoul as South Korea's main expat haven.

The central district rising from the port to Yongdu (Dragon's Head) Mountain is cramped and gritty in places, a tangle of office blocks, shopping arcades, and wet markets that's an intriguing—if not the most livable—part of town. More expatriates prefer to congregate in Seomyeon to the north, where the intersection of Busan's two subway lines has created a newer downtown of sorts. This is a heavily built-up buzzing area of neon-lined streets, shopping complexes, and crammed nightspots, perfect for those who want to be at the heart of the action. Most of the housing here is in sizable apartment blocks, with semifurnished two-bedroom units in newer structures such as the Majestower renting for around 800,000 won per month after a 5-10 million won deposit. Apartment prices in the area start at around 200 million won.

The Haeundae district, bordering the beach of the same name, is a fairly recent creation that has quickly become a favorite of expatriates and upwardly mobile locals. While it's some distance from the traditional city center, it's connected to other parts of town via the subway and has so many amenities of its own that venturing outside the area is never a necessity. In addition to beach access, Haeundae offers international schools, an eye-popping range of restaurants and bars, and Busan's newest and flashiest retail spaces, including the colossal Centum City complex, dubbed the largest department store in the world. The towering new condominiums here, with their sweeping sea views, are widely seen as the city's best, and they bear impossibly posh names like Trump or Zenith. Despite that, they're not outrageously priced, at least compared to similar developments in Seoul. New two- to three-bedroom units of around 170 square meters can be rented for about 1-2 million won per month with a 20 million

© RUFINA K.E. PARK

coastal trail, Busan

won deposit. Reasonably nice apartments fairly close to the beach can be found for as little as 300 million won, but when it comes to prices, the sky's the limit.

Those on tighter budgets should head for the Pusan National University and Kyungsung University neighborhoods, which are full of largely low-rise villas divided into smaller apartment units that rent fairly cheaply, as well as lively low-cost eateries and clubs set up to cater to the student-heavy population. Rents for one- and two-bedroom units in these areas range 400,000-800,000 won, with minimal deposits of 5 million won, and they can be purchased for 100-150 million won or so. Both locations are about equidistant from Haeundae Beach and the old city center and are also quite convenient in transportation terms with good subway connections.

Culture

City authorities have spared no expense over the past few years in their effort to make Busan an arts as well as a maritime center, and while it's far too early to say whether they'll succeed, the results are encouraging. The biggest event on the Busan cultural calendar is the Busan International Film Festival held each fall, which in the last decade has become one of the more prominent gatherings on the global film circuit. When it's happening, it's nearly impossible to escape, with movies screened all over the city, the famous and their fans crowding all the top hotels, and a laundry list of premieres and parties thrown each night.

The city also stages a contemporary art festival every two years, the Busan Biennale, and has several well-stocked galleries and museums, including the Busan Museum of Art. It has also managed to maintain a handful of historic assets, including Beomeosa, a tranquil mountaintop temple compound, and sections of the Geumjongsanseong, a partially restored fortress that dates back some three centuries and provides some fantastic hiking opportunities.

BUSAN'S "LITTLE RUSSIA"

One of the first things that strikes many visitors to Busan, especially if they arrive by train and wander the streets near the station, is the abundance of Caucasians walking the street and the signs in the Cyrillic alphabet. This area, Jungang-dong, is the heart of Busan's Russian community.

While only a few hundred Russians reside here permanently, their numbers are boosted substantially by sailors and traders who travel on the ships that now run regularly between Busan and the ports of the Russian far east. Many make a living by buying up South Korean clothing, electronics, and cosmetics in bulk and reselling them at a substantial markup in the remote communities that dot Russia's Pacific frontier. A sizable network of shops, nightclubs, and restaurants have sprung up to serve these visitors, and in the evening it's possible to walk stretches of the neighborhood and believe you're in another country as tables full of people huddle together over bottles of vodka or steaming bowls of borscht.

Interestingly, the Russians were far from the first foreign arrivals to frequent this area. As the name of one of its main drags—Texas Street—implies, it was once the preferred playground of U.S. soldiers looking to blow off steam, a bawdy stretch of raucous bars, street food vendors, and peddlers of counterfeit goods. Even further back, it was part of one of the country's first officially designated foreign settlements, opened as a trading post for Japanese merchants some 400 years ago.

Some vestiges of the area's 20th-century seediness remain, but the vendors are now focused on a new batch of customers. City authorities seem to have endorsed the district's quirkiness, and continue the tradition of abandoning it to non-Koreans, by naming the former Texas Street a special "shopping street for foreigners" where all sorts of low-priced delights and exotic experiences await travelers. So far, the Russians appear to be the only people who have really taken notice.

Daily Life

According to official statistics there are over 40,000 foreign nationals living in Busan. It's not a massive foreign population, but it's certainly an active one. The city has a good range of support networks and associations for non-Koreans, including clubs for activities such as sailing, hiking, and shooting, groups for expatriate women and spouses of South Koreans, even a branch of the Democrats Abroad. There are also several churches, Buddhist temples, and small mosques that run services for foreign residents. The expat community even has its own publication in *Busan Haps,* a bimonthly magazine that's a clearinghouse of news and information on events, foreign food enclaves, and nightlife, and a handful of community websites, including Busan Awesome and Koreabridge.

Much of the expatriate social scene revolves around the internationally themed pubs, clubs, and restaurants of Haeundae, although there are also popular meeting places in Seomyeon, Gwangalli, and the Pusan National University district, which tends to draw a younger crowd.

Health

Like other major South Korean cities, Busan has clinics and pharmacies on nearly every corner that can address minor health issues, and a few major hospitals with international clinics or English-speaking staff to handle larger ones. These include Pusan National University Hospital, Wallace Memorial Baptist Hospital, and Maryknoll Medical Center.

Schools

Several international schools have been set up to cater to Busan's expanding foreign community, including the Busan International Foreign School, which has a new campus on the city's outskirts, near Songjeong Beach, and offers both U.S. and British-based curricula; and the Busan Foreign School, which follows the U.S. curriculum and is located in Haeundae. Both institutions offer classes from preschool through high school, with tuition rates topping out at just over 20 million won. There are also independent schools for Japanese and Chinese residents.

Shopping

Busan offers a healthy mix of old and new-style shopping opportunities, with the aging port area dominated by markets but neighborhoods like Haeundae and Seomyeon home to high-end department stores and big-box retail chains like Home Plus and E-mart. The Lotte Department Store in Seomyeon and Haeundae's Centum City complex are the city's top shopping destinations, and both have a sufficient range of foreign apparel and delicacies to temporarily console the homesick expat.

Transport

The Busan subway consists of four very long lines that connect most major points in the city and extend well into its outskirts. The trains are fast, user-friendly, and cheap—the maximum fare is 1,400 won—but unfortunately shut down shortly before midnight, which means night owls may find themselves resorting to taxis a lot. Thankfully these are also quite inexpensive, with fares starting at 2,200 won and rarely exceeding 20,000 won even for longer trips such as Busan Station to Haeundae. The city also has a bus fleet that plies the main roads, with fares similar to the subway. However as English-language information on bus routes is limited and buses are more subject to the whims of traffic, most residents find themselves sticking to the train.

DAEGU 대구

For centuries Daegu has been a vital transportation center, situated near South Korea's geographic heart in a bowl-like mountain valley at the confluence of two major rivers and along the first major road to link Seoul and Busan. These days it helps keep things on the move in an entirely different way as a major producer of automobile parts. Textiles are the other key industry, and the local government nurtures ambitions (as yet largely unrealized) of Daegu becoming a fashion capital à la Milan. The city's hasty expansion over the past few decades have left it with little to distinguish it visually, but the authorities have worked hard to boost its charm with environmental and beautification projects, and Daegu now has a higher ratio of parks per person than any other metropolis in South Korea.

The foreign population, about 22,000 strong and growing at a rate of around 8 percent per year, is a mix of factory workers, teachers, executives, and military personnel. Most find Daegu a pleasant—if not spectacularly exciting—home, with a small-town feel that belies its 2.5 million or so population. The city has some lively entertainment districts, excellent hiking in the surrounding hills, ample cultural resources, and swift transport connections to other parts of the peninsula.

Like Daegu itself, the expatriate community is fairly spread out, but Suseong-gu, just southeast of the city center, seems to be the preferred district for locals and foreign residents alike. Suseong is a high-density area of mostly spanking-new high-rise apartments but also boasts lovely tree-lined streets, top-notch sports facilities, and public gardens. Nicer three-bedroom apartments in the 30 *pyeong* (100 square meter) range rent for around 700,000 won per month, with deposits of about 10 million won, and carry average selling prices of around 300 million won. There are also a significant number of foreigners in the Kyungpook National University area in north Daegu, which is a mix of newer apartment blocks and older lower-rise villa housing. Accommodations in this area are significantly cheaper, with monthly rents from around 300,000 won for a studio or 500,000 won for a small two-bedroom unit after deposits of about 5 million won.

Culture

Daegu's cultural infrastructure is limited, and most foreign residents have to travel to Seoul or Busan for truly world-beating events or exhibitions, but there are some local attractions worth a look, including an arts house and opera center with regular performances, and museums in Suseong district and Kyungpook University with extensive collections of local crafts and relics. The mountains surrounding Daegu also house several important historic and religious sites, such as Donghwasa Temple and the Gatbawi Buddha.

Daily Life

Some basic information on accommodation options and medical and other services in Daegu is available at the city hall in the central (Jung-gu) area. There are also a number of expat-oriented clubs and interest groups to join, including hiking groups, a rugby team, and friendship and language exchange groups designed to bridge the gaps between the local and foreign communities. *Daegu Compass* is the latest title to take a stab at the challenging English-language magazine market, and also runs a website with good maps and tips on promising local nightspots and events. The epicenter of the expat social scene is probably the buzzing Rodeo Street-Samdeok Fire Station zone in downtown Daegu, a few busy streets that manage to cram in a surprising collection of restaurants and bars, from curry houses to German-style microbreweries.

Health

Several Daegu hospitals have established international clinics catering to non-Korean speakers, all with very high standards of medical care. Keimyung University's Dongsan Medical Center, just west of the city center, is the best-known. In Suseong district, Hyosung Hospital runs an international center with a particular focus on women's health issues.

Schools

Daegu has a few international education options, most affiliated with religious groups.

The Daegu International School runs classes based on the U.S. curriculum from kindergarten through high school, with tuition rates of about 15-20 million won annually. The Daegu American School, located on the Camp George U.S. military base, primarily serves the children of U.S. service members but occasionally accepts outside students if space permits. There's also a Chinese school for Mandarin speakers.

Shopping

Though imported goods are generally in shorter supply than in Seoul or Busan, there are a number of superstores sprinkled throughout the city, such as E-mart, Home Plus, and even a Costco, that carry a good range of foreign food mainstays as well as local produce. For trendy clothing and higher-end retail goods, the department stores and boutiques of Dongseong-no, a street running through the heart of central Daegu, is a good place to start. Seomun Market is one of the largest traditional-type bazaars in the country and offers some great bargains on fabrics, household items, and seafood.

Transport

Daegu has a modern two-line subway system that does a good job of linking most of the city's key districts. Fares are a flat 1,200 won, with a small discount given to passengers using prepaid smart cards. The subway is supplemented by dozens of bus routes, but only a few key buses serving busy downtown streets such as Dongseong-no display route information in English. There are also plenty of taxis trawling the city streets; fares are in line with other cities. Many contain sheets with major destinations listed in Korean and English that you can point to if other means of communication fail.

ULSAN 울산

Few places embody South Korea's postwar progress as much as Ulsan, which was little more than a windswept fishing community three or four decades ago but has since become the country's industrial capital. The main base of operations for Hyundai Motor Group and the world's largest shipbuilders, as well as a key refining and petrochemical site, this city of just over one million has the highest per-capita wealth of any town in South Korea, and is home to a number of foreign engineers, experts, and managers working for its highly successful corporations. While it's not going to win any prizes for its beauty, the city's lingering reputation for uninspiring factory architecture and pollution is somewhat unfair. Some prosperous-looking, carefully planned districts have sprung up to serve an increasingly affluent population, and Ulsan's coastal and mountain outskirts boast some of the nicest scenery in South Korea. Bisected by the Taehwa River and meticulously planned (at least in the newer districts), it has a pleasant setting and is easily navigable, with a good array of shopping, recreational activities, and cuisine. Ulsan has lured talented graduates from all over South Korea, resulting in a fairly young and fun-loving population.

The area with the highest proportion of non-Koreans is probably the aptly named "foreigners' compound" in Bangojin, a fairly quiet seaside neighborhood in Dong-gu (East District). This is primarily a housing development for employees or customers of the burgeoning Hyundai Heavy Industries shipyard nearby. Although it's a fair distance of 8 kilometers (5 miles) from the city center, this collection of aging apartment blocks and bungalows is fairly self-sufficient, with its own school, shops, and social club, and many foreign residents enjoy the community feel. However, it's generally accessible only to those employed by or doing business with Hyundai, who will have their housing arranged for them.

Nam-gu, specifically the relatively new upscale apartment developments of the Samsan-dong area, is steadily eclipsing the old downtown of Jung-gu (Central District) to the north as the preferred home of expatriates, though Jung-gu's cramped old buildings are also being replaced by sleek ultramodern condo developments in places. Ulsan's prosperity has pushed property prices steadily upward to the point where they rival Seoul's, but as it's not as crowded, buyers and renters tend to get more space for their money. Two-bedroom units in newer developments in Nam-gu and Jung-gu rent for around 1 million won per month with a 20 million won deposit; a unit of similar size in villas in the east or Ulsan University district will go for around half that. Sizable apartments of 120 square meters and up in popular developments such as the Jung-gu Prugio cost 350 million won or more.

Culture

It is industry and not the arts that has always been Ulsan's forte, but the city isn't a cultural desert. There are two cultural and art centers maintained by the city government and Hyundai (of course) that regularly stage concerts and musicals and host foreign visual arts exhibitions. The outskirts of the city are home to several important Confucian academies, temples, and shrines, and the ancient Silla capital of Gyeongju is just 40 minutes or so away.

Daily Life

As in other cities, Ulsan City Hall and district offices have some bare-bones information in print and online for new residents that covers things like renting a home and garbage separation. The foreigners' compound runs occasional events and has some on-again, off-again sporting groups, such as the Hash House Harriers and an expat football league, which nonresidents are welcome to join—check at the clubhouse for the latest information. While there's no English-language print media of note, the Ulsan Online website contains some helpful mini-guides to the city and events listings. The old downtown (Seongnam-dong) and Ulsan University districts house several pubs and restaurants regularly frequented by foreign residents.

Health

Dongkang Medical Center in the city center and Ulsan University Hospital both have some English-speaking staff and are well equipped to address most medical issues, although foreign nationals in need of more personal or long-term care tend to head down south to one of the specialist international clinics in Busan.

Schools

The only international school of any note in Ulsan is the Hyundai Foreign School in the Bangojin foreigners' compound, which currently offers a British-based curriculum for students ages 2 to 14. Parents not associated with Hyundai are welcome to send their children to the school provided they've spent an ample amount of time abroad. It's a fairly small but tight-knit institution with reasonable fees, by international school standards, of about 8-16 million won per year. Some parents have their children commute to schools in nearby Busan.

Shopping

South Korea's big-box retailers, including Lotte Mart, E-mart, and Home Plus, are all well represented in Ulsan. The mammoth Lotte and Hyundai department stores in Samsan-dong are the places to go for pricey brand-name clothing and imported food and spirits. The New Core outlet mall in the old city center offers some brand-name goods at knockdown prices and is surrounded by a host of interesting boutiques and accessory vendors. There's also a "furniture street" downtown that groups dozens of shops displaying the full range of imported and locally produced household goods—the perfect place to start filling up a new home.

Transport

The government is apparently working on it, but transport is one place where Ulsan tends to fall short of some other cities. While the roads are for the most part spacious, well-maintained, and blessedly free of traffic compared to Seoul, the city is very spread out and lacks a rapid transit system. There's a fairly extensive and inexpensive bus network, but it can be hard for non-Korean speakers to negotiate as almost no English-language route information is available and buses run fairly infrequently. Most expatriate residents regularly resort to taxis, which start at 2,200 won and end up costing 6,000-8,000 won for most inner-city trips, or buy a car or scooter to get around.

GANGWON-DO 강원도

It's not for those who crave big-city stimulation, require the company of a lot of other expatriates, or constantly yearn for imported goods. But in a crowded, highly urbanized nation, the northeastern Gangwon-do is the perfect home province for those searching for open spaces, access to the outdoors, and a slower pace of life. Gangwon is a thinly populated place of small and medium-sized towns set among dramatic coastlines, soaring mountain ranges, and the country's densest forests. It's South Korea's uncontested recreation capital, with the country's finest ski slopes, hiking, white-water rafting, and rock climbing, and for the less active, natural scenery. The air is clean, the local produce is top-notch, and the cost of living is low, but the downsides are also obvious enough. The expatriate presence is small, cultural and after-dark distractions are limited, and public transit is thin on the ground. Whether the positives will outweigh these shortfalls is a matter of preference, but even in the depths of the province, residents are hardly at the ends of the earth. The provincial capital, Chuncheon, is around an hour by high-speed rail from Seoul and all its delights. Job opportunities for foreigners are obviously more limited than in busier places but do exist, most notably in the language teaching and hospitality sectors.

Gangwon's small expatriate population, with a few exceptions, is split among Chuncheon; the southwestern city of Wonju, the province's largest; and the coastal town of Gangneung. All have populations of around 300,000 with 1,000 or so foreign residents apiece. While the cities are similar in terms of size and appearance with sedate, fairly low-rise town centers surrounded by the ubiquitous apartment blocks, each has unique features and advantages. Gangneung makes summer beach outings easy,

old and new housing in Gangwon-do

whereas Chuncheon and Wonju offer far quicker access to Seoul. Chuncheon is famed for its many lakes and festivals, while Gangneung is a better gateway to Seoraksan, the crown jewel of South Korea's national parks. Accommodations in all three cities are inexpensive compared to South Korea's major centers, but landlords are generally less used to Western-style tenancies, and the traditional system of large deposits with minimal or no monthly rent (*jeonse*) is more common. The deposit on a typical partially furnished two-bedroom apartment of around 80-90 square meters is 70-90 million won with no monthly rent; smaller deposits of 10-15 million won, if accepted, will usually result in rents of around 500,000 won per month. Apartment prices hover around the 150 million won range, even in the central districts of Chuncheon.

Culture

Barring the odd annual celebration, such as Chuncheon's International Mime Festival, international-class displays of contemporary art or music are uncommon in Gangwon-do. However, there's certainly no shortage of historical sites to explore; national parks such as Seoraksan and Taebaeksan have long lists of temples, tombs, and hermitages with hundreds of years' worth of legends behind them.

Daily Life

There are few organized expatriate groups or activities in Gangwon-do beyond a few Facebook-based associations, such as Gangneung Open Mic. Foreign residents inevitably tend to meet each other and form bonds quickly due to their relative rarity. Strangely enough, Seoul-based companies and clubs such as Adventure Korea, which runs regular hiking and rafting trips in Gangwon, seem most active in planning excursions for foreign residents of the province.

Shopping

Major retailers such as E-mart have a limited presence in Gangwon-do, with most concentrated on the outskirts of Wonju and Chuncheon. All cities have traditional-style markets, however, usually open on five- or seven-day cycles, that offer a staggering array of fresh local produce, textiles, and household necessities, all at extremely low prices (although some bargaining and knowledge of Korean may be required). Pungmul Market in Chuncheon and Wonju's Munmak Market are among the liveliest.

Transport

Most of the government's efforts have been poured into road building, and as of yet there are no major public transportation networks in Gangwon beyond the rapid buses and trains that cart travelers to and from larger cities like Seoul and Daegu. Chuncheon, Wonju, and Gangneung all have limited public bus services, but these are generally inefficient and tough for the non-Korean speaker to navigate. As the province is a major tourism center, there's a disproportionately large number of taxis available for hire; fares generally start at 2,200 won. Long-term residents usually find that a private vehicle is the only choice for anyone wanting constant access to transport or to explore the province's remote corners.

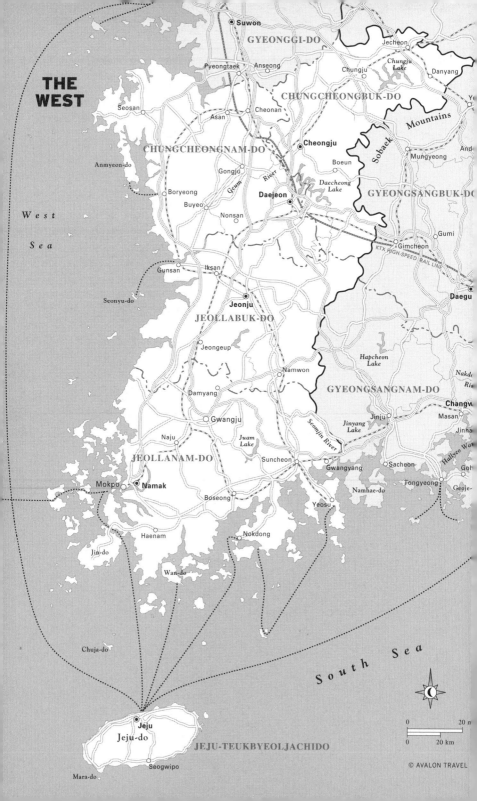

THE WEST

The relationship between South Korea's western provinces and the rest of the country hasn't always been a harmonious one. The region's fish-rich waters and fertile emerald plains made it the nation's primary breadbasket, but its slower, heavily agricultural way of life caused it to be viewed as something of a backwater by the more industrious commerce-minded capital and eastern provinces. This meant the west was frequently an afterthought, or neglected outright, in national development drives, and it was not until quite recently that South Koreans managed to elect a native of the region to the country's highest office. Not surprisingly, there's a streak of resentment in this part of South Korea that has occasionally boiled over into serious incidents, such as a 1980 revolt in Gwangju against the then-ruling dictatorship.

These days, however, the rivalry between the west and the rest of the country is a low-level affair, confined to competition for investment or the sports arena—perhaps because the region has become a force in its own right. Agriculture is still an essential industry, but boomtowns like Daejeon and Gwangju have become centers of far more cutting-edge trades, including biotechnology, robotics, and the arts.

The fact that much of the region escaped the industrialization that gripped the rest of South Korea in the 1970s and 1980s means pockets are less prosperous than the national average, but also that more of its landscape and traditions have been left

© BRIAN DEUTSCH

intact. This has made the west fertile ground for foreign residents with a serious interest in Korean culture and the arts, and it continues to produce more celebrated writers, painters, and sculptors per capita than anywhere else in the country. On the whole it's more conservative and less outward-looking than the Seoul area or the heavily trafficked ports of the southeast, and anyone looking for the cosmopolitan shades or pulse-pounding excitement of those kinds of places is bound to be disappointed here. But those who see leisurely living as more important or who crave rural scenery, fresh produce—even Seoulites are forced to admit this area has the country's best food—and frank, friendly people, or who simply want a less adulterated Korean experience, should give the west serious consideration.

The Lay of the Land

Western South Korea is divided into three provinces, all of which are bordered to the west by the Yellow Sea. Jeollanam-do (South Jeolla Province) takes up the peninsula's southwestern corner and has a population of almost two million, excluding the metropolitan city of Gwangju, which lies at its center but due to its size (1.5 million people) is governed independently. Its northern stretches are home to ample river-fed plains, and it is flanked on the east by one of the peninsula's steepest mountain ranges, but the province is most renowned for the breadth and diversity of its marine resources. The broad bays of the southwest coast shelter important ports such as Yeosu and Mokpo and lead out to a group of around 2,000 islands, many uninhabited, that are the stomping grounds of a staggering variety of seafood.

Directly to the north, Jeollabuk-do (North Jeolla Province) is dominated by its fertile western plains, blessed with abundant rainfall and single-handedly responsible for much of South Korea's rice, barley, and cotton crops. In the middle of this expanse

© BRIAN DEUTSCH

rice paddies

is the provincial capital of Jeonju, one of the country's last true outposts of historic architecture.

Chungcheongnam-do (South Chungcheon Province) is squeezed between Jeollabuk-do to the south and Gyeonggi Province and suburban Seoul to the north. Like its southern neighbor, this is an agriculturally rich province of low hills, wide fields, and jagged coastline, but it is also distinguished by being the former heart of the Baekje kingdom and is home to a number of relics, traditional arts, and festivals that proudly display this noble legacy. Daejeon, the province's largest and the country's sixth-largest city, has steadily earned a reputation as South Korea's research and development powerhouse.

CLIMATE

The west shares the temperate climate of the rest of the country, with mild springs and autumns and chilly winters. Summers, however, are generally warmer, slightly longer, and punctuated by more rainfall than in other areas, lending the region its optimum growing conditions.

Where to Live

DAEJEON 대전

Daejeon's roots as a small collection of farms are still apparent in the city's name, which literally means "big rice field." The rice paddies are still visible on the outskirts of the city, as are the jade mountains that surround it and the three rivers that divide Daejeon's main districts. But since rail links made it a major north-south transportation hub in the 1900s, the town has become a lot less bucolic. It was named provincial capital soon after, and served as the new home for some national government agencies in the late 1990s in the struggle to ease the concentration of bureaucrats in Seoul.

More recently its sizable array of specialized schools and postgraduate degree holders have earned Daejeon the moniker of South Korea's Silicon Valley. The catalyst was probably the granddaddy of South Korean scientific exploration, the Korea Advanced Institute of Science and Technology (KAIST), which was basically alone when it set up here more than 30 years ago. But districts such as Daedeok Innopolis now house dozens of public and private institutes busily studying everything from robotics to nuclear fusion and wireless broadband standards, all staffed by some of the country's top minds. This has fostered a sizable foreign community of more than 14,000, including students, academics, and tech experts as well as the usual language teachers and family types.

With much of the city a relatively recent creation, Daejeon is orderly and tidy by South Korean standards, with easily navigable streets, parks, and riverside paths. This applies particularly to the Dunsan-dong area, which has sprung up just west of the old downtown, and as it's now home to most new apartments, offices, and even City Hall, has effectively replaced it. This neighborhood and nearby Mannyeon-dong are popular with foreign residents for their convenience and proximity to shopping, dining, and nightlife—most of Daejeon's top restaurants and retailers are here. Housing is also on the new side and of good standards, if somewhat high-density. Studios or one-bedroom

INTERVIEW: BRIAN DEUTSCH

© BRIAN DEUTSCH

Brian Deutsch

Former Jeollanam-do resident Brian Deutsch was an English instructor but better known (at least in the foreign community) as the voice behind the "Brian in Jeollanamdo" blog, which served as an informative guide to the region as well as an excellent barometer of some of the issues facing Korea and foreign teachers on the whole. The blog is still up and running at http://briandeutsch.blogspot.com, though Deutsch returned to the United States a couple of years ago.

Q: *Can you explain what brought you to Jeollanam-do as opposed to Seoul, where just about everyone seems to congregate?*

A: I actually spent a year in Bundang, a trendy district in a satellite city of Seoul, before coming down here. Looking back, I think it was actually a little more, well, culture shocking going to Bundang than Jeollanam-do because of the appearance of close similarity up there. I'm sure there's a proper term for it, but the closest I can get is to say, "Look up *Uncanny Valley* and apply it to Christmas, coffee, and pizza."

Q: *How long were you there, and what kinds of changes in the living environment did you notice over that time?*

A: I was in Jeollanam-do for three years, in Suncheon for two. A huge change was in the number of people, of teachers, online, and what that has meant for the collective knowledge base. Before I came, I couldn't even find things like pictures or population figures for most of the counties. Now a few minutes online can get you just about whatever you need.

Q: *Jeolla is known to be a pretty traditional region—what would you say are the biggest pluses of living there from the point of view of the foreigner, and the biggest minuses? Are culture shock and isolation major issues?*

A: South Korea looks pretty similar, regardless of the region. However, Jeollanam-do is quite unique in its politics. It is considered the birthplace of Korean democracy, and it has the battle scars to prove it. In the 2007 presidential election it voted overwhelmingly against the former president, Lee Myung-bak. What is considered "progressive" and "liberal" in Korean politics often runs counter to the sensibilities of some foreigners.

Isolation can indeed be a major issue.

units in the area's newer complexes of 10-15 *pyeong* (33-50 square meters) can be rented for around 400,000 won per month with a 5-10 million won deposit; family-friendly apartments of about twice that size are in the 700,000-800,000 won range. Smaller apartments can be bought outright for 100 million won or so, but 200 million won and up is a more reasonable budget for newer, more spacious units. There are fewer villas and detached houses available for rent in this area, and most tend to be aging or in poor condition; when they are on offer, rents tend to be slightly lower than apartments.

During my year in Gangjin County, for example, people would sometimes do a double-take on seeing a white face, and I can assure you I had the same reaction each time I saw a person aged 18 to 35. There are practically no jobs for young people, and the populations of rural areas are quickly declining, being replaced somewhat by mail-order brides and their children.

Jeollanam-do does have a lot going for it. I found the people generally warmhearted, and the pace of life slower and more relaxed than farther north. The food is great, and once you try the kimchi there, you won't want to eat it anywhere else. The area is very green, and even the cities juxtapose urban and rural. There is a lot of history, a lot of tradition kept alive, but the rural lifestyle is becoming more and more exotic, even for Koreans.

Q: *What would be your main recommendations to a foreign national moving to Jeollanam-do, or anywhere in South Korea, really, to help them have a more positive experience?*

A: The most important thing to remember is to keep your priorities in mind and not let anything interfere with them. If you come to teach, then teach. If you come to study the language, then study the language. If you come to learn more about Buddhism, or Confucianism, or K-pop, then learn.

If you're coming here as a teacher, learn as much about teaching in Korea as you can. Adjusting to the Korean idea of what a native speaker of English is supposed to be is, in my opinion, the biggest challenge you'll face. The other things, the regional differences, the cultural issues, will sort themselves out.

Finally, be patient and understanding. It is you that will have to come to terms with Korea, not the other way around.

Q: *Having recently made the transition back to your home country, what kind of advice would you give expatriates in Korea contemplating the same?*

A: Moving back to the United States was a challenge for a number of reasons. A lot of the amenities I had gotten used to in Korea—convenient public transportation; safe, walkable neighborhoods; cheap, no-hassle health care—are hard to find back home. Job-hunting was a very long process and 4.5 years abroad wasn't really seen as an asset. And the excitement of living and working in a foreign country was replaced by boredom from the dullness of contemporary American culture. I was 29 when I left but felt much older, as if I had just retired and suddenly switched off a huge part of my life.

An expat planning to move back will need to start preparing early. Start browsing job sites today to see what's available, what looks interesting, and what qualifications you'll need to get into the field you want. Talk to people currently in that field to see if they have advice for putting your overseas experience to use. It's not easy for expats to find work back home after years teaching abroad, and it's definitely not easy for former teachers in Korea to find ESL-teaching work in the United States without additional qualifications. These things take a while to learn and acquire, so starting well before you buy that return ticket will save you a lot of time and energy later.

The westernmost district, Yuseong-gu which contains the Daedeok Innopolis and most of the city's other major research facilities, also has a reasonable expatriate presence, most working at the nearby institutes or venture firms. Units in newer developments with a good range of amenities, such as Daedok Techno Valley, are usually handed out by employers but can also be rented for around 800,000 won per month for a two-bedroom, with deposits of around 10 million won. The average selling price is about 300 million won.

Culture

It'd be hard to argue that Daejeon is a cultural mecca, but it's no wasteland either. The excellent Daejeon Culture and Arts Center in Mannyeon-dong, a futuristic five-story structure surrounded by a park, has a solid collection of visual art and impeccably designed performance spaces that have hosted distinguished local and international acts such as the New York Philharmonic. Appropriately, given its focus on science, the city also has several museums concentrating on areas like the intersection of technology and art and natural phenomena, including the National Science Museum. The mountains on Daejeon's outskirts are home to several important Buddhist temples, and several key archaeological sites from the ancient Baekje kingdom are a short distance away.

Daily Life

Daejeon's expatriate community is small enough to be accessible but large and diverse enough to support a good range of interests. Most of the foreign restaurant and nightlife scene is focused in the new town of Dunsan-dong. Gung-dong, the neighborhood surrounding Chungnam National University, also has a number of edgy clubs and is popular with the younger foreign and local crowd, while the area around KAIST has a few haunts frequented by the institute's foreign researchers.

There's no foreign-language media to speak of in Daejeon beyond the newsletters that organizations like KAIST occasionally produce for employees or students. The city government publishes some helpful guides and information on foreign-language services, available on its website and usually at district offices. There are also a few active multinational clubs, including a soccer team and a salsa group. There are at least half a dozen churches of various denominations in the city with English-language services, including the Christian International Church and the Daejeon Onnuri English Ministry, and Buddhist temples and monasteries in the surrounding mountains also welcome foreign practitioners, although their English-language resources are more limited.

Health

Two of Daejeon's major hospitals—Chungnam National University and Daejeon St. Mary's—have large numbers of English-speaking doctors and nurses and therefore tend to be favored by foreign residents, but virtually all the city's medical facilities offer a high standard of care and have at least a few multilingual professionals on hand. The city government maintains a helpful list of smaller clinics and pharmacies with English-speaking staff.

Schools

Surprisingly, given its obvious esteem for learning and abundance of postgraduates, there's very limited educational infrastructure for foreign nationals in Daejeon. There's currently only one international school in the city, Daejeon Christian International School, that offers a U.S.-based curriculum for students from preschool through high school, and it is also one of the only institutions in South Korea running the International Baccalaureate program, held in high esteem by universities worldwide. It's a quality institution, but of course this quality comes at a price; tuition fees start at around 20 million won per academic year for the lower grades and rise to around 30 million at the high school level. As it's only 50 minutes to Seoul via the KTX high-speed train, some parents consider sending older children to schools in the capital, although the daily commute can grow tiring.

Shopping

As in other sizable South Korean cities, major retail chains such as E-mart and Home Plus have branches throughout Daejeon. The Galleria Timeworld and Lotte Department Store in Dunsan-dong and the Say Department Store in the old city center are Daejeon's highest-end retail spaces, with dozens of boutiques, designer outlets, even galleries and health clubs. While they've grown somewhat less active, merchants also regularly flock to traditional agricultural and wholesale markets, which are an unparalleled source of fresh low-cost produce. Jungang Markets, in the eastern district of the city, is one of the largest and most active.

Transport

Daejeon currently has a limited single-line subway system that links most areas of importance—City Hall and the old downtown, for example—but leaves many northern and southern neighborhoods uncovered. This is supplemented by a highly efficient city bus network, with stops on nearly every corner equipped with LED screens displaying route information and arrival times—almost always in Korean only, of course. Both the bus and the subway cost about 1,000 won per trip, and fares can be paid via cash or the local smart card (Hankkumi). Taxis are also abundant, with fares starting at 2,200 won.

GWANGJU 광주

The undisputed economic and cultural center of South Korea's southwest, Gwangju is a bustling city of around 1.5 million with a tragic past and vibrant present. Long a refuge for artists, dissidents, and intellectuals who fell out of favor with the ruling class in the north, the city has a reputation for dissent, as exhibited in a 1929 uprising against Japanese rule and a pro-democracy rebellion in 1980 that was brutally suppressed but marked a pivotal shift in South Korea's struggle against dictatorship. These memories may hang heavily on Gwangju, but it has nonetheless managed to blossom into a prosperous outpost of culture and industry, with a disproportionate number of writers, sculptors, and musicians and a brisk trade in businesses like high-tech components and photonics. It has a tight, friendly, and relatively diverse foreign community that tends to appreciate Gwangju's manageable size, easygoing people, and excellent local cuisine, as well as a contemporary art scene that belies its size and out-of-the-way location. Gwangju is, however, strategically positioned a short distance from some of the most beautiful parts of South Korea, including the bamboo forests of Damyang and the Boseong tea plantations, and is well-connected to Seoul via air and high-speed rail.

Encircled by lush fields and the rolling Mudeung mountain range, the city enjoys a picturesque location, but developed so rapidly that it is a rather chaotic tangle of buildings and apartment blocks. The newer segments of Gwangju in the west (Seo-gu and Gwangsan-gu) and north (Buk-gu) are newer and better-planned, with more stretches of green space, and have tended to attract the most foreign residents. These are also more convenient than the original city center in Dong-gu (East District) for people working in the many western industrial parks. Apartments in newer complexes

© BRIAN DEUTSCH

Chonnam University in Gwangju

will generally require large deposits—10 million won and up—as most landlords are more comfortable with the local system of renting, but rents themselves are quite low, around 300,000 won for a 15-20 *pyeong* (50-66 square meter) unit suitable for one or two people, and in the 500,000-700,000 won range for large 30-40 *pyeong* (100-130 square meter) units with enough space for a family. Apartment prices in these districts are typically in the 100-150 million won range.

Culture

The biggest event on Gwangju's cultural calendar is the Gwangju Biennale, the first contemporary arts festival of its kind in Asia. This one-month festival typically draws around 500 artists from all over the world who exhibit works tackling themes like race, industrialization, and ecology; it's a must-see for anyone with an interest in modern visual art, but unfortunately, as the name indicates, takes place only once every two years. The city is also home to a branch of the Platoon Kunsthalle, the brainchild of a Berlin-based art collective that creates malleable exhibition spaces with a focus on street art, graphic design, and live performances. There are also several museums highlighting local history, art, and folk traditions, and older assets, such as pavilions, ancestral shrines, and, on nearby Mudeung Mountain, temples and Buddhist relics.

Daily Life

Gwangju's expatriate population is a few thousand strong and includes a smattering of executives, students, language teachers, foreign spouses, and factory workers. The city government is more helpful than most and supports a very active International Center, which in addition to offering advice on settling in as well as legal and employment consultation services, publishes a monthly magazine (*The Gwangju News*) for the foreign population. The center is a good place to touch base with the city's international clubs, which cover activities such as football, Frisbee, and martial arts.

It also puts on language classes and events such as movie screenings and lectures on Korean cultural topics.

Most of the foreign socializing takes place in Chungjangno, a neighborhood in the old downtown that's largely pedestrianized and bursting with restaurants, pubs, and clubs. Gwangju has several churches and an Islamic center that offer multilingual services, as well as a few Buddhist temples that accept foreign nationals for short or long stays.

Health

Gwangju has over a dozen well-equipped hospitals and many more neighborhood clinics. Chonnam University Hospital and Honam Medical Center are two of the major institutions with designated international facilities in place for non-Korean speakers, but every sizable hospital will have at least some English-speaking doctors on hand.

Schools

Beyond the local system, the only educational options in Gwangju are the Kwangju Foreign School, which is U.S.-accredited and accepts students from elementary through high school, and a Chinese school. Tuition rates at Kwangju Foreign School are around 13-15 million won per year depending on the age of the child.

Shopping

Gwangju has a few interesting shopping options beyond the standard big-box retailers and department stores. Art Street, a 300-meter avenue in the Chungjangno area, is lined with shops and galleries that are a treasure-trove of paintings, calligraphy, art supplies, and ceramics new and old, and is also a common venue for outdoor exhibitions and performances. Chungjangno is also home to boutiques and an underground shopping complex with a decent range of imported goods. The sprawling Kumho World complex in the west of the city is a great place to browse for electronics.

Transport

Public transport is not one of Gwangju's strong points. The single east-west subway line is clean and efficient enough but doesn't extend to vast swaths of the north and south. City buses cover more ground but, apart from a few key routes, can be infrequent and crowded. Fares for both the bus and subway are around 1,000 won per trip and can be paid in cash or via a local "e-money" smart card known as "Bitgoeul."

Many foreign residents find themselves purchasing a vehicle or relying on taxis, which are readily available and fairly cheap, starting at 2,200 won and rarely exceeding 10,000 won even for trips from one end of town to the other. There are also frequent rail, road, and air connections to Seoul, and the city has a small international airport that handles a few flights from neighboring Japan and China.

JEONJU 전주

Conflict, rapid-fire industrialization, and a seemingly inexhaustible appetite for standard-issue apartment blocks have wiped out many of the historical structures in South Korean cities, but Jeonju has remained something of an exception and is now famous as a result. The city has no major industry to speak of, but in addition to being the capital of North Jeolla Province and a significant educational center, has preserved more traditional architecture than any other major settlement in the country. Much of central Jeonju is taken up by a *hanok* (Korean house) village, block after block of graceful wooden homes with hidden courtyards and topped with distinctive curled roofs. The city is also dotted with old gates, cathedrals, and shrines, and is crisscrossed by parks and streams, giving it a soothing cultured air that even the slapdash newer construction in many areas can't detract from.

This respect for the old extends beyond the buildings; Jeonju's people are very proud of their roots even by South Korean standards, and it's something of a magnet for historians, scholars, and others interested in Korean traditions. Arts that have fallen out of favor elsewhere in South Korea, such as the making of *hanji* (Korean paper) and home-brewed wines, still command a healthy following here. It's a unique and in spots charming place that seems to have more "soul" than a lot of other towns, and is ideally suited to culture buffs, students of Korean arts, or those who don't mind the quieter life.

Despite the city's traditional air, most accommodations on offer are in average high-rise apartments, which are fairly inexpensive, with rents for a midsize (around 100 square meters) units typically about 500,000 won with a deposit of 2-5 million won, and selling prices starting in the 130 million won range.

Culture

In many ways the whole city of Jeonju is a museum, and it also has a very large number of cultural outlets for its limited (by South Korean standards) population of about 600,000. The largest are the Sori Arts Center, which includes a massive theater and exhibition halls, and the Traditional Cultural Center in Wansan-gu, which regularly stages performances with an emphasis on indigenous music and opera. Dozens of smaller museums and galleries cluster around the *hanok* village, devoted to everything

© GONIL MOON/123RF.COM

Jeonju's *hanok* village

from calligraphy and Asian medicine to the battle for Korean independence, and the village also contains several homes of famous artists or political figures that are open to the public. Annual events include festivals celebrating local arts such as classical music and papermaking, as well as a film festival that has quickly picked up speed.

Daily Life

Jeonju simply doesn't have the commercial or educational infrastructure to attract massive numbers of expatriates—foreign businesspeople will find few job opportunities, and families will find a lack of schools geared toward non-Korean children. But there is a tight-knit foreign community of a few thousand here, many of them teachers or students lured by the city's traditional assets or relaxed feel. The Jeonju Hub Internet site is the best source of information for new residents to the city and contains a wealth of information on where to source English-language services. There are clubs for French speakers, soccer players, basketball enthusiasts, and more, as well as half a dozen or so foreign-oriented restaurants and bars in the Chonbuk National University area.

Health

English-language care is available at several Jeonju hospitals, including Chonbuk National University Hospital and Namgang Hospital.

Schools

At the time of writing there were no international school options in Jeonju, though plans for new institutions are said to be in the offing.

Shopping

Jeonju has a branch of large retailer E-mart and a Lotte Department Store. Most boutiques and specialty shops are located in the city center near the historic Gaeksa Gate, and there are also a few agricultural markets in the area with a wide variety of fresh produce and herbs. The *hanok* village is an excellent place to hunt down ceramics, paper art, teas, and crafts.

Transport

There has been talk of a light-rail network, but for now public transit in Jeonju consists of a bus system that is limited and rather confusing for non-Korean speakers. Given the city's compact size, taxis are usually a less stressful and only slightly more expensive option, and many expatriates eventually prefer to drive themselves around. Jeonju is also linked to the high-speed KTX rail network, which puts the rest of the country within easy reach.

PRIME LIVING LOCATION

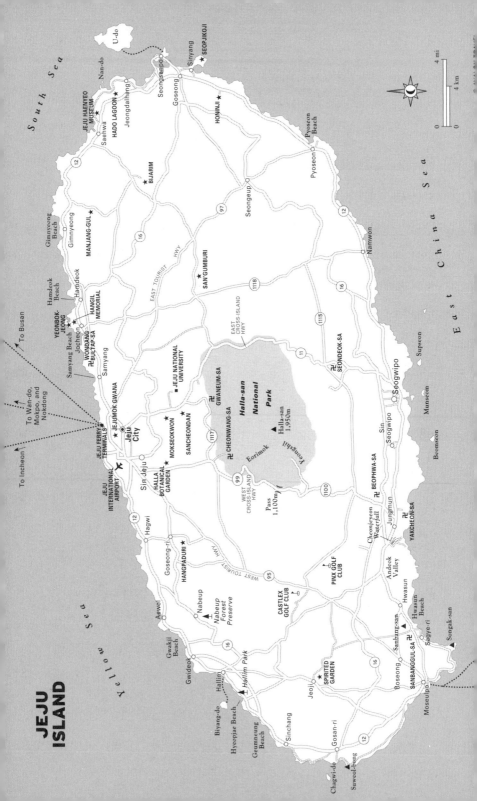

JEJU ISLAND 제주도

Asia's Hawaii, Honeymoon Island, the Island of the Gods—few places capture the South Korean imagination or attract as many superlatives as Jeju Island. Located about 100 kilometers (60 miles) from the mainland in the Korea Strait, it is the nation's preeminent leisure destination, with balmy weather, lovely beaches, and thanks to its volcanic origins, striking natural features, including Hallasan, South Korea's highest peak. Jeju's isolation has allowed a culture, dialect, and legends to take root that remain quite distinct from those found in the rest of the country, and it is the nation's only "autonomous" province, retaining to this day a measure of independence and a certain air of mystery.

Tourism has been the backbone of the island's economy for decades, but in recent years it has taken off in earnest, with a sharp spike in visitor numbers from elsewhere in Asia and beyond. Jeju's infrastructure is being built up to match, with the airport expanding, plush resorts springing up, and new attractions being developed. The provincial government has also unveiled ambitious plans to capitalize on the island's natural resources, strategic location, and growing renown to transform it into an international zone along the lines of Hong Kong or Singapore, with low taxes, a liberal investment regime, and foreigner-friendly schools, condominiums, and shopping complexes.

How successful this initiative will be remains to be seen, but some expatriates have

© ANNE HILTY

JEJU'S TRIPLE THREAT

One of the more commonly bandied-about expressions concerning Jeju Island is that it has *sam da* or "three abundances"–wind, rocks, and women.

When it comes to wind, the saying rings true. Atmospheric pressures caused by the interplay of sea and land regularly push average wind speeds above eight meters per second (18 mph)–about the force needed to topple a small boat–from fall to late spring each year, making fishing for the island's justifiably famous seafood a sometimes dangerous pursuit. On the other hand, the gusts have also fostered a thriving wind-sport industry, with enthusiasts packing the island's beaches for the country's best windsurfing and its highlands for hang gliding. Unsurprisingly, Jeju is also home to South Korea's first large-scale wind farm, the Hangwon Wind Power Generation Complex.

As for stone, the island's dark volcanic rock has been put to all sorts of uses, including building fences and farming implements, altars, and pagodas. Perhaps no creation is as instantly recognizable as the *dol hareubang* or "stone grandfather," a squat wide-eyed statue topped with a large bowler-like hat that was traditionally placed in front of villages to ward off disease and evildoers. They are found nowhere else in Korea.

The women–and this may prove disappointing to the young single men out there–is a reference to Jeju's renowned women divers. Carrying on a centuries-old tradition, these formidable ladies plumb the depths of the ocean surrounding the island for seaweed and shellfish without the benefit of standard scuba gear. Though they're now a major tourist draw and have even been named potential candidates for United Nations heritage status, their numbers are dwindling as fewer young women set out to learn this difficult and daring trade. Recent government surveys have counted around 5,000 women divers on the island, a third of the numbers seen in the 1970s, and over two-thirds are in their 60s or older.

found that Jeju, with its natural beauty, relaxed atmosphere, and outstanding recreational facilities, already offers a very favorable living environment. Unfortunately, outside of teaching and some segments of the tourism industry, there are relatively few employment opportunities on the island, but it's a compelling alternative to the mainland for the self-employed, retirees, and those fortunate enough to land a job there.

The Lay of the Land

Jeju is South Korea's largest island, a rough oval of about 1,800 square kilometers (695 square miles). Situated where the South and East China Seas meet, it is nearly as close to Shanghai as to Seoul. The by-product of a series of volcanic eruptions, the island is a place of lush forests, plunging waterfalls, and wave-battered cliffs, dominated by the snow-dusted crater of Hallasan at its center.

The north half of the island is home to Jeju City, the largest settlement in the province, and with the nearby international airport and ferry terminal, its main transportation gateway. Many of the island's more well-trammeled attractions, including major museums, botanical gardens, and the odd lava formation of Yongdu-am (Dragon's Head Rock) are also in the Jeju City vicinity.

© ANNE HILTY

sea view near Seogwipo

Jeju's southern half is comparatively more sedate, with its main city, the harbor town of Seogwipo, akin to Jeju City's sleepier cousin. But it may not stay that way for long. The sprawling Jungmun Resort Complex, which contains several luxury hotels, pristine beaches, and golf courses, is also on the island's south coast, which seems to be the focus of some of the larger planned retail and housing development projects, such as the Berjaya Jeju Resort.

CLIMATE

Jeju lies in a subtropical climate zone and definitely enjoys warmer temperatures on average than the South Korean mainland, but to imagine it as a sort of sultry paradise is a bit of a stretch. Though winters are relatively short and mild, temperatures still drop to close to freezing (though rarely below that, at least at lower elevations). Summers are hotter than in other provinces, especially in the southern half of the island, with temperatures topping out at around 35°C.

The island tends to receive stronger winds and more precipitation than the peninsula nearly year-round. It's also more susceptible to typhoons in the summer, though fortunately these usually dish out relatively little damage.

LANGUAGE

Though many provinces and cities have distinct accents, Jeju Island is probably the only place in South Korea where it could be argued that a full-blown separate language has been maintained. The local dialect shares some vocabulary and basic sentence structures with standard Korean, but still makes use of archaic expressions that either aren't used on the mainland anymore or were never used there at all, many of which exhibit strong Mongolian and Manchu influences. One example is *oreum,* the Jeju-dialect word for mountain or hill, which sounds a lot like the Mongolian for the same thing but apparently has nothing in common with the standard Korean *me* or *san.*

PRIME LIVING LOCATIONS

INTERVIEW: ANNE HILTY

© ANNE HILTY

Anne Hilty

American scholar and psychologist Anne Hilty was captivated by Jeju's natural beauty and heritage on her many visits to the island, and moved there permanently after stints in Seoul and Hong Kong. As well as offering counseling and support to the local expatriate community, she focuses on research of Jeju's unique cultural legacy, and has become a tireless advocate of its preservation. Hilty is also the author of

Jeju Island, Reaching to the Core of Beauty, published in 2011 by Seoul Selection. For more on her work visit http://drannehilty. wordpress.com.

Q: *What do you see as Jeju's biggest draws? Is the environment for expatriates improving or declining, and how so?*

A: Major advantages of living on Jeju Island include its natural splendor and related activities, Jeju's many initiatives to become an internationally oriented location, and the openness of its people to foreigners. In terms of Jeju as "Free International City" (the "free" referring to its economic zone and visa-free policy), it has a Foreign Advisory Committee within the government, is developing an international health care facility and foreigner help center, has an international education zone with three such schools thus far and contracts with a few others, has a recently renovated international airport, and is generally focused on making life here appealing to foreign residents–and, investors.

Q: *What are the job opportunities on Jeju like? And how would you describe the foreign community?*

A: Unless you are a foreign investor looking to set up or partner with a major business, jobs are primarily available in education–as a visiting professor, certified teacher at an international school, or foreign-language teacher in the public or private systems. As for the foreign community–"communities," in reality–there are approximately 10,000 foreigners on Jeju:

Unique as it might be, the Jeju dialect isn't likely to present any extra difficulties for the foreign resident. It's falling out of fashion with the young weaned on Seoul-produced TV, and Jejuites for the most part speak it only to each other and are quite capable of switching to standard Korean when interacting with outsiders.

CULTURE

There's no denying that Jeju's greatest assets are natural rather than constructed, but it would be a mistake to dismiss it as a cultural desert. There's an excellent national

9,000 Chinese or Korean Chinese [Chinese citizens of Korean heritage], 500 from other Asian countries, and 500 from non-Asian ("Western") nations. The non-Asian foreign community is very small, and its members socialize regularly with one another. Integration among Jeju native, mainland Korea native, and nonnative communities is still minimal.

Q: *Any particular difficulties or local sensitivities new arrivals in Jeju should look out for?*

A: For new arrivals to Jeju who have lived on the Korean mainland, or others who have knowledge of Korean culture, they should suspend most of what they know about Korea in recognition of Jeju's very distinct culture (it feels "foreign" to most visitors from the Korea mainland, actually)—including distinct regional accent and even local dialect. Local sensitivities include the current controversy over the development of a naval base on Jeju's southern coast—newcomers should realize that the issue is far more complex than it would seem at first glance, and that it is illegal and grounds for deportation to become involved in any political protest. Newcomers might also want to be aware that the relationship between Jeju and the mainland has been a difficult one for 1,000 years already, and that not all native people of Jeju embrace Korean identity. Come with open eyes, heart, and mind, and it will serve you well.

Q: *You offer free crisis services to expatriates—what kind of issues do people commonly grapple with? Any advice on dealing with the transition to Korean life/culture shock?*

A: I established this option via my website as I'm a PhD-trained psychologist and there are no counselors or counseling services on the island provided by a native English speaker. There has not been a great call for this, I'm glad to report, though of course the issues that expats encounter would be the same in living abroad anywhere—depression or anxiety associated with uprooting oneself and living in a culture distinctly different from one's own, as well as potential exacerbation of any underlying mental health condition for which one is already in treatment. Moving abroad can be destabilizing in the short term, and some struggle to cope with this. The best advice I can give is (a) awareness of this possibility—it isn't all adventure!, (b) exploring various stress-reduction and coping options, and (c) regularly talking with family as well as friends, both in the new location and back home, for support.

Q: *How long do you think you'll remain on Jeju? Any post-Jeju plans?*

A: Having grown up in New York City, I view myself as a "global citizen," with ties to numerous parts of the world. I've established a home for myself here on Jeju, however, and involved myself broadly and deeply with the Jeju native community with the intention of remaining indefinitely.

museum in Jeju City that focuses on excavations from nearby archaeological sites, a serviceable cultural center that hosts concerts, plays, and film screenings, as well as a striking new provincial art museum and several galleries highlighting the work of island artists, a good number of whom have found fame on the peninsula and farther afield. The island is dotted with Buddhist temples, botanical gardens, folk villages, and independent museums honoring everything from green tea to teddy bears. People requiring regular exposure to anything more obscure or sophisticated would do better to pack their bags for Seoul.

Where to Live

It's not unheard of for foreign residents to settle in smaller towns, or, if they're working for hotels, in resort complexes, but the vast majority of expatriates live in or around Jeju City or Seogwipo.

JEJU CITY 제주시

With over 400,000 people, Jeju City is the largest city on the island by a long shot, and consequently has the greatest range of choices when it comes to things like shopping, entertainment, and health care. If quick access to the South Korean mainland and other countries in the region is important, it's probably the only living location that should be considered because it is the main jumping-off point and port of arrival for the island. Even by South Korean standards, Jeju City has developed dramatically over the past decade, and every year there are fewer and fewer things that residents need to leave the town to hunt down. With so many overseas visitors, it has a worldly air for a South Korean metropolis of its size, with a host of attractions and recreational opportunities that are bound to appeal to residents as well.

There are, of course, downsides—Jeju City is a fairly busy and built-up place, much like its counterparts on the mainland and with little of the quaint charm touted in tourist brochures. In peak months it can seem overrun, with visitors outnumbering locals in many areas. Whether these faults are outweighed by the city's advantages will depend on what kind of conveniences prospective residents need and how deeply they want to entrench themselves in traditional island life.

Jeju City is not that large, and neighborhoods don't differ radically from one to the next, but a fair number of foreign nationals settle in the Shinjeju (New Jeju) area, which roughly covers the zone west of downtown toward the airport. The city's political and

former government complex, Jeju City

© ANNE HILTY

commercial center, it is a well-appointed area crammed with facilities and fairly modern apartment buildings. Two- to three-bedroom units of around 100 square meters at newer apartment complexes such as the Mideum Adriae can be rented for a *jeonse* deposit of around 100-150 million won, or bought outright for around 400 million won. With a smaller deposit—5-10 million won—monthly rents in Shinjeju should be in the 700,000 to 1.5 million won range.

SEOGWIPO 서귀포

Seogwipo is not all that far from Jeju City—a mere 45 minutes or so by road—but in some ways seems to exist in a different time. The town itself is a small bucolic outpost clinging to the rocky coast bordering the East China Sea and surrounded by picturesque peaks, waterfalls, and islets. "Downtown" consists of a few streets that wind down from the outlying hills toward the harbor, which is usually filled with bobbing fishing and pleasure craft. The dramatic setting and easygoing air have made it a favorite destination of newlyweds and day-trippers, and have convinced more than a few people to settle in for the long haul.

It obviously can't compete with Seoul or even Jeju City when it comes to things like excitement, imported groceries, art galleries, or educational facilities, but with so many resorts and parks as well as a coastline within spitting distance, Seogwipo's got the edge when it comes to laid-back lifestyle and outdoor pursuits. The diving, golf, and hiking in the area are all excellent, and it has also got a well-deserved reputation for fine produce, fresh seafood, and the warmest weather in the country. With so much development planned for the Seogwipo area, much of it specifically designed to attract foreign money and talent, it's also a place that bears watching, since some of its infrastructure shortcomings may well be addressed over the next few years.

The selection of housing available in Seogwipo is relatively limited; there are just a few recently built apartment complexes and villas, and stand-alone homes are rarely

PRIME LIVING LOCATIONS

© ANNE HILTY

swimming hole near Seogwipo

advertised, though it always pays to check with local real estate agents. Those apartments that are on the market are quite good value by South Korean standards; a typical *jeonse* deposit on a two- to three-bedroom unit of around 100 square meters in a mid-range building like the Gangcheon-dong Daelim Yeollim would be about 80 million won, and would rarely exceed 100 million won even in newer, flashier complexes. Prices to buy an apartment range about 100-150 million won.

Daily Life

There are around 8,500 foreign nationals living on Jeju Island, most in or around Jeju City. The expatriate population isn't really large enough to have taken over entire neighborhoods, but there are a few bars and restaurants on the island where the foreign community tends to congregate, including Gecko's in the Jungmun Resort Complex near Seogwipo and Winnie's Brunch and Pub near Jeju City Hall.

Not surprisingly, given the island's mostly balmy weather and abundance of nature, many of the expatriate clubs and associations are centered on outdoor activities, such as soccer, sailing, and Ultimate Frisbee. The *Jeju Weekly* is the island's sole English-language publication of note but does an admirable job covering local social issues and travel and cultural opportunities. Foreign residents also tend to connect and plan activities on the Internet through websites such as Facebook or the very informative Jeju World Wide (www.jejuworldwide.com).

SCHOOLS

Government efforts to encourage international schools to set up shop in Jeju seem to have borne fruit in recent years, with several institutions already establishing branch campuses and more on the way. Among those already active are the North London Collegiate School Jeju, which follows the British curriculum, and the Korea International School Jeju Branch. Tuition at both institutions runs from about 17-30 million won per year, depending on grade level. Both also offer boarding facilities.

HEALTH

The standard of health care in Jeju is quite high, and with several modern well-equipped hospitals on the island, there's rarely a need to go elsewhere for medical attention. The provincial health authority has designated several general hospitals, including Jeju National University Hospital, Halla General, and Hanmaeum General in Jeju City and the Seogwipo Medical Center in Seogwipo, foreigner-friendly facilities, and all offer services in English, Chinese, or Japanese.

SHOPPING

Much like any sizable city on the mainland, Jeju City has several department stores and branches of big-box retailers such as E-mart where expatriates can pick up a fair variety of local and international produce. Seogwipo also has an E-mart branch and a well-trafficked market district with a spectacular selection of fresh fruit, vegetables, and seafood. Prices of the many things not produced on the island tend to be higher than in other South Korean cities, partially a result of the cost of shipping goods over

Yongyeon Bridge, Jeju City

but also because many shops cater to free-spending tourists. For major purchases of clothes, electronics, and the like, it's often well worth organizing a trip to Busan or Seoul, even when the cost of getting there and back is factored in.

TRANSPORT

Getting to and from the island is easy; three or four domestic airlines offer multiple flights daily between Jeju City and virtually every major city on the mainland, with Seoul and Busan served most frequently. Fares are typically in the 60,000-80,000 won range and rise on weekends and holidays. There are also daily ferry services to Incheon, Busan, and Mokpo, many of which allow passengers to bring vehicles aboard. A handful of international airlines fly directly between Jeju and cities such as Tokyo, Shanghai, and Hong Kong.

On the island itself, public transportation is limited to a few bus routes serving Jeju City, Seogwipo, and the coastal road that rings the island, with fares ranging about 1,000-4,000 won, depending on distance. Taxis are also readily available in Jeju City and Seogwipo, with fares starting at 2,200 won. Many of the island's nicer spots can easily be reached only by private vehicles, and many long-term foreign residents end up buying cars or motorcycles to get around.

RESOURCES

Consulates and Embassies

IN THE UNITED STATES

EMBASSY OF THE REPUBLIC OF KOREA IN THE UNITED STATES
2320 Massachusetts Ave. NW, Washington, DC 20008
tel. 202/939-5663
fax 202/342-1597
http://usa.mofat.go.kr

KOREA CONSULATE GENERAL IN HONOLULU
2756 Pali Highway, Honolulu, HI 96817
tel. 808/595-6109
fax 808/595-3046
http://usa-honolulu.mofat.go.kr

KOREA CONSULATE GENERAL IN LOS ANGELES
3243 Wilshire Blvd., Los Angeles, CA 90010
tel. 213/385-9300
fax 213/385-1849
http://usa-losangeles.mofat.go.kr
Districts: Southern California, Nevada, Arizona, New Mexico

KOREA CONSULATE GENERAL IN SAN FRANCISCO
3500 Clay St., San Francisco, CA 94118
tel. 415/921-2251
fax 415/921-5946
http://usa-sanfrancisco.mofat.go.kr
Districts: Northern California, Colorado, Utah, Wyoming

KOREA CONSULATE GENERAL IN SEATTLE
2033 6th Ave., Suite 1125, Seattle, WA 98121
tel. 206/441-1011
fax 206/441-7912
http://usa-seattle.mofat.go.kr
Districts: Washington, Oregon, Idaho, Montana

KOREA CONSULATE GENERAL IN ATLANTA
229 Peachtree St., Suite 2100, Atlanta, GA 30303
tel. 404/522-1611
fax 404/521-3169
http://usa-atlanta.mofat.go.kr
Districts: Georgia, Florida, Alabama, Tennessee, South Carolina, North Carolina

KOREA CONSULATE GENERAL IN HOUSTON
1990 Post Oak Blvd., Suite 1250, Houston, TX 77056
tel. 713/961-0186
fax. 713/961-3340
http://usa-houston.mofat.go.kr
Districts: Texas, Arkansas, Louisiana, Oklahoma, Mississippi

KOREA CONSULATE GENERAL IN BOSTON
1 Gateway Center, 300 Washington St., Suite 251, Newton, MA 02458
tel. 617/641-2830
fax 617/641-2831
http://usa-boston.mofat.go.kr
Districts: Massachusetts, New Hampshire, Vermont, Maine, Rhode Island

KOREA CONSULATE GENERAL IN NEW YORK
335 E. 45th St., 4th floor, New York, NY 10017
tel. 646/674-6000
fax 646/674-6023
http://usa-newyork.mofat.go.kr
Districts: Connecticut, Delaware, New York, New Jersey, Pennsylvania

IN CANADA
EMBASSY OF THE REPUBLIC
OF KOREA IN CANADA
150 Boteler St., Ottawa, ON K1N 5A6
tel. 613/244-5010
fax 613/244-5043
http://can-ottawa.mofat.go.kr

IN GREAT BRITAIN
EMBASSY OF THE REPUBLIC OF
KOREA IN THE UNITED KINGDOM
60 Buckingham Gate, London SW1E 6AJ
tel. 020/7227-5500
fax 020/7227-5503
http://gbr.mofat.go.kr

IN AUSTRALIA
EMBASSY OF THE REPUBLIC
OF KOREA IN AUSTRALIA
113 Empire Circuit, Yarralumla, ACT 2600
tel. 02/6270-4100
fax 02/6273-4839
http://aus-act.mofat.go.kr

IN SOUTH KOREA
United States
UNITED STATES EMBASSY
188 Sejong-daero, Jongno-gu, Seoul 110-710
tel. 02/397-4144
fax 02/397-4101
http://seoul.usembassy.gov

UNITED STATES
CONSULATE IN BUSAN
Rm. 612, Lotte Gold Rose Building, #150-3,
Yangjung-dong, Busanjin-gu
tel. 051/863-0731
http://busan.usconsulate.gov

Canada, Great Britain,
and Australia
CANADIAN EMBASSY
21 Jeongdong-gil, Jung-gu, Seoul 100-662
tel. 02/3783-6000
fax 02/3783-6112
www.canadainternational.gc.ca/korea-coree

BRITISH EMBASSY
24 Sejong-daero 19-gil, Jung-gu, Seoul
100-120
tel. 02/3210-5500
fax 02/725-1738
http://ukinrok.fco.gov.uk/en

AUSTRALIAN EMBASSY
11F, Kyobo Building, 1 Jongno 1-ga, Jongno-gu,
Seoul 110-714
tel. 02/2003-0100
fax 02/722-9264
www.southkorea.embassy.gov.au

Planning Your Fact-Finding Trip

VISIT KOREA
http://english.visitkorea.or.kr
Government information site for visitors, with a wealth of information on sights, shopping, and cuisine, as well as maps, suggested itineraries, and links to tour packages.

KOREA HOTELS
www.koreahotel.com
Discount hotel booking engine; often has much more favorable rates than those quoted by hotels directly.

Housing and Real Estate Agents

SANTA FE RELOCATION SERVICES
www.santaferelo.com
Relocation specialist with offices in 14 countries in the region, including South Korea.

NICE RENT
www.nicerent.com
Company specializing in rentals for expatriates in Seoul or beyond; also offers relocation assistance services. Website includes some property listings.

CENTURY 21 SEOUL REALTY
www.c21seoul-realty.com
South Korea branch of the international real estate agents. Also provides pre- and postrelocation services to help new residents settle in.

BUDONGSAN 114
www.r114.com
Arguably South Korea's largest, busiest, and most useful property search portal. Listings and the latest price trends for the entire country, but unfortunately in Korean only.

Making the Move

LIVING IN SOUTH KOREA
KOREA4EXPATS
www.korea4expats.com
Excellent online resource on most elements of expatriate life in South Korea. Regularly updated with current event listings.

WAYGOOK
www.waygook.org
Named after the Korean word for foreigner, Waygook is an online community made up mainly of English-language instructors, but its forums are a helpful source of living information and advice for expats of all stripes.

MEETUP
www.meetup.com
Search your Korea location on this global networking site to find what kind of clubs and interest groups there are in your area. Seoul alone has dozens focusing on everything from hiking to language exchange, dining out, and urban farming.

MOVING COMPANIES
ASIAN TIGERS GROUP
www.asiantigersgroup.com
Specialist in moves to the region, with a South Korean presence.

ALLIED PICKFORDS
http://kr.alliedpickfords.com
Major global movers' network covers the United States, Canada, Great Britain, and Australia, as well as South Korea.

INTERNATIONAL MOVERS
www.internationalmovers.com
Use this site to request quotes from multiple movers, and get some helpful tips on relocating in general.

Language and Education

LANGUAGE SCHOOLS
Seoul
SEOUL KOREAN LANGUAGE ACADEMY
7F K&Y Hi-tech Bldg., 649-2 Yeoksam-dong, Gangnam-gu 135-080
tel. 02/563-3226
fax 02/563-3227
http://seoul-kla.com

LANGUAGE TEACHING RESEARCH CENTER
2F Sun Tower, 1-158 Sinmunro 2-ga, Jung-gu, 100-101
tel. 02/735-0039
fax 02/734-6036
www.ltrc.co.kr

YONSEI UNIVERSITY KOREAN LANGUAGE INSTITUTE
50 Yonseiro, Seodaemun-gu, 120-749
tel. 02/2123-8550
fax 02/2123-8662
www.yskli.com

SOGANG UNIVERSITY KOREAN LANGUAGE EDUCATION CENTER
1-1 Sinsu-dong, Mapo-gu, 121-742
tel. 02/705-8088
fax 02/701-6692
http://klec.sogang.ac.kr/root/index.php?lang=english

Busan
KOREAN LANGUAGE SCHOOL FOR FOREIGNERS
388-12 Jangjeon 1-dong, Geumjeong-gu
tel. 051/513-0131
www.kliff.co.kr

PUSAN NATIONAL UNIVERSITY INSTITUTE OF INTERNATIONAL EXCHANGE AND EDUCATION
San 30, Jangjeon 3-dong, Geumjeong-gu
tel. 051/510-1983
http://ili.pusan.ac.kr/

Other Cities
YEUNGNAM UNIVERSITY KOREAN LANGUAGE INSTITUTE (DAEGU)
280 Daehakro, Gyeongsan, Gyeongsangbuk-do 712-749
tel. 053/810-7860
fax 053/810-4702
http://kli.yu.ac.kr/

UNIVERSITY OF ULSAN KOREAN LANGUAGE PROGRAM
93 Daehakro, Nam-gu, Ulsan 680-749
tel. 052/220-5959
fax 052/224-2061
www.ulsan.ac.kr/eng/international/korean.aspx

CHONNAM NATIONAL UNIVERSITY LANGUAGE EDUCATION CENTER
300 Yongbong-dong, Buk-gu, Gwangju 500-757
tel. 062/530-3631
fax 062/530-3629
http://language.jnu.ac.kr

COLLEGES AND UNIVERSITIES
Seoul
SEOUL NATIONAL UNIVERSITY
1 Gwanak-ro, Gwanak-gu, 151-742
tel. 02/880-4447
fax 02/880-4449
www.useoul.edu

YONSEI UNIVERSITY (OFFICE OF INTERNATIONAL AFFAIRS)
50 Yonseiro, Seodaemun-gu, 120-749
tel. 02/2123-3486
fax 02/2123-8636
www.yonsei.ac.kr

KOREA UNIVERSITY
145 Anamro, Seongbuk-gu 136-701
tel. 02/3290-1152
www.korea.edu

Health

KOREA INTERNATIONAL MEDICAL ASSOCIATION
www.koreahealthtour.co.kr
Government-backed agency promoting medical tourism to South Korea. Has a helpful search facility for foreign-friendly facilities and doctors.

NATIONAL HEALTH INSURANCE CORPORATION
www.nhic.or.kr
Website of the government insurance provider with contact information for regional offices.

Nationwide emergency hotline (accidents, injury, fire, etc.; interpretation services available): 119

Employment

INVEST KOREA
www.investkorea.org
Website of the government foreign investment promotion agency; has loads of information on the rules and regulations around setting up a business or investing in South Korea.

SEOUL GLOBAL CENTER JOB SITE
http://jobs.seoul.go.kr

JOB POT
www.jobpot.com
Search engine for job-seekers.

KOREA BUSINESS CENTRAL
www.koreabusinesscentral.com

Online community for professionals in (or doing business with) South Korea. Has job listings and a wealth of other resources.

WORK N' PLAY
http://worknplay.co.kr
Hundreds of jobs listings, regularly updated. Focuses mainly on language teaching positions, though others come up.

DAVE'S ESL CAFE
www.eslcafe.com
Job listings and advice for English-language teachers.

Finance

Banks

KOREA EXCHANGE BANK
www.keb.co.kr
Website of a bank offering a range of expatriate-friendly services.

SHINHAN BANK
www.shinhan.co.kr
Part of one of South Korea's largest financial groups, this bank has a dedicated "global center" in Seoul that exclusively serves foreign nationals and companies.

CITIBANK KOREA
www.citibank.co.kr
South Korea division of the U.S. bank; has a significant local presence.

Brokerages and Other Services

SAMSUNG SECURITIES
www.samsungsecurities.com
South Korea's biggest brokerage.

SAMSUNG ECONOMIC RESEARCH
www.seriworld.org
Research and insight on the South Korean economy and beyond.

KIM & CHANG
www.kimchang.com
Major law firm with one of the country's largest tax practices.

Communications

POST
KOREA POST
www.koreapost.go.kr

INTERNET SERVICE PROVIDERS
KT
www.kt.com

SK BROADBAND
www.skbroadband.com

LG U+
www.uplus.co.kr

PHONE COMPANIES
SK TELECOM
www.sktelecom.com

KT
www.kt.com

LG U+
www.uplus.co.kr

NEWSPAPERS AND MAGAZINES
THE KOREA HERALD
www.koreaherald.com

THE KOREA TIMES
www.koreatimes.co.kr

THE JOONGANG ILBO
http://koreajoongangdaily.joinsmsn.com

KOREABANG
www.koreabang.com
An entertaining site dedicated to English-language translations of the hottest stories making the rounds of the Korean Internet, and the ensuing online debates—often more interesting than the stories themselves.

10 MAGAZINE
http://10magazine.asia
English-language magazine that tries to keep readers abreast of events nationwide, although emphasis inevitably ends up on Seoul.

TELEVISION AND RADIO
KOREAN CABLE TV ASSOCIATION
www.kcta.cor.kr

SKYLIFE
www.skylife.co.kr

Travel and Transportation

KOREA RAIL
www.korail.com

KOREAN AIR
www.koreanair.com

ASIANA AIRLINES
http://flyasiana.com

EXPRESS BUS LINES ASSOCIATION
www.kobus.co.kr
Online bus schedules and terminal information, but does not cover all routes.

Prime Living Locations

SEOUL
General
SEOUL METROPOLITAN GOVERNMENT
http://english.seoul.go.kr

SEOUL GLOBAL CENTER
25 Taepyeongno 1-ga, Jung-gu, 100-750
tel. 02/1688-0120
fax 02/723-3206
http://global.seoul.go.kr
One-stop shop for efficient—and free—information and assistance on any number of issues that can crop up for foreign residents of Seoul, from applying for a credit card to starting a business. Has branches in several expat-favored neighborhoods, including Itaewon and Gangnam.

Housing
STAR PARKS REALTY
5F Fire Insurance Assn. Bldg., Yeouido-dong, Yeongdeungpo-gu 150-101
tel. 010/6275-9494
fax 02/783-0886
www.nearsubway.com
Wider range of properties than many real estate agents have serving the foreign community, which tend to focus on the Yongsan district. Also has listings for short-term (under one year) rental contracts.

CRAIGSLIST SEOUL
http://seoul.craiglist.org
Popular online classified site has real estate listings for Seoul, nearby suburbs, and occasionally beyond.

Medical
YONSEI UNIVERSITY SEVERANCE HOSPITAL
250 Seongsanno, Sodaemun-gu
tel. 02/2228-5800
www.yuhs.or.kr

SAMSUNG MEDICAL CENTER
81 Ilwonro, Gangnam-gu 135-710
tel. 02/3410-0200
www.samsunghospital.com

JASENG HOSPITAL OF ORIENTAL MEDICINE
635 Sinsa-dong, Gangnam-gu
tel. 02/3218-2167
www.jaseng.net

Organizations
AMERICAN CHAMBER OF COMMERCE IN KOREA
www.amchamkorea.org

BRITISH CHAMBER OF COMMERCE IN KOREA
www.bcck.or.kr

CANADIAN CHAMBER OF COMMERCE IN KOREA
www.canchamkorea.org

AUSTRALIAN CHAMBER OF COMMERCE IN KOREA
www.austchamkorea.org

ROYAL ASIATIC SOCIETY, KOREA BRANCH
www.raskb.com

SEOUL INTERNATIONAL WOMENS' ASSOCIATION
http://siwapage.com/

International Schools
YONGSAN INTERNATIONAL SCHOOL OF SEOUL
San 10-13 Hannam 2-dong, Yongsan-gu 140-210
tel. 02/797-5014
fax 02/797-5224
www.yisseoul.org

SEOUL FOREIGN SCHOOL
55 Yeonhui-dong, Sodaemun-gu 120-113
tel. 02/330-3100
fax 02/335-2045
www.seoulforeign.org

DULWICH COLLEGE SEOUL
5-1 Banpo 2-dong, Seocho-gu 137-800
tel. 02/3015-8500
fax 02/501-9748
www.dulwich-seoul.kr

DWIGHT SCHOOL SEOUL
1582-1 Sangam-dong, Mapo-gu 121-835
tel. 02/6920-8600
fax 02/6920-8700
www.dwight.or.kr

FRANCISCAN FOREIGN KINDERGARTEN
707 Hannam-dong, Yongsan-gu 140-210
tel. 02/798-2195
fax 02/798-6171
www.franciscanfk.com

ECLC INTERNATIONAL KINDERGARTEN
5-3 Hannam-dong, Yongsan-gu
tel. 02/795-8418
fax 02/795-8439
www.eclcseoul.com

GYEONGGI-DO
General
GYEONGGI PROVINCIAL GOVERNMENT
http://english.gg.go.kr

RESOURCES

**INCHEON METROPOLITAN
CITY GOVERNMENT**
http://english.incheon.go.kr

SUWON CITY GOVERNMENT
http://eng.suwon.ne.kr/

Housing
RPARK REALTY
Rm. 210 Yangwoo Dramacity, 854-1
Janghang-dong, Ilsan-gu, Goyang
tel. 031/901-8300
fax 031/901-8355

CHOICE R.E.
#101 Cheonji Bldg, 270-3 Seohyun-dong,
Bundang-gu, Seongnam
tel. 031/706-5205
fax 031/706-5206

TOP REAL ESTATE OFFICE
#108, Kumho Apt. Shop, 932-2 Pyeongchon-
dong, Dongan-gu, Anyang
tel. 031/383-1999
fax 031/383-1318

SONGDO STAR REALTY
78, 4-1 Songdo-dong, Incheon
tel. 032/835-7766
www.realestatesongdo.com

Medical
**AJOU UNIVERSITY
MEDICAL CENTER**
San 5, Wonchon-dong, Yeongtong-gu, Suwon
443-721
tel. 031/219-4311
fax 031/219-5432
http://hosp.ajoumc.or.kr

INHA UNIVERSITY HOSPITAL
7-206 3-ga Sinheung-dong, Jung-gu, Incheon
400-711
tel. 032/890-2455
www.inha.com

ST. MARY'S HOSPITAL UIJEONGBU
65-1 Geumo-dong, Uijeongbu
tel. 031/820-3636
fax 031/820-3665
www.cmcujb.or.kr/eng/main/index.jsp

International Schools
SEOUL INTERNATIONAL SCHOOL
388-14 Bokjeong-dong, Sujeong-gu,
Seongnam 461-200
tel. 031/750-1200
fax 031/759-5133
www.siskorea.org

KOREA INTERNATIONAL SCHOOL
373-6 Baekhyun-dong, Bundang-gu,
Seongnam 463-420
tel. 031/789-0505
fax 031/255-0505
www.kis.or.kr

**CHADWICK INTERNATIONAL
SCHOOL**
17-4 Songdo-dong, Yeonsu-gu, Incheon
406-840
tel. 032/250-5000
fax 032/252-2007
www.chadwickinternational.org

**INTERNATIONAL CHRISTIAN
SCHOOL UIJEONGBU**
P.O. Box 23, Uijeongbu, 480-600
tel. 031/855-1276
fax 031/855-1278
www.ics-ujb.org

THE EAST
General
**BUSAN METROPOLITAN
CITY GOVERNMENT**
http://english.busan.go.kr

**DAEGU METROPOLITAN
CITY GOVERNMENT**
http://english.daegu.go.kr

ULSAN METROPOLITAN CITY GOVERNMENT

http://english.ulsan.go.kr

GANGWON PROVINCIAL GOVERNMENT

http://eng.gwd.go.kr

BUSAN HAPS

http://busanhaps.com
Website of Busan's main English-language magazine.

BUSAN AWESOME

http://cityawesome.com
Expat-oriented website includes articles, area guides, and event listings.

GEOJE FOREIGN RESIDENTS ASSOCIATION

www.gfra.net
Website of an association dedicated to foreign residents of Geoje, an island community near Busan where the shipyards employ many non-South Koreans.

DAEGU COMPASS

www.daegucompass.com
Community website for foreigners in Daegu.

ULSAN ONLINE

www.ulsanonline.com
Online publication Ulsan's expat community, regularly updated with articles and events.

Housing

BUSAN REALTY CONSULTING

1F, 1224-2 Jung-dong, Haeundae-gu, Busan
tel. 051/731-1114
fax 051/747-7333
www.busanrealty.com

JOEUN REALTY AGENCY

156 Zenith Square, 147 U 1-dong, Haeundae-gu, Busan
tel. 051/747-5555
fax 051/746-2288
www.joeunrealty.co.kr

KOOL HOUSE REALTY

665-1 Bongduk 3-dong, Jung-gu, Daegu
tel. 053/474-7921
fax 053/473-7922
www.kool-house.com

Medical

PUSAN UNIVERSITY HOSPITAL

179 Gudeokro, Seo-gu, Busan 602-739
tel. 051/240-7970
fax 051/248-2669
www.pnuh.co.kr

KEIMYUNG UNIVERSITY DONGSAN MEDICAL CENTER

56 Dalseongro, Jung-gu, Daegu, 700-712
tel. 053/250-7303
fax 053/250-7795
www.dsmc.or.kr

ULSAN UNIVERSITY HOSPITAL

290-3 Cheonha-dong, Dong-gu, Ulsan 682-714
tel. 052/250-7000
www.uuh.ulsan.kr

International Schools

BUSAN INTERNATIONAL FOREIGN SCHOOL

50 Gijangdaero, Gijang-gun, Busan 619-902
tel. 051/742-3332
fax 051/742-3375
www.bifskorea.org

BUSAN FOREIGN SCHOOL

67 Daechonro, Haeundae-gu, Busan 612-853
tel. 051/747-7199
fax 051/747-9196
www.busanforeignschool.org

DAEGU INTERNATIONAL SCHOOL
1555 Bongmu-dong, Dong-gu, Daegu 701-170
tel. 053/980-2100
fax 053/980-2101
http://dis.or.kr

HYUNDAI FOREIGN SCHOOL
Hyundai Foreigners' Compound, 260 Seobu-dong, Dong-gu, Ulsan 682-808
tel. 052/250-2851
fax 052/232-3220
www.hyundaiforeignschool.com

THE WEST
General
DAEJEON METROPOLITAN CITY GOVERNMENT
www.daejeon.go.kr

DAEJEON INTERNATIONAL COMMUNITY CENTER
www.dicc.or.kr

GWANGJU METROPOLITAN CITY GOVERNMENT
http://eng.gwangju.go.kr

GWANGJU INTERNATIONAL CENTER
www.gic.or.kr

JEONJU CITY GOVERNMENT
www.jeonju.go.kr

THE JEONJU HUB
http://thejeonjuhub.com
News and networking site for Jeonju expatriates.

Medical
CHUNGNAM NATIONAL UNIVERSITY HOSPITAL
282 Munhwaro, Jung-gu, Daejeon 301-721
tel. 042/280-8429
fax 042/280-8423
www.cnuh.co.kr

CHONNAM NATIONAL UNIVERSITY HOSPITAL
42 Jaebongro, Dong-gu, Gwangju 501-757
tel. 062/220-5114
fax 062/220-8330
www.cnuh.com

International Schools
TAEJEON CHRISTIAN INTERNATIONAL SCHOOL
77 Yongsan 2-ro, Yuseong-gu, Daejeon 305-500
tel. 042/620-9000
fax 042/620-9038
www.tcis.or.kr

KWANGJU FOREIGN SCHOOL
106 Samsoro, Buk-gu, Gwangju, 500-480
tel. 062/575-0900
fax 062/575-0902
www.kwangjuforeignschool.org

JEJU-DO
General
JEJU PROVINCIAL GOVERNMENT
http://english.jeju.go.kr

THE JEJU WEEKLY
www.jejuweekly.com
Website of Jeju's English-language newspaper.

JEJU WORLD WIDE
www.jejuworldwide.com
Online news information resource for expatriates.

Medical
HALLA GENERAL HOSPITAL
65 Doreong-no, Jeju City
tel. 064/740-5000
fax 064/743-3110
www.hallahosp.co.kr

SEOGWIPO MEDICAL CENTER
1530-2 Dongheung-dong, Seogwipo
tel. 064/730-3106
fax 064/733-4320
http://jjsmc.or.kr

International Schools
NORTH LONDON COLLEGIATE SCHOOL JEJU
San 1-6, Gueok-ri, Daejung-eup, Seogwipo
699-931
tel. 064/793-8000
www.nlcsjeju.co.kr

KOREA INTERNATIONAL SCHOOL JEJU
San 11, Gueok-ri, Daejung-eup, Seogwipo, 699-931
tel. 064/741-0509
http://kis.ac/

Glossary

aigo   common expression of exasperation or astonishment, rough equivalent of "my goodness"

agasshi   young woman

ajeossi   middle-aged man

ajumma   middle-aged woman

banmal   casual speech

bojunggum   housing deposit

bon   clan or roots

budongsan   real estate agent

buk   traditional barrel drum

bukhan   South Korean name for North Korea

bunuigi   the atmosphere of a place or situation

chaebol   conglomerates that still dominate most segments of the economy

chatjip   old-style teahouses

chemyeon   "face" or reputation

chodeunghakgyo   elementary school

chuseok   lunar harvest festival or "Korean Thanksgiving," usually falls in September or October. One of the most important holidays on the Korean calendar along with *seollal.*

daechong   porch

daechu-cha   jujube tea

daegum   traditional large flute

dalkgalbi spicy marinated chicken

ddeok   rice cakes

do   province

dol hareubang   statue used to ward off evil

dong   neighborhood

gayageum   traditional musical instrument like a zither

godeunghakgyo   high school

goseok   express bus

goshiwon   dormitory accommodation

gu   district within a city

gun   county

gut   shamanic ritual

gwangyeoksi   metropolitan city

gyopo   term for Korean person living overseas

hagwon   private academies to supplement studies after school hours

hallyu   the "Korean Wave" of South Korean films, TV serials, and music popular in other Asian countries

han   an emotional state

hanguk   abbreviation for **daehanminguk,**   local name for South Korea

hanguk-o or *hanguk-mal*   the Korean language

hangul   the Korean script

haniwon   Asian medicine clinic

hanja   borrowed Chinese characters

hanjeongsik   Korean banquet

hanji   Korean paper

hanok   traditional houses with a yard and curling eaves

hanyak   traditional medicine

hasukjip or *hasuk*   homestay

ho   class, when referring to trains

hoesik   pronounced "way-shik,"

RESOURCES

virtually mandatory (and usually raucous) office parties

hwangsa   dust that carries pollutants from China

hyeongum yeongsujung   cash receipt system

imdae   for rent

jangma   the local name for a seasonal monsoon

jeondaenmal   formal speech

jeong   trust or enduring bond

jeonse   full-deposit system, the traditional way to rent an apartment in which a large sum of money is deposited with the landlord but no or minimal monthly payment is made

jeonse daechul   housing deposit loan

joseon   dynasty that preceded Japanese rule and World War II; frequently used as an adjective to denote Koreans or Korean-ness.

jikhaeng   intercity bus

junghakgyo   middle school

kibun   a person's mood

kimbap   Korean version of the California roll, a common lunch or snack

kimchi   frequently spicy fermented cabbage that accompanies almost all meals

Konglish   the often odd local take on English most commonly heard and seen in songs and advertising

mae-mae   real estate term meaning the company has property for sale and can also connect sellers with property buyers

makgeolli   rice wine

minbak   guesthouse

minsokjujom   traditional pub

mobum   deluxe taxis

mudang   a medium, usually female

mugunghwa   "eternal flower," rose of Sharon

nongak   traditional agricultural music

nunchi   "eye measure," the ability to accurately gauge the mood of a person or the atmosphere of a place or situation

ondol   networks of pipes that carry hot water under homes, warming the floors

panchan   side dishes of seasoned or pickled vegetables, seaweed, eggs, and the like

ppali ppali   literally, "hurry, hurry," or "me first"

pungsu   Korean pronunciation of "feng shui," the Chinese art of geomancy

pyeong or **pyong**   unit of measurement, equivalent to around 3.3 square meters

pyojunmal   standard Korean

san   mountain

seollal   lunar New Year

seon   known as **chan** in Chinese, or Zen in Japanese, a form of Buddhism

si   city

ssanghwa-cha   "double harmony," medicinal tea

ssirum   form of wrestling

supa   miniature supermarkets

supyo   preprinted checks

teukbyeolsi   special city title

tukshil   first class train car

uchaeguk   post office

waeguk-saram or **waeguk-in**   foreigner; literally "outside country person"

wolse   monthly payments to rent an apartment, like the system used in the West

won   South Korean (and North Korean) currency unit

yakguk   pharmacy

yangban   wealthy nobility

yeogwan   inn or motel

yobosaeyo   expression used when answering the telephone

Phrasebook

Korean translations by Yu-kyoung Moon

PRONUNCIATION

The romanization provided generally follows the government transliteration system, with a few exceptions where alternatives better mimic the standard pronunciations. The English alphabet can only approximate some of the sounds found in hangul, and the transliterations found here should be viewed as a rough guide.

The Korean "g" is somewhere between the "g" and "k" sound in English, "d" is between "d" and "t," and "b" could be "b" or "p." "U" and "i" can be read as the "oo" in "moon" and "ee" in "meek," respectively. For vowel combinations, "eo" sounds like the short "u" in "bus," and "oe" and "ae" something like the short "ay" in "way."

NUMBERS

Korean Numbers

English	Romanized Korean	Korean
1	hana	하나
2	dul	둘
3	set	셋
4	net	넷
5	tasot	다섯
6	yosot	여섯
7	ilgop	일곱
8	yodolp	여덟
9	ahop	아홉
10	yeol	열
50	shween	쉰
90	ahun	아흔

Sino-Korean Numbers

English	Romanized Korean	Korean
1	il	일
2	i	이
3	sam	삼
4	sa	사
5	o	오
6	yuk	육
7	chil	칠

8	pal	팔
9	gu	구
10	ship	십
50	oship	오십
100	baek	백
500	obaek	오백
1000	cheon	천
5000	ocheon	오천
10,000	man	만
100,000	shipman	십만
1 million	baekman	백만
100 million	eok	억
1 billion	shipeok	십억

DAYS OF THE WEEK

English	Romanized Korean	Korean
Monday	wolyoil	월요일
Tuesday	hwayoil	화요일
Wednesday	suyoil	수요일
Thursday	mogyoil	목요일
Friday	gumyoil	금요일
Saturday	toyoil	토요일
Sunday	ilyoil	일요일

TIME

English	Romanized Korean	Korean
yesterday	eojae	어제
today	onul	오늘
tomorrow	naeil	내일
minute	bun	분
hour	shigan	시간
second	cho	초
10 o'clock	yeolshi	열시
10:30	yeolshi samshipbun	열시 삼십분
morning	achimae	아침
afternoon	ohu	오후
night	bam	밤
last week	jinanju	지난주
next week	daumju	다음주

this week	ibonju	이번주
month	wol	월
six months	yukkaewol	육개월
year	nyon	년
last year	chagnyeon	작년
this year	olhae	올해
next year	naenyeon	내년
early	iljik	일찍
late	nutgae	늦게
now	chigeum	지금
later	najungae	나중에

GREETINGS AND PLEASANTRIES

English	Romanized Korean	Korean
hello	annyong hasaeyo?	안녕하세요?
goodbye (person leaving)	annyonghi kesaeyo	안녕히 계세요
goodbye (person staying)	annyonghi kasaeyo	안녕히 가세요
Nice to meet you.	bangapsumnida.	반갑습니다.
How are you?	chal chinnaesoyo?	잘 지냈어요?
I'm fine.	chal chinnaesoyo.	잘 지냈어요.
yes	yae/nae	예/네
no	aniyo	아니오
maybe	amado	아마도
thank you	kamsahamnida	감사합니다
That's OK.	kwenchanayo.	괜찮아요.
Excuse me.	shillaehamnida.	실례합니다.
I'm sorry.	mianhamnida.	미안합니다.
Do you speak English?	yeongo halsu issoyo?	영어할 수 있어요?
I don't understand.	chal morugesseoyo.	잘 모르겠어요.
I don't speak Korean.	hangukeo mothamnida.	한국어 못합니다.
Please give me ____	____ jusaeyo	____ 주세요
this	igot	이것
that	cheogot	저것
I like ____	____ choayo	____좋아해요
I don't like ____	____ anchoayo	____안좋아해요
more	to	더
little	chogum	조금
a lot	mani	많이

GETTING AROUND

English	Romanized Korean	Korean
bus	beosu	버스
train	gicha	기차
subway	chihacheol	지하철
taxi	taeksi	택시
ticket	pyo	표
station	yeok	역
north	buk	북
east	dong	동
west	seo	서
south	nam	남
Please take me to ___	___ gajusaeyo	____로 가주세요
on the left	wenchoguro	왼쪽으로
on the right	orunchoguro	오른쪽으로
straight	chikchin	직진
downtown	shinae	시내
slowly	cheoncheonhi	천천히
fast	ppali	빨리
Stop here, please.	yeogi-ae sewojuseyo.	여기에 세워주세요.
How much do I owe you?	olmayaeyo?	얼마예요?

ACCOMMODATIONS

English	Romanized Korean	Korean
hotel	hotael	호텔
motel/inn	motael/yeogwan	모텔/여관
guesthouse	minbak	민박
room	bang	방
Western-style room	yangshil	양실
Korean-style room	hanshil	한실
Is there a room available?	bang issumnika?	방 있습니까?
We're full.	tajassumnida.	다 찼습니다.
Can I see the room?	bang jom poyeojushigesseoyo?	방 좀 보여주시겠어요?
How much is it per night?	hanbakae olmayaeyo?	박에 얼마예요?

FOOD

English	Romanized Korean	Korean
restaurant	restorang/shikdang	레스토랑/식당
rice	bap	밥
noodles	guksu	국수
meat	gogi	고기
fish	saengson	생선
vegetables	yachae	야채
soft drinks	umryosu	음료수
beer	maekju	맥주
water	mul	물
glass	chan	잔
spoon	sutgarak	숟가락
chopsticks	cheotgarak	젓가락
over here please (to get server's attention)	yeogiyo	여기요
I'm a vegetarian.	cheonun chaeshikchuicha imnida.	저는 채식주의자입니다.
Can I see a menu?	Menyu jeom polsuissulkayo?	뉴 좀 볼 수 있을까요?
Is there an English menu?	Yeongomenyuga itnayo?	영어메뉴가 있나요?
I'd like to order __ please.	___jusaeyo.	____ 주세요.
Can I have a fork please?	poku hana jushigesseoyo?	포크 하나 주시겠어요?
The bill, please.	gyaesanseo jusaeyo.	계산서 주세요.
That was great. (lit. "I ate well.")	chalmogossumnida.	잘먹었습니다.

SHOPPING

English	Romanized Korean	Korean
department store	baekhwajeom	백화점
market	shijang	시장
superstore/hypermarket	daehyeong matu	대형마트
grocery store	supeo	수퍼
convenience store	pyonhuijeom	편의점
Do you have ___?	___ issoyo?	___ 있어요?
Where can I find ___?	___ odiaeyo?	___ 어디에 있어요?
How much is ___?	___ olmayaeyo?	___ 얼마예요?
cheap	ssayo	싸요
expensive	pissayo	비싸요
Can you go a bit lower?	jogumman kakajusaeyo?	조금만 깍아주세요?
I'll take it.	salkaeyo.	살께요.

HEALTH AND EMERGENCIES

English	Romanized Korean	Korean
Help!	teowajuseyo!	도와주세요
Stop bothering me.	kuijankae hajimasaeyo.	귀찮게 하지 마세요.
Go away.	cheolikasaeyo.	저리가세요.
thief	doduk	도둑
police	gyeongchal	경찰
doctor	uisaweon	의사
dentist	chikwauisa	치과의사
ambulance	aembyulensu	앰뷸런스
hospital	byeongwon	병원
pharmacy	yakguk	약국
prescription	jeobangjeon	처방전
medicine	yak	약
painkiller	jintongjae	진통제
antibiotic	hangsaengjae	항생제
antihistamine	hanghistamin	항히스타민
antacid	chaesanchae	제산제
birth control	piimyak	피임약
condom	condom	콘돔
I feel nauseous.	soki misukoryeoyo.	속이 미슥거려요.
My ___ hurts.	___ apayo.	___가(이) 아파요.
head	mori	머리
stomach	pae	배 / 위
tooth	ipal	이빨
arms	pal	팔
legs	dal	다리
back	heori	허리
body	mom	몸
fever	yeol	열
cold	kamgi	감기
cough	gichim	기침
indigestion	sohwabulryang	소화불량
diarrhea	seolsa	설사
allergy	aleoji	알러지
I'm allergic to ___.	___ aleojiga isseoyo.	___알러지가 있어요.

Suggested Reading

HISTORY

Cumings, Bruce. *Korea's Place in the Sun: A Modern History*. New York: W.W. Norton, 2005. Excellent overview of Korean history concentrating on the last tumultuous century. Noticeably more sympathetic to the North Korean point of view than other works on Korea's recent past.

Oberdorfer, Don. *The Two Koreas: A Contemporary History*. New York: Basic Books, 2002. Political history of the two Koreas since the 1970s from a former soldier and foreign correspondent.

GENERAL

Breen, Michael. *The Koreans*. New York: St. Martin's Griffin, 2004. Still the definitive work on the Koreans and what makes them tick from one of Seoul's most seasoned expatriates.

Burgeson, J. Scott. *Korea Bug*. Seoul: Eunhaeng Namu, 2005. Eclectic and entertaining collection of pieces from an old zine writer that covers history, pop culture, expatriate life, and more.

Coyner, Tom, and Song-Hyon Jang. *Doing Business in Korea: An Expanded Guide*. Seoul: Seoul Selection, 2010. Good primer on South Korean business culture with advice for would-be entrepreneurs and frank discussion of pitfalls that need to be avoided.

Tudor, Daniel. *Korea: The Impossible Country*. Tokyo: Tuttle Publishing, 2012. A Seoul-based journalist takes an insightful and affectionate look at the phenomena shaping contemporary South Korean society, from competition to K-pop.

FICTION AND POETRY

Lee, Chang Rae. *A Gesture Life*. New York: Riverhead, 2000. Second work from a Korean American novelist explores themes of the Japanese colonial period.

Lee, Krys. *Drifting House*. New York: Penguin Books, 2012. Spanning South Korea and the United States, this haunting collection of short stories examines the impact of the country's troubled history on the Korean psyche and the immigrant experience.

Lee, Peter, ed. *Flowers of Fire: 20th Century Korean Stories*. Honolulu: University of Hawaii Press, 1986. One of the first, and still one of the best, introductions to modern Korean literature available in English.

Shin, Kyung-sook. *Please Look After Mom*. New York: Vintage, 2012. A tale of a mother's sacrifices for her family stands as testament to the high cost of South Korea's rapid modernization.

Un, Ko. Translated by Brother Anthony of Taize. *10,000 Lives*. Los Angeles: Green Integer, 2005. Broad and exquisite collection of work from the Nobel Prize-nominated poet.

LANGUAGE

Choo, Miho, and William O'Grady. *Handbook of Korean Vocabulary*. Honolulu: University of Hawaii Press, 1996. Helpful book that groups Korean

RESOURCES

expressions by their Chinese-character roots.

Revere, Stephen. *Survival Korean.* Seoul: Nexus, 2005. Good introduction to the language and script with an emphasis on practical everyday expressions.

Suggested Films

JSA. Directed by Park Chan-wook, 108 min., CJ Entertainment, 2000. A Korean take on the Hollywood-style action blockbuster set along the tense North-South Korea border.

Memories of Murder. Directed by Bong Joon-ho, 132 min., CJ Entertainment, 2003. Taut, masterfully paced detective thriller that successfully evokes the confusion of 1980s South Korea.

Seopyeonje. Directed by Im Kwon-taek, 112 min., Taehung Pictures, 1993. Heartrending film from South Korea's master director about traditional opera (*pansori*) singers struggling to make a living in the modern world.

Spring, Summer, Fall, Winter...and Spring. Directed by Kim Ki-duk, 103 min., Korea Pictures, 2003. A visually striking exploration of Buddhist themes.

Index

A

accidents, traffic: 106, 153
accommodations: fact-finding trip 60-63;
    see also housing
accounts, bank: 127
address system: 79
agriculture: 11, 29
airlines: 143
Airport Railroad (AREX): 50
air quality: 96, 102
air travel: 143
alcohol: 71, 96, 104
alien registration cards: 68
alphabet, Korean: 88
Andong: 58
Andong Mask Dance Festival: 49
animals: 13
apartment complexes: 77
Apple: 30
archaeological sites: 182
architecture: apartment complex
    architecture 77; traditional Korean
    architecture 53, 58, 76, 81
Arirang Festival: 59
arts, the: general discussion 41-44;
    festivals 212; Leeum Samsung Museum
    of Art 54
assault: 105
ATM cards: 47, 128
attire: 46, 116
authors: 41
auto travel: 151-153
autumn: 47
autumn festivals: 158
A visas: 67

B

babies: 71
baggage claim: 48
Bangojin: 58
banking: 125-129
bargaining: 53, 74
bars: 124
Baru: 60
baseball: 44
bathing culture: 56
benefits, job: 117
Beomeosa Temple: 58
bicycling: 147
big business: 29, 32
boat travel: 146-147
Bongeunsa Buddhist temple: 55

books: 73
Boryeong Mud Festival: 49
boy bands: 41
Breen, Michael: 112
broadband: 136
Buddhism: 39
budgets: fact-finding trip 46; monthly
    budget 121; see also costs
Bukchon Hanok Village: 53
bureaucracy: 66
Busan: daily life 194-197; fact-finding trip
    57, 62; gay culture 37; geography 11;
    language schools 91
Busan Cinema Center: 57
Busan Foreign School: 57, 197
Busan International Film Festival: 49
Busan Sea Festival: 158
business cards: 34, 46
business contacts: 113
business opportunities: 114
bus travel: Gyeonggi-do 189; Seoul 50,
    146, 177; smart card 122

C

cabs: 50, 124, 149, 177, 189
car, travel by: 151-153
cash: 47
cash receipt system (hyeongum
    yeongsujung): 74
cats: 72
Caucasians, social treatment of: 16
cell phones: 133
ceremonies, shamanistic: 38
Chang-wook, Park: 44
Cheonggyecheon: 53, 166
cherry blossoms: 158
children: moving with children 69-71;
    packing for children 73; safety of
    children 106; school for foreign
    children 92
China: cultural influences 31; historic
    contact with China 15
Chongryon: 25
Christianity: 40
Chuncheon: 58
Chungcheong Province: 160, 207
Chung-hee, Park: 24, 29
Chungju World Martial Arts Festival: 49
city buses (Seoul): 149
City Hall (Seoul): 53, 169
class, social: 32
climate: 46

clinics: 98-99
clothing: 46, 73, 116
coastal geography: 11
colleges: 92
commissions, real estate agent: 82
communications: 133-140
competition: 34, 92
compliments: 34
condos: 61
Confucianism: 26, 33, 36, 118
conglomerates (chaebol): 32
constitution: 26
consulates: 228
corruption, governmental: 27
cosmetics: 73
Costco: 122
costs: buying a car 151; cost of living 85,
    121-125; starting a business 114-115; tips
    for cutting costs 122
counties: 12
country divisions: 12
Craigslist: 80
credit cards: 47, 128
crime: 104
culture: 31-44; arts 41-44; Busan 195;
    culture shock 69, 208, 221; Daegu
    198; economy and cultural awareness
    30; employee culture 118; etiquette,
    social 33-35; gender roles 36-37;
    Gyeonggi-do 182; introducing children
    to culture 70; Jeju Island 221; political
    turmoil 19; regard of children 70;
    religion 38-40; Seoul 168; social
    climate 20; social values 36; sports 44;
    Ulsan 200
currency: 47, 125, 126-127
customs: immigration 48; shipped goods
    75

D

Daedeok Innopolis zone: 56
Daegu: daily life 197-199; fact-finding trip
    56, 62; geography 11
Daegu International School: 199
Daehangno: 55
Daejeon: 56, 62, 207-211
Dalmaji Hill: 58
dance: 49
dating: 104
Demilitarized Zone (DMZ): 11, 179, 183
democracy: 24, 26
demonstrations: 104, 137
Deutsch, Brian: 208
dialects: 90-91
dining: 35

directions: 79
disabilities, access for people with: 102
discount programs: 74
discrimination, workplace: 119
doctors: 98
documentation: banking requests 126;
    fact-finding trip 46; medical records
    100; visa requirements 67
dogs: 72
Do Ha Gun: 61
Dongbinggo-dong: 174
Dongdaemun Market: 53
Dongdaemun Station: 53
Dongducheon: 188
dormitories: 80
double taxation: 130
dress: 46, 116
drinking: 96, 104
driver's licenses: 152
driving: 106, 151-153
drug offenses: 105
drugs, prescription: 100
Dulwich College: 170
Dunsan-dong district: 56
D visas: 67
Dwight School: 170

E

eastern provinces: 191-203
economy: general discussion 29-30;
    education 86; investments 131
education: general discussion 92-95;
    economy 86; education reform 113;
    resources 231; see also schools
elders: 33, 35
electricity: 75, 85
electronics: 73
E-mart: 123
embassies: 228
emergency care: 98
employee culture: 118
employers: expectation of expat workers
    116, 118; help with visas/residency
    process 66; vetting prospective
    employers 110
employment: 108-119; health insurance
    99; job hunting 115-118; labor laws 119;
    self-employment 111; visa complications
    68; work environment 118
English language: 108, 109-111, 220
entertainment costs: 123
ethnic groups: 10, 32-33
etiquette, social: 33
events, annual: 49
E visas: 67

exams: 94
exchange rates: 122
executive branch: 27
expats: Busan 57, 196; business start-up advice 113; Chongryon 25; cultural awareness and economy 30; executives 115; government 28; increasing numbers 113; neighborhoods 122; population 17-18; villas 78; returning home 209; Russian 196; Seoul 54, 82; social treatment 15-17; Ulsan 58; see also foreigners
expenses: see costs
exporters, major: 29
express buses: 146

F
face (chemyeon): 36
fact-finding trip: 45-63; arrival customs 48; itineraries for 52-59; practicalities 60-63; preparation for 46-48; resources 230
fall: 13, 47, 158
family names: 32-33
family roles: filial piety 14; jeong 34; social formality 33
fauna: 13
ferries: 146
festivals: 49, 158
filial piety: 14
film: 42, 49, 57
finance: 120-133; banking 125-129; saving guide 122; living costs 121-125; taxes 130-131; wages 117
flora: 13
fluency, Korean: 87
folk beliefs: 38
food: Bukchon Hanok Village 53; dining customs 35; food poisoning 102; giving to children 70; grocery costs 121, 122, 123; local cuisine 96; major exports 30; packing 73; seafood 57, 58, 62
foreign embassies: 228
foreigners: 15-17; banking 120; clinics 99; deporting 101; safety 104; international banks 126; northern cities 188; police leniency 105; real estate 84; remittances 129; see also expats
formality: 33, 46, 89
Fraser Suites: 60
F visas: 67-68

G
Gaesong: 59
games: 44
Gangbuk: 166

Ganghwa-do: 182
Gangjin Celadon Festival: 49
Gangnam district: 54, 166, 172, 176
Gangneung: 58
Gangwon-do: 161, 193, 201-203
gay culture: 37
Gecko's Terrace: 63
gender disparity: 17-18
gender roles: 36-37
geography: 11, 166
Geunhye, Park: 37
gifts: 34
globalization: 31
Gojoseon: 20
Goryeo Dynasty: 21
government: general discussion 26-28; big business 29; regional government 91
Goyang: 188
GPS: 79
gratuities: 124
greetings: 34
grocery costs: 121
Gwangju: 11, 33, 211-213
Gyeongbokgung Palace: 53, 166
Gyeonggi-do: 179-190; daily life 183-184; geography 181; living locations 185-189; map 180; overview 159; transportation 189
Gyeongju: 58
Gyeongsang: overview 160; regional rivalries 33
Gyeongsangbuk-do: 193
Gyeongsangnam-do: 193

H
Hadong Wild Tea Cultural Festival: 49
Haeundae Beach: 57, 58
Hahoe village: 58
han concept: 34
hangul script: 21, 88, 89
Hannam-dong: 174
Han River: 165, 166
health: 96-107; Busan 196; environmental factors 102-103; Gyeonggi-do 184; superstitions 101; hospitals 98-99; insurance 99; Jeju Island 224; prescriptions 100; Seoul 169
hepatitis: 101
hierarchy, social: business 113; doctors 98; elder respect 14; language formalities 89
high school: 93
hiking: 55, 188, 201
Hilty, Anne: 220
hiring process: 117
HIV-positive expats: 101

holiday travel: 48, 122
homes, stand-alone: 79
homestays: 80
homogenous society: 32
homosexuals: 37
hospitality: 15
hospitals: 98-99
Hotel Riviera: 62
hotels: 61
hot springs: 56
housing: 76-85; cutting costs 122;
    expenses 85, 121; pet considerations
    72; purchasing 84; renting 80-84;
    resources 230; types 77-80
Hwang, Yi: 127
Hyatt Regency: 63
Hyundai Asan Company: 59
Hyundai Engineering and Construction:
    29
Hyundai Foreign School: 200
Hyundai Motor Group: 29, 59

I

I, Yi: 127
Ichon-dong: 174
Ilsan: 55
immigration: fact-finding trip 48; pets 72
imported goods: 73
Incheon: 58, 181, 185
Incheon International: 50, 143
income: 29
income tax: cash receipt system
    (hyeongum yeongsujung) 74; South
    Korean income tax 130; U.S. income
    tax 130
industry: 58
information resources: 56
Insa-dong: 168, 173
insurance, health: 99
international clinics: 99
international schools: general discussion
    92, 94-95; Busan 197; Daegu
    198; Daejeon 210; Gwangju 213;
    Gyeonggi-do 184; Jeju Island 224;
    Seoul 170; Ulsan 200
Internet: banking 128; cafés 138; cost 85,
    121; service 136-138
intolerance: 14
investing: 131-132
invitations: 35
Inwangsan: 55
IP Boutique Hotel: 60
iPhones: 30
Itaewon strip: 54, 169

J

Jagalchi Market: 57, 62
Japan: criticism 16; cultural influences
    31; historic contact 21, 22-24; Korean
    population 25
Jegyu, Kand: 43
Jeju City: 218, 222-223
Jeju Island: 217-225; fact-finding trip
    59, 63; map 216; overview 161; social
    climate 33
Jeju Springflower Guesthouse: 63
Jeolla: geography 206; overview 160;
    regional rivalries 33
Jeollabuk-do: 206
Jeollanam-do: 206
Jeongbalsan: 55
jeong concept: 34
Jeonju: 11, 213-215
Jewel in the Palace: 41
Jinh: 158
Jinhae Cherry Blossom Festival: 158
Jinju Lantern Festival: 49
Jinmimyeongga: 63
job hunting: 115-118, 209
Jogye order: 39
Jongno-gu: 172
Joseon Dynasty: 22, 32, 40, 166
journalism: 112
judicial branch: 26, 113
Jung-gu: 56, 58, 172
justice system: 113

K

KAL Hotel: 63
Kasantobang: 63
Ki-duk, Kim: 44
kimchi: 16
kindergarten: 171
Korea Advanced Institute of Science and
    Technology (KAIST): 56
Korea Composite Stock Price Index
    (KOSPI): 132
Korea Culture and Information Service:
    69-71
Korea Exchange: 132
Korea Exchange Bank (KEB): 126
Korean medicine (hanyak): 97
Korean Peninsula: 11
Korean War: 23-24, 106
Korea Railroad Corporation (Korail): 144
Korea Telecom (KT): 134
Korea Tourism: 70
Korea Train Express (KTX): 144
Koryo Tours: 59
Kumgang Mountains: 59

Kyobo Building: 53
Kyung-ni, Park: 42
Kyungpook National University: 56

L

labor: costs 17; laws 119
Lake Park: 55
landlines: 134
language: English 87, 108, 109-111; Jeju
    Island 219; Korean dialects 90-91;
    Korean schools 91-92; politeness 89;
    real estate terms 77; resources 231;
    Yonsei University 55
law enforcement: 105
laws, labor: 119
leaf-peeping: 158
leases: 82
Leeum Samsung Museum of Art: 54
legal issues: 18
legends: 20
legislative branch: 27
lesbian culture: 37
LG (company): 29
literature: 41
"Little Russia": 196
living costs: 121-125
loans: 128
Lone Star: 30
long-term rentals: 83
Lotte Hotel: 62
love hotels: 61
luxury goods: 124

M

magazines: 139-140
Mahayana Buddhism: 39
mail services: 138
maintenance fees: 85
map, country: 142
Mapo-gu: 172-173, 175
markets: Jagalchi Market 57; Seoul 53;
    shopping 74, 124-125; stock markets
    132
marriage: foreign brides 18; interracial
    15, 32
martial arts: 49
mask dances: 49
meals: 35
media: 139-140, 169
medical care: 98-99
medical insurance: 46
medical records: 100
medications: 46, 98, 100
medicine: Korean 97; see also health
mediums, shamanistic: 38

men, safety for: 104
men's roles: 36-37
Metro system: 148
minbak accommodations: 61
Mindan: 25
minorities: 32
Miracle on the Han River: 29
missionaries, Christian: 40
mobile app development: 30
mobile phones: 133, 171
Mokpo: 59
money: see finance
Monteith, Andrew: 110-111
mountains: 11
Mount Halla: 11
movies: 41, 42, 49
Muhak: 166
music: pop 41, 42; traditional 42
Myeong-dong district: 53
Myung-bak, Lee: 26, 137

N

Nakdong River: 11
Namdaemun Market: 166
Namsan Guesthouse: 60
Namsan Park: 54
National Health Insurance Corporation
    (NHIC): 99
National Tax Service (NTS): 74
natural disasters: 106
Naver: 137
newspapers: 139-140
nightlife: 57
North Korea: 23; border area 182, 188;
    Demilitarized Zone (DMZ) 11, 179, 183;
    overland travel 143; excursions 59;
    military conflict 106-107; social ideas 14
Novotel Daegu City Center: 62

OP

obligation: 34
officetels: 80, 173
online banking: 128
online services: 136-138
packing: 73
painting: 42
Palgongsan Mountain: 56
passports: 46, 109
pensions: 61, 131
pets: 72
pharmaceuticals: 73
pharmacies: 100
phone costs: 85
phone service: 134-136
phrasebooks: 46

plane travel: 143
plants: 13
police: 105
politeness: 89
politics: government 26-28; Jeolla 208;
    online 137; twentieth century 24;
    women 37
pollution, industrial: 11
pop culture: 30, 41
population: 17, 76
POSCO: 29
postal service: 138-139
pottery: 42, 49
poverty: 14, 19
precipitation: 12
pregnancy: 37
prehistory: 20
prejudice: 14, 17, 28, 119
preschoolers: 71, 171
prescriptions: 100
president: 26
preteens: 71
primary school: 93
prime living locations: 155-225; the east
    191-203; Gyeonggi-do 179-190; Jeju
    Island 217-225; overview 157-162; Seoul
    163-178; the west 204-215
prime minister: 26
private institutes (hagwon): 109
prosperity: 54
provinces: 12
public phones: 135
public transportation: 148
Pyongyang: 59

QR

quarantine: 72
railways: 144-145
Rakkojae: 60
real estate: purchases 84; rental agents
    80-82; resources 230; Seoul 54; terms
    77
recreation: 201
recruiters, job: 116
regional dialects: 90-91
regional rivalries: 33
relationship: 33
religion: 38-40
remittances: 129
rental cars: 151
rental homes: 80-84, 121
respectability: 36
restaurants: 124
Rhee, Syngman: 24
rivers: 11

road conditions: 141
road rules: 152
road safety: 106
rock climbing: 201
Royal Anchor: 63
rudeness: 33
Russian expats: 196

S

safety: 51, 104-107
Saimdang, Shim: 127
salaries: 117
Samcheong-dong district: 53
Samsan-dong: 58
Samsung Electronics: 29
Samwon Garde: 60
sanitation: 102
Santa Claus: 63
saving: 122
scarcity: 34
schools: Busan Foreign School 57;
    colleges/universities 92; entrance
    92; Gyeonggi-do 184; international
    92; Seoul 170; testing 94; see also
    international schools
script, hangul: 21, 88, 89
sea travel: 146-147
seasonal highlights: 158
seasons: 12
security guards: 124
Sejong, King: 21, 88, 127
Sejong-daero: 53
self-employment: 111
Seogwipo: 223
Seollal (Lunar New Year): 48
Seomyeon: 57
Seongbuk-dong: 173
Seongbuk-gu: 173
Seongnam: 187
Seoraksan: 158
Seoraksan National Park: 58
Seoul: 163-178; city layout 166-167;
    climate 167; culture 168; daily life 169-
    172; fact-finding trip 52-56, 60-61; gay
    culture 37; geography 11, 166; language
    schools 91; map 164; neighborhoods
    172-177; overview 158-159; shopping
    172; transportation 50, 145, 177-178
Seoul Foreign School: 170
Seoul Forest: 55
Seoul Global Center: 56
Seoul International School: 171
Seoulist: 170, 171
shamanism: 38
Shilla: 63

Shin, Kyung-sook: 42
Shinchon area: 55
Shinchon/Hongdae: 55
Shinhan Bank: 126
Shinsegae Centum City: 57
shipbuilding: 29
shipping: 75, 138
shopping: general discussion 124; Busan 197; Gangnam district 55; Gyeonggi-do 184; Jeju Island 224; customs 74; Seoul 172
short-term rentals: 82
short term visas: 67
Silla Dynasty: 20-21
skiing: 201
smartphones: 29, 30
smoking: 96, 102
soap operas: 41
Sobaek Mountains: 58
soccer: 44
social climate: 14-18
social networks: 136
society: see culture
Sogang University: 91
Sokcho: 58
Song, Yaeri: 170
Soyo-san: 188
spirituality: 38-40
spoken Korean: 90
sports: 44
spring: 12, 47
spring festivals: 158
stand-alone homes: 79
start-up businesses: 114
state council: 26
Stay Korea Guesthouse: 60
stock markets: 132
stonework: 218
storms: 218
subway: general discussion 148; Gyeonggi-do 189; Seoul 53, 177; smart card 122
suicide, teen: 94
summer festivals: 158
supermarkets: 123
superstitions: 39, 101
surnames: 32-33
Suwon: 58, 186

T
Taebaek Mountains: 11, 193
Taebaeksan Snow Festival: 158
Taejo, King: 166
taekwondo: 44, 49
Tang Dynasty: 21

Tap and Tapas: 63
taxes: general discussion 130-131; income 74; workers rights 119
taxis: 50, 124, 149, 177, 189
teaching English: 109-111, 220
teahouses (chatjip): 168
teenagers: 71, 94
Tehran-ro: 54
telephone service: 134-136
temperatures: 12
temporary visas: 67
testing: 94
theft: 104
Three Kingdoms Period: 20
tipping: 124
tobacco: 71, 96, 102
toiletries: 73
tourism: 171, 217
tourist visas: 67
Toyoko Inn: 62
tradition: closed society 14; cultural 31; education 86; Gyeongju and Andong 58; Korean medicine 97; office 118
traditional home (hanok): 76, 81
traffic accidents: 106
traffic laws: 152
train travel: 50, 144-145
transportation/travel: general discussion 141-153; costs 123; fact-finding trip 50; guides 46; holiday 122; smart card 122; travel times 145
traveler's checks: 47
tuition: 94, 95, 171

UV
Uijeongbu: 188
Ulsan: general discussion 199-201; fact-finding trip 58, 62; geography 11
Ulsan Hotel: 62
Ulsan University: 58
Un, Ko: 42
UNESCO World Heritage Site: 182
United States: criticism 16; income tax 130
universities: general discussion 92; Seoul 55; language study 91
urbanization: 29
utility costs: 121
vaccinations: 46, 101
Vatos Urban Tacos: 61
vegetation: 13
villas: 78
visas: employment 115, 119; long-term 67; North Korea 59; re-entry 68; tourist 67
visual arts: 42
volcanic rock: 218

WXYZ
wages: 117, 130
war: 23-24
water costs: 85
water quality: 96, 102
wealth gap: poverty 14; social class 32
weather: 12, 218
western provinces: 160, 204-215
Westin Chosun Busan: 62
wheelchair access: 102
white-water rafting: 201
wildlife: 13
wind: 218
winter: 13
winter festivals: 158
Winter Sonata: 41

women: business 117; Jeju Island divers
    218; safety 104; social roles 36-37
won currency: 126
Wonju: 58
work: see employment
workers rights: 119
work visas: 115, 119
wrestling: 44
written Korean: 88
Yoido Full Gospel Church: 40
Yongdusan Park: 57
Yongsan: 54, 172, 174
Yongsan International School: 170
Yonsei University: 55, 59, 91
Yuseong-gu: 209
Yuseong Hot Springs: 56

www.moon.com

DESTINATIONS | ACTIVITIES | BLOGS | MAPS | BOOKS

MOON.COM is ready to help plan your next trip! Filled with fresh trip ideas and strategies, author interviews, informative travel blogs, a detailed map library, and descriptions of all the Moon guidebooks, Moon.com is all you need to get out and explore the world—or even places in your own backyard. While at Moon.com, sign up for our monthly e-newsletter for updates on new releases, travel tips, and expert advice from our on-the-go Moon authors. As always, when you travel with Moon, expect an experience that is uncommon and truly unique.

KEEP UP WITH MOON ON FACEBOOK AND TWITTER
JOIN THE MOON PHOTO GROUP ON FLICKR

MAP SYMBOLS

▦ Expressway	○ City/Town	✗ Airfield	▰ Archaeological Site
▦ Primary Road	◉ State Capital	✈ Airport	⚲ Church
▦ Secondary Road	⊛ National Capital	▲ Mountain	⛽ Gas Station
┄ Unpaved Road	★ Point of Interest	♣ Park	Mangrove
⋯ Ferry	■ Other Location	⛷ Skiing Area	Reef
▰ Railroad			Swamp

CONVERSION TABLES

$°C = (°F - 32) / 1.8$
$°F = (°C \times 1.8) + 32$

1 inch = 2.54 centimeters (cm)
1 foot = 0.304 meters (m)
1 yard = 0.914 meters
1 mile = 1.6093 kilometers (km)
1 km = 0.6214 miles
1 fathom = 1.8288 m
1 chain = 20.1168 m
1 furlong = 201.168 m
1 acre = 0.4047 hectares
1 sq km = 100 hectares
1 sq mile = 2.59 square km
1 ounce = 28.35 grams
1 pound = 0.4536 kilograms
1 short ton = 0.90718 metric ton
1 short ton = 2,000 pounds
1 long ton = 1.016 metric tons
1 long ton = 2,240 pounds
1 metric ton = 1,000 kilograms
1 quart = 0.94635 liters
1 US gallon = 3.7854 liters
1 Imperial gallon = 4.5459 liters
1 nautical mile = 1.852 km

°FAHRENHEIT / °CELSIUS

230 / 110
220 / 100 WATER BOILS
210
200 / 90
190
180 / 80
170
160 / 70
150
140 / 60
130 / 50
120
110 / 40
100
90 / 30
80
70 / 20
60
50 / 10
40
30 / 0 WATER FREEZES
20 / -10
10
0 / -20
-10
-20 / -30
-30
-40 / -40

INCH 0 1 2 3 4

CM 0 1 2 3 4 5 6 7 8 9 10

MOON LIVING ABROAD IN SOUTH KOREA

Avalon Travel
a member of the Perseus Books Group
1700 Fourth Street
Berkeley, CA 94710, USA
www.moon.com

Editor: Leah Gordon
Series Manager: Elizabeth Hansen
Copy Editor: Ashley Benning
Graphics Coordinator: Elizabeth Jang
Production Coordinator: Elizabeth Jang
Cover Designer: Elizabeth Jang
Map Editor: Kat Bennett
Cartographer: Paige Enoch
Indexer: Rachel Kuhn

ISBN-13: 978-1-61238-632-4
ISSN: 1948-5980

Printing History
1st Edition – 2010
2nd Edition – September 2013
5 4 3 2 1

Front cover photo: Cheonggyecheon, the restored stream that runs through central Seoul. The lanterns are strung up for Buddha's Birthday. © klaigungwaan photography/Craig D.C. Lewis

Title page photo: Yakcheonsa (temple), Jeju © Anne Hilty

Interior color photos: p. 4 cherry blossoms in Gyeonggi-do © Jonathan Hopfner; p. 5 bridge in Seoul © Hyunsu Kim/123rf.com; p. 6 (inset) lion statue © Craig D.C. Lewis, (bottom) Buddhist lanterns © Rufina K.E. Park; p. 7 (top left) river outside Chuncheon, Gangwon-do © Rufina K.E. Park, (top right) War Memorial, Seoul © Craig D.C. Lewis, (bottom left) Buddha statue © Craig D.C. Lewis, (bottom right) autumn tree and outdoor sculpture, Han River, Seoul © Craig D.C. Lewis; p. 8 (left) children wearing traditional dress at the Changing of the Guard, Gyeongbokgung Palace in Seoul © danscandal/123rf.com, (right) autumn foliage © Sungjin Kim/123rf.com

Back cover photo: Buddha, Namsan (mountain), Gyeongju © Jonathan Hopfner

Printed in Canada by Friesens

KEEPING CURRENT

Although we strive to produce the most up-to-date guidebook that we possibly can, change is unavoidable. Between the time this book goes to print and the time you read it, the cost of goods and services may have increased, and a handful of the businesses noted in these pages will undoubtedly move, alter their prices, or close their doors forever. Exchange rates fluctuate—sometimes dramatically—on a daily basis. Federal and local legal requirements and restrictions are also subject to change, so be sure to check with the appropriate authorities before making the move. If you see anything in this book that needs updating, clarification, or correction, please drop us a line. Send your comments via email to feedback@moon.com, or use the address above.